I0753653

MESSAGES OF HOPE – MEDITATIONS, AFFIRMATIONS & PRAYERS

Premier Edition Published in 2015 in the United States of America

Sources: All Bible verses paraphrased from a multitude of various scriptures including: the Geneva Holy Bible, New King James, The Torah, Catholic Public Domain, Orthodox Jewish Bible, NIV Anglicized, among many others.

WWW.MYDOVESONG.COM

ISBN-13: 978-0615977843
ISBN-10: 0615977847

MESSAGES OF HOPE

Meditations, Affirmations & Prayers

D. ASHANTI-DUBOIS

My Dove Song
MYDOVESONG
PUBLISHING

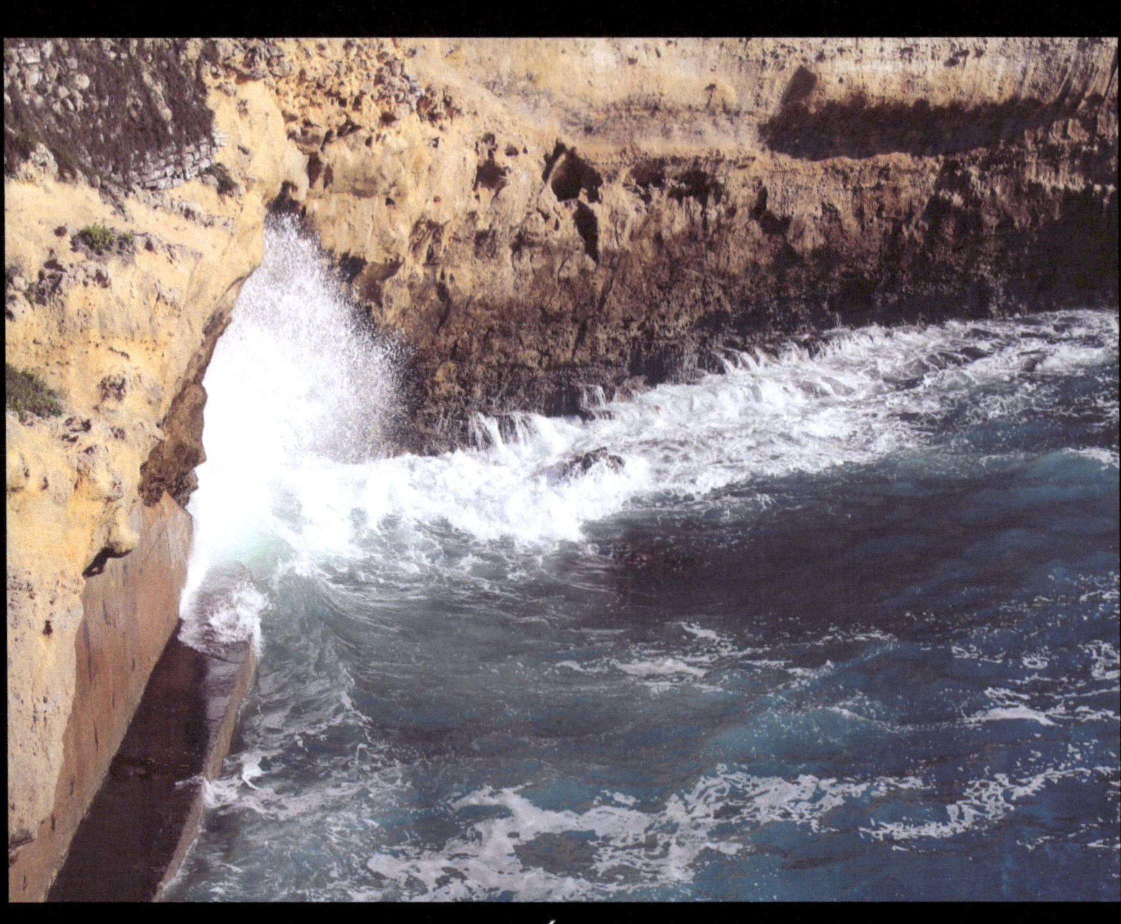

MESSAGES OF

AFFIRMATIONS TO EMPOWER YOUR LIFE

HOPE

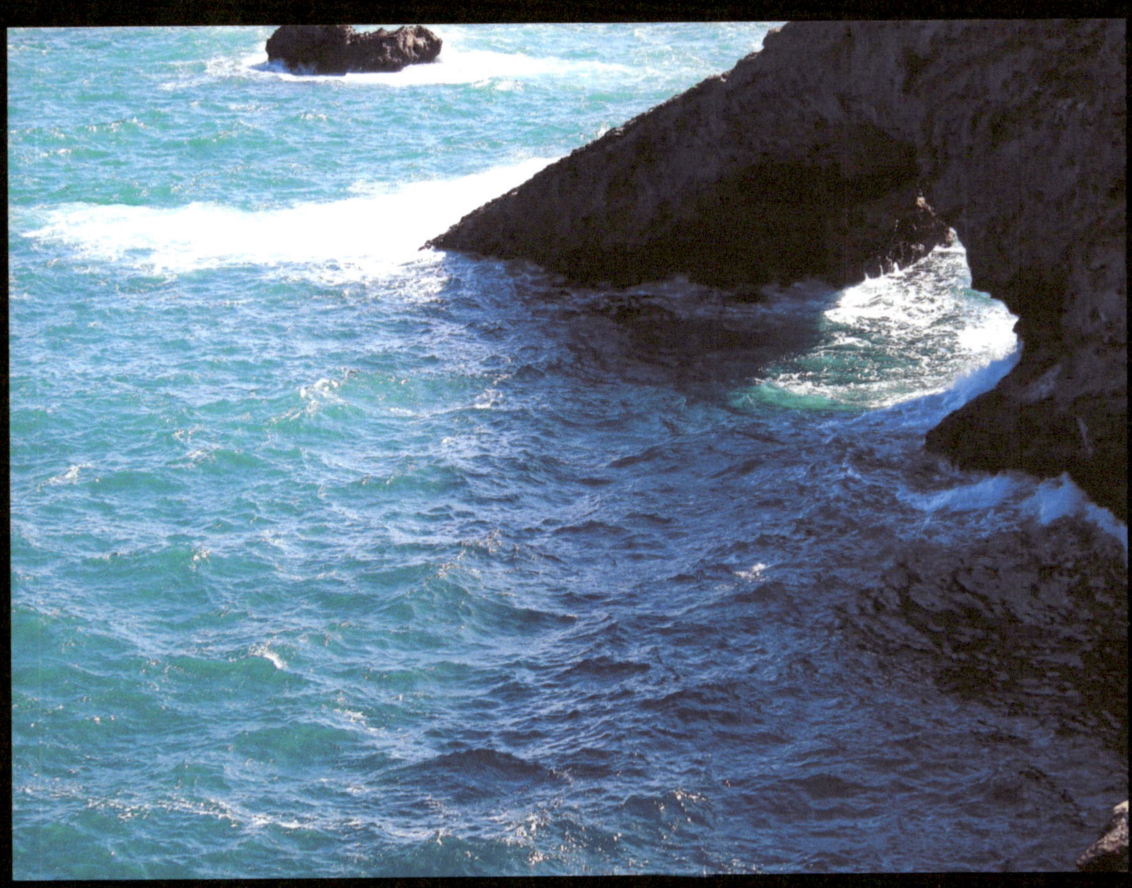

Divine Holy One, Come into my life so that I may live all that I wish to live and be all that I desire to be. Please take away all that stands between me and you and my hopes and dreams. Fulfill my daily needs, and empower me to be courageous, determined, loving, joyful, and prosperous. Manifest a miracle in me today.
In the name of the Holy One, Jesus Christ, I pray... Amen.

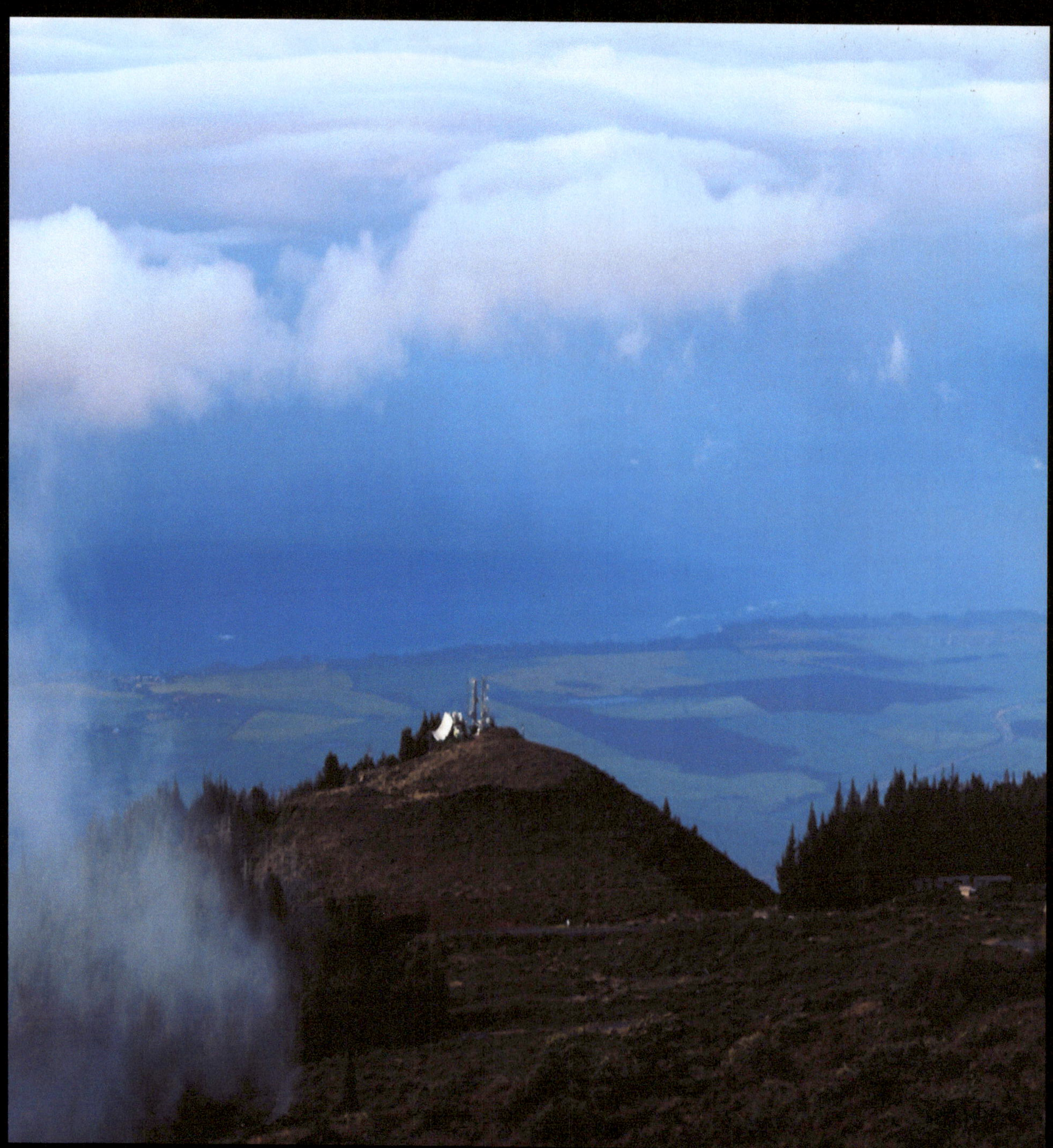

Island of Maui, Hawai'i

My life is a true miracle in the making.
Every challenge, crisis, and hardship I face, makes me stronger in my heart, my spirit, and mind.
I am courageous, I am victorious, and I shall stand.

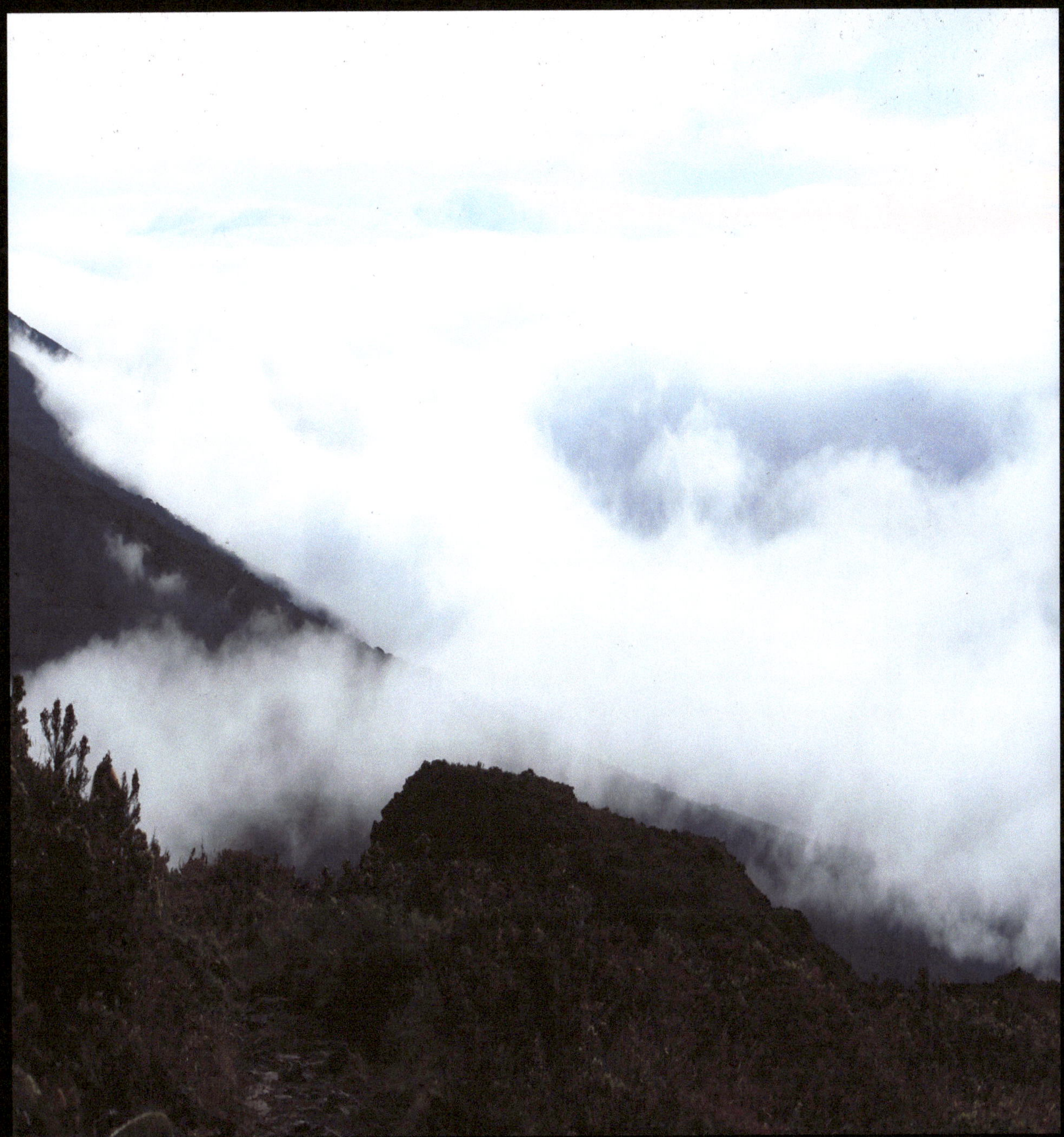

Haleakala State Park - Maui Hawai'i

It is my Divine right to live my dreams and I claim them without fear.
I believe in them. I will work for them, and they are mine.

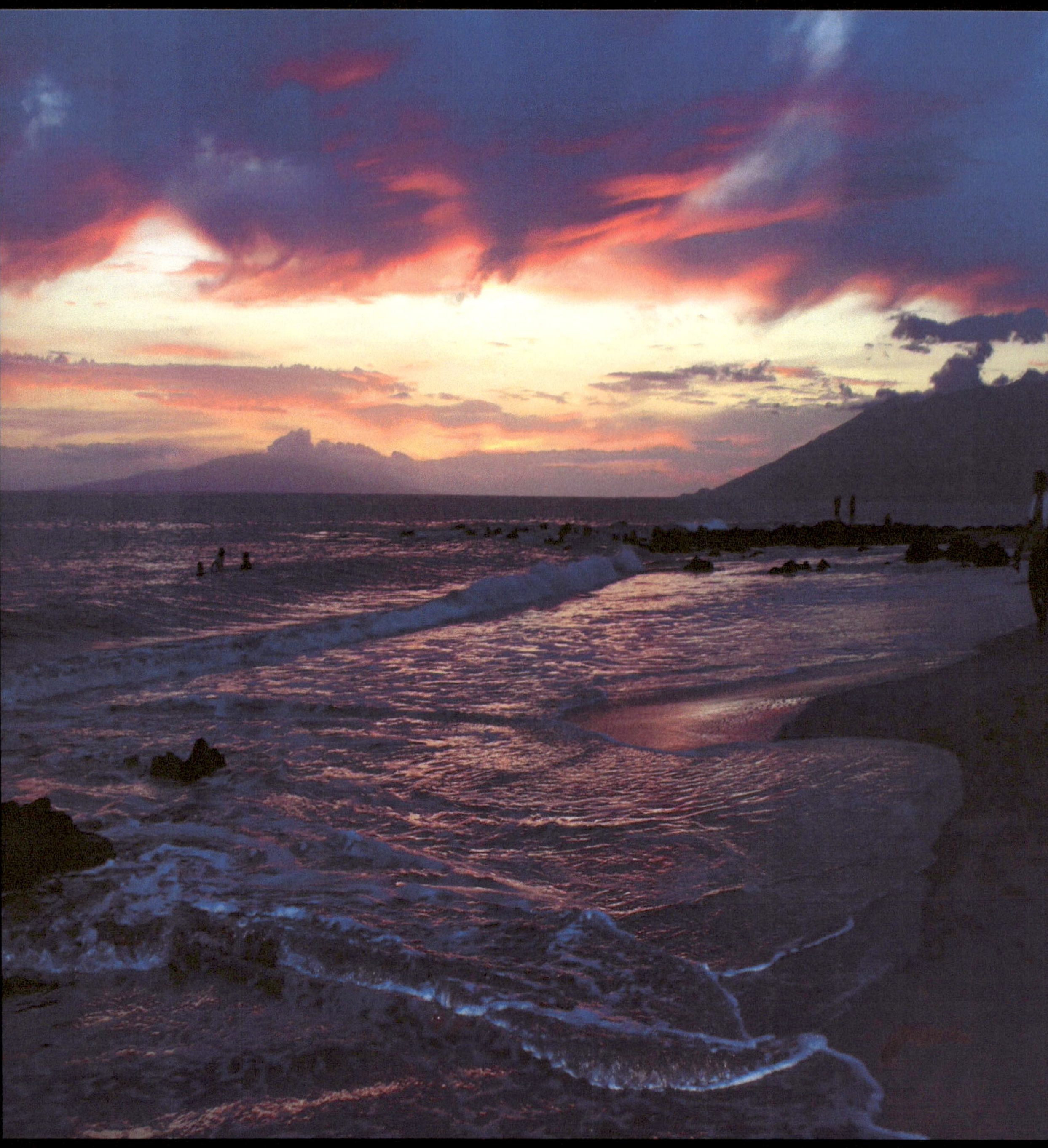

Kamaole Beach III - Maui, Hawai'i

I am loved beyond measure because the Divine loves me.

I am protected. I am accepted. I am sheltered. I am blessed.

I am in the arms of the Divine.

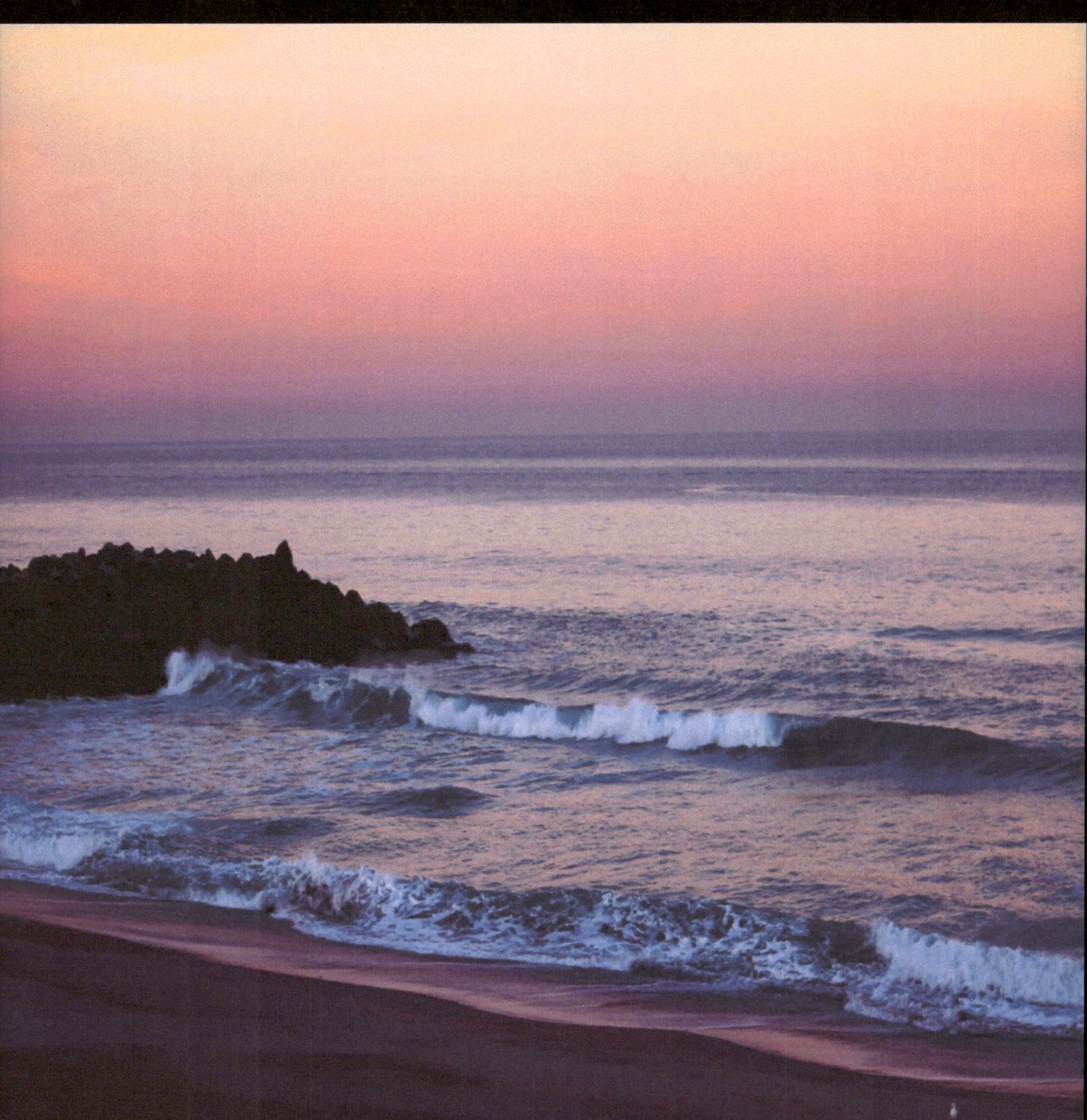

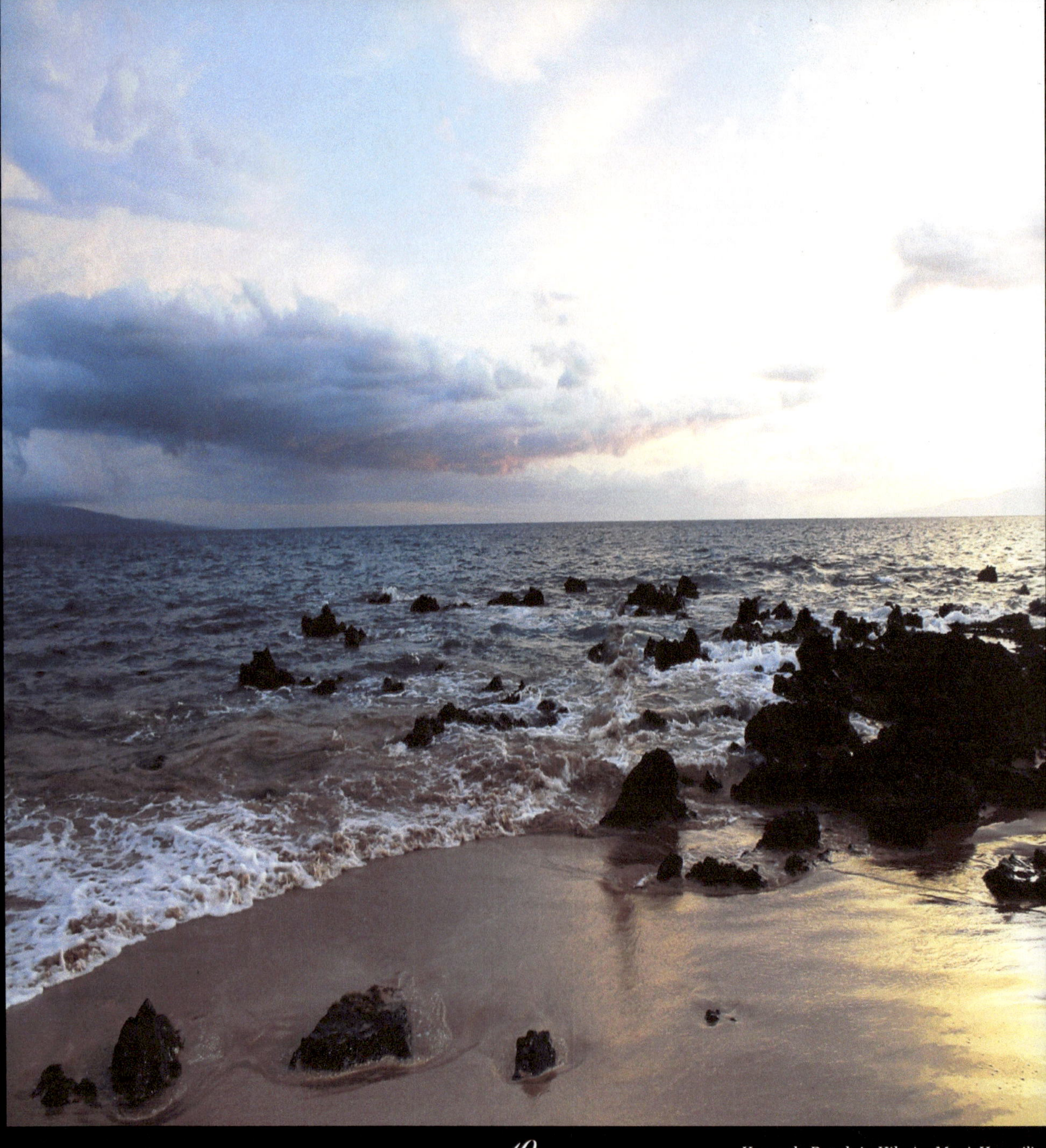

Kamaole Beach in Kihei - Maui, Hawai'i

Today is the day I fulfill my dreams and I will not cease until it is done.
I will accomplish something today.

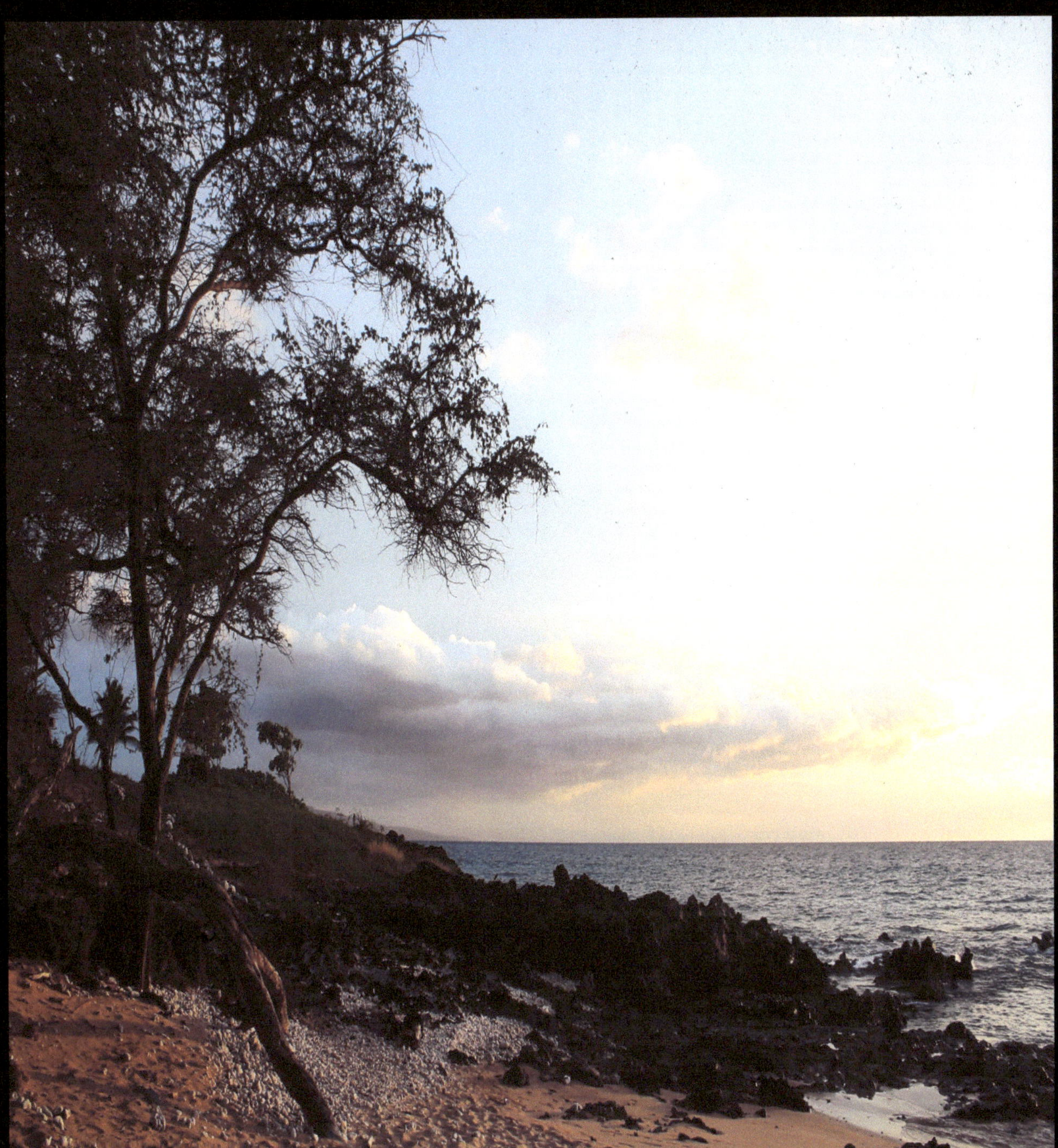

Kamaole Beach II - Maui, Hawai'i

I choose to let go of all things that hurt me. I do not fear change.

I do no worry for the future. I am not sorry for the past.

I did not give up; I let go of these things.

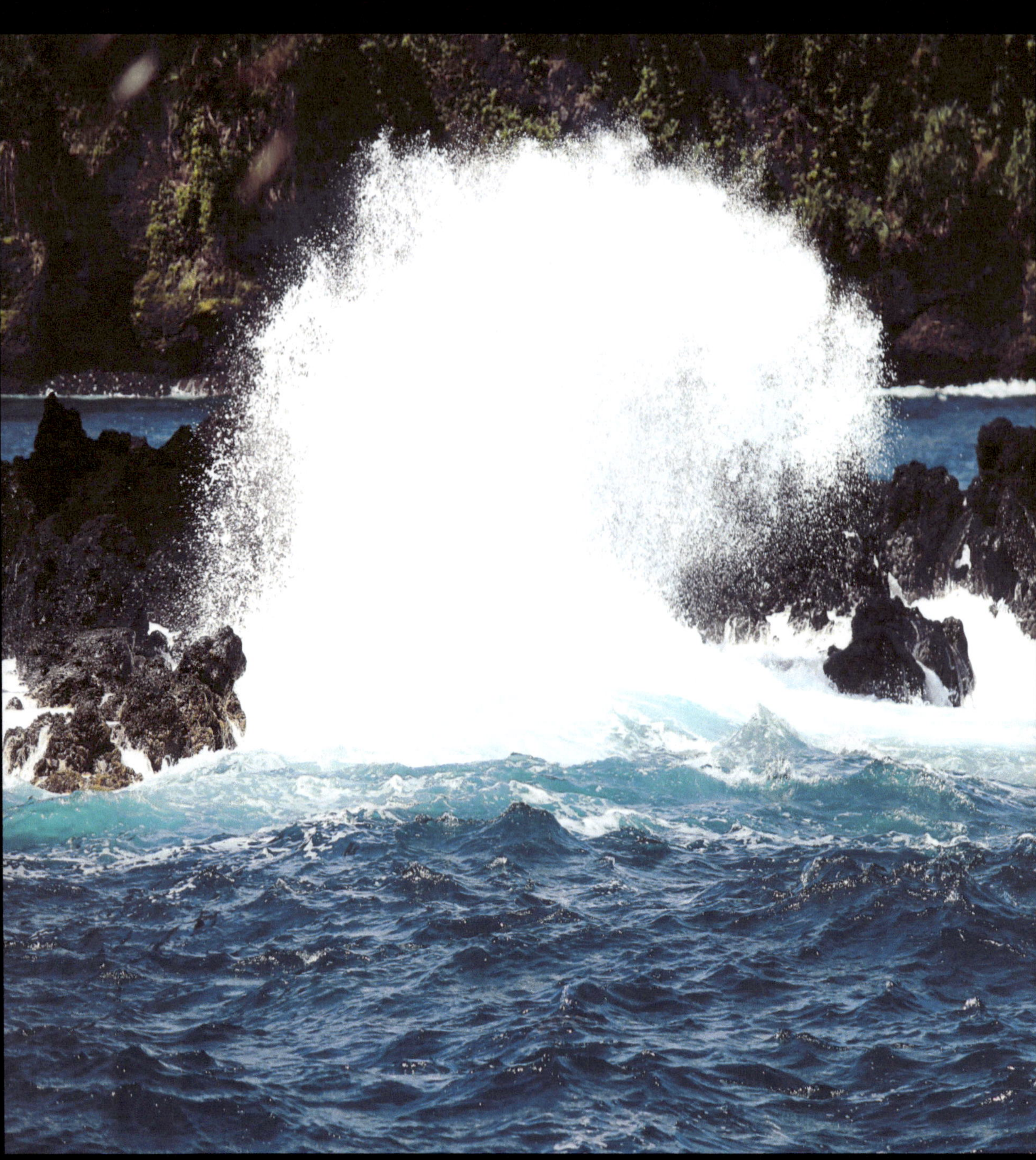

Maui, Hawai'i

I have the power within me to manifest my dreams and change my life.

I see it. I feel it. I believe it. It is possible. It is done.

I already have everything I need to be happy.

Love lies within me. I am complete.

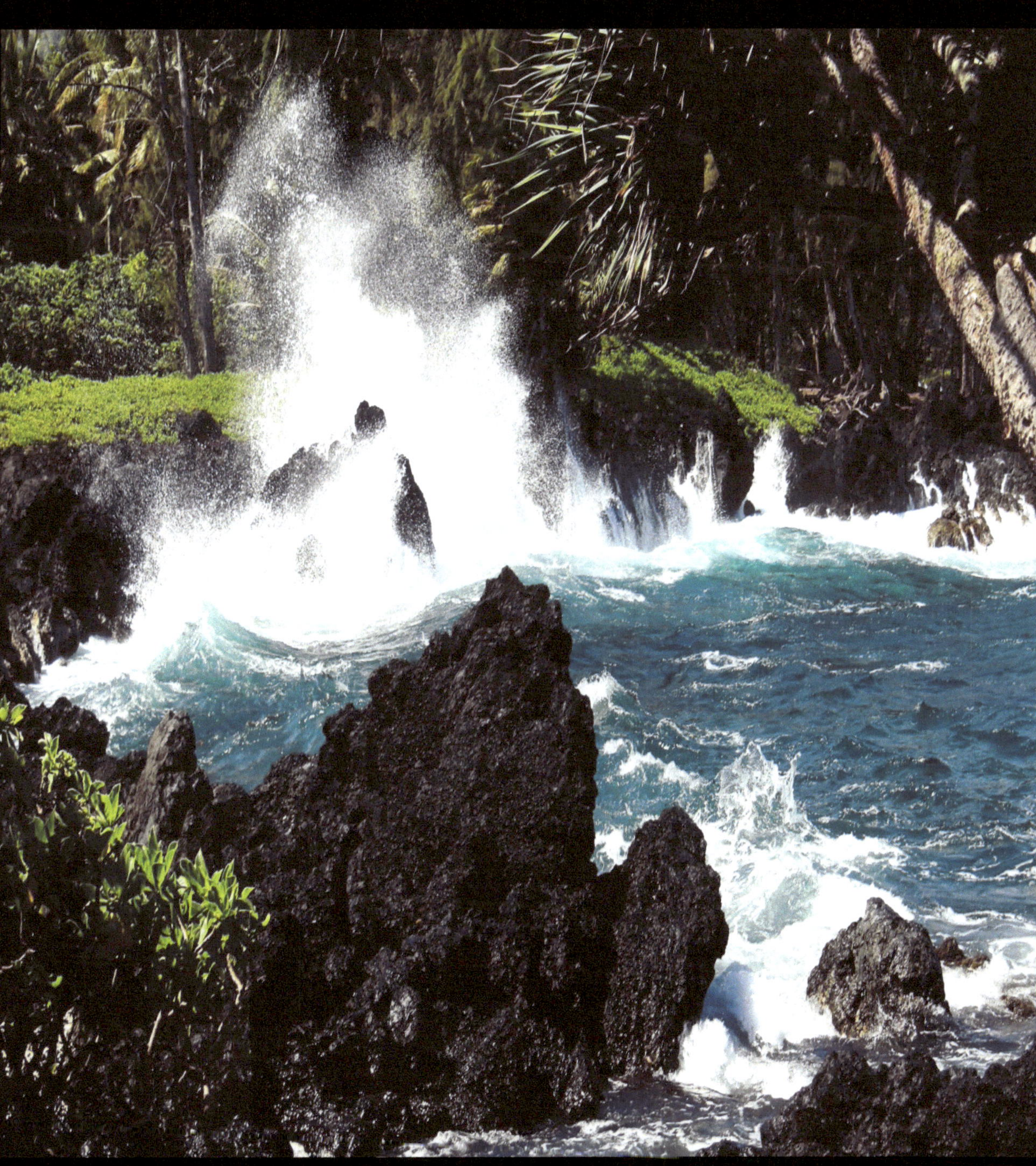

Island of Maui, Hawai'i

All the good I desire will come to me.

And by faith, I will do all that is necessary to achieve my goals.

My faith is the promise of great things to come.

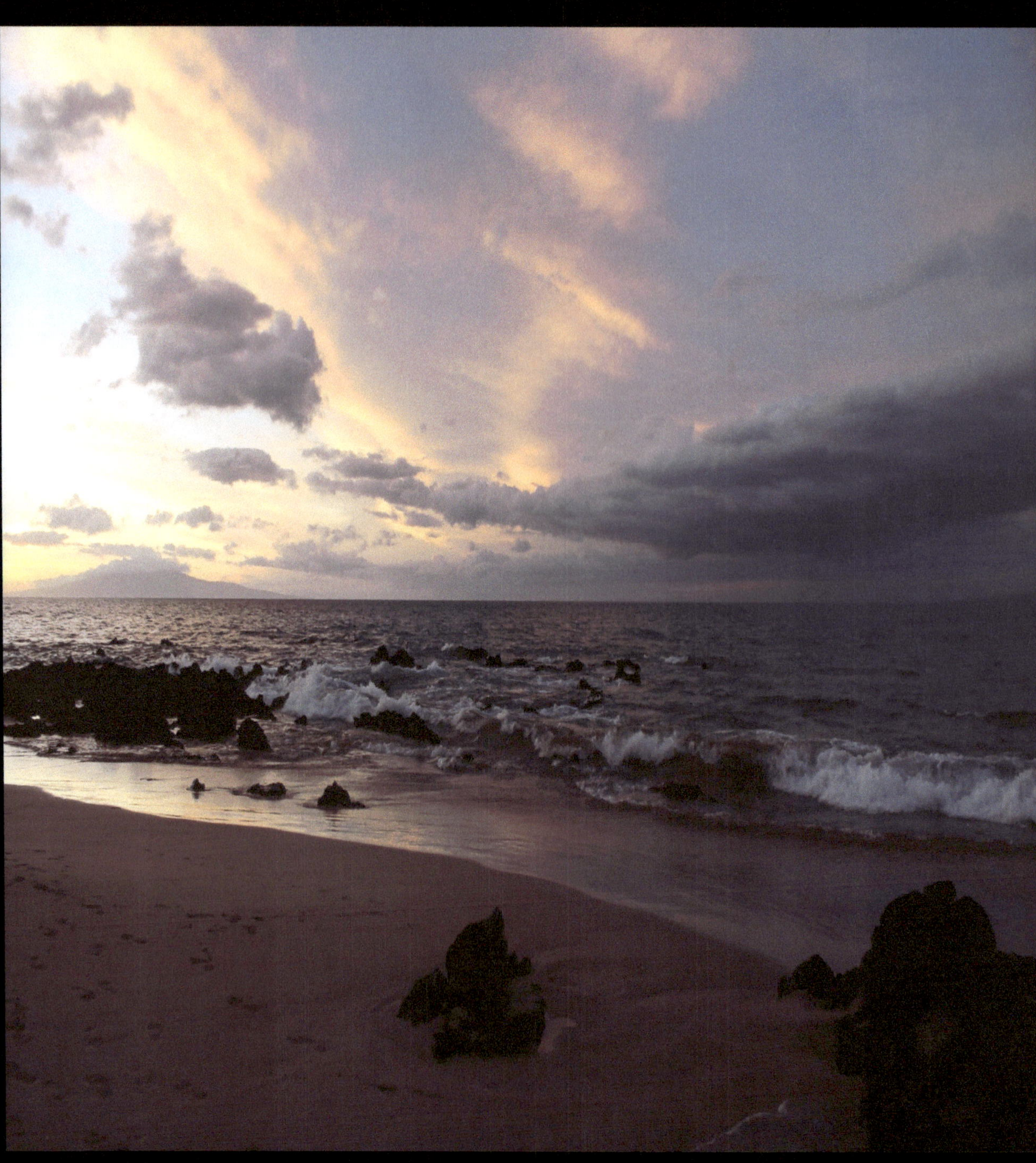

Chambre d'Amour - Anglet , France

I am free from my past and I choose to live without guilt, regret, or pain.

I will not go back, but shall move forward. And I leave all of yesterday in the hands of the Divine.

I stand on the promises of GOD.

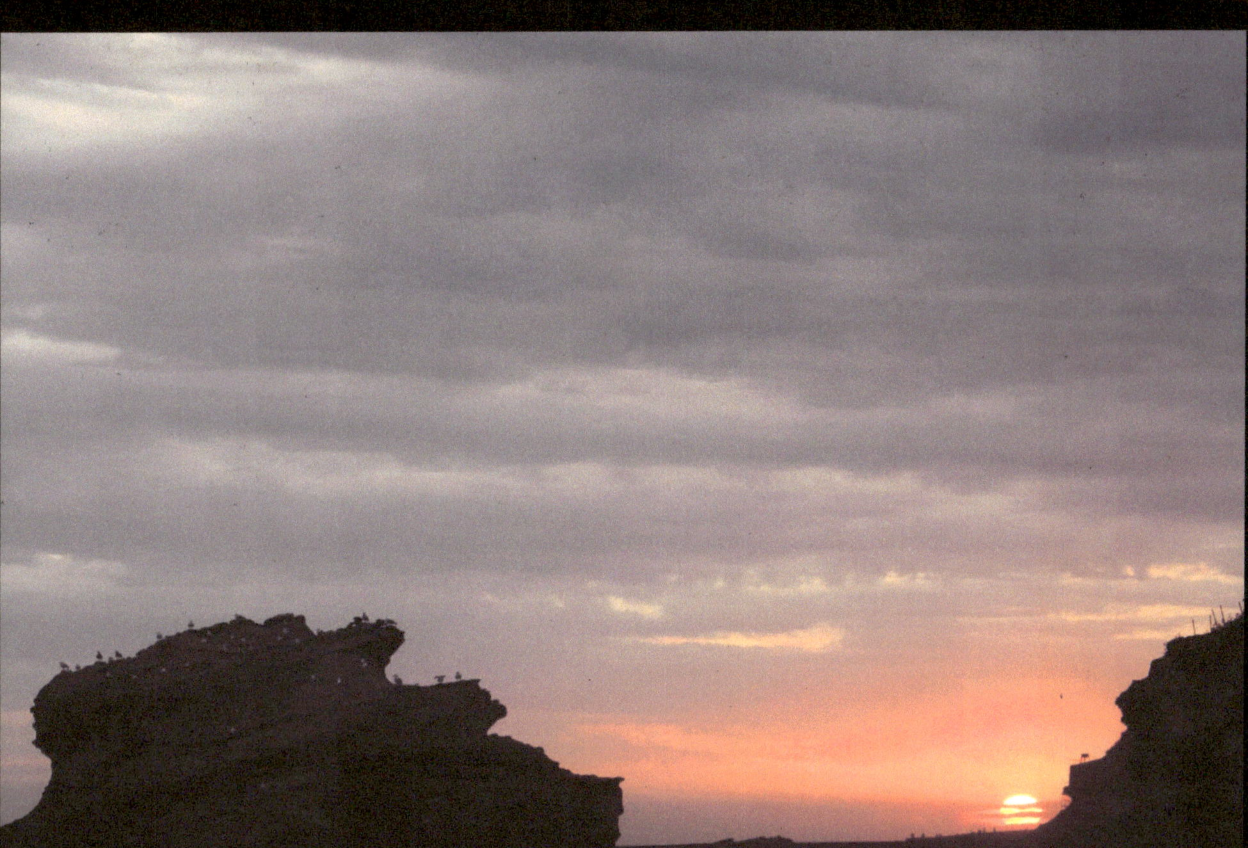

I let go of the pain of yesterday, I have no fear of tomorrow.
Today is a day of new beginnings. I expect great things.

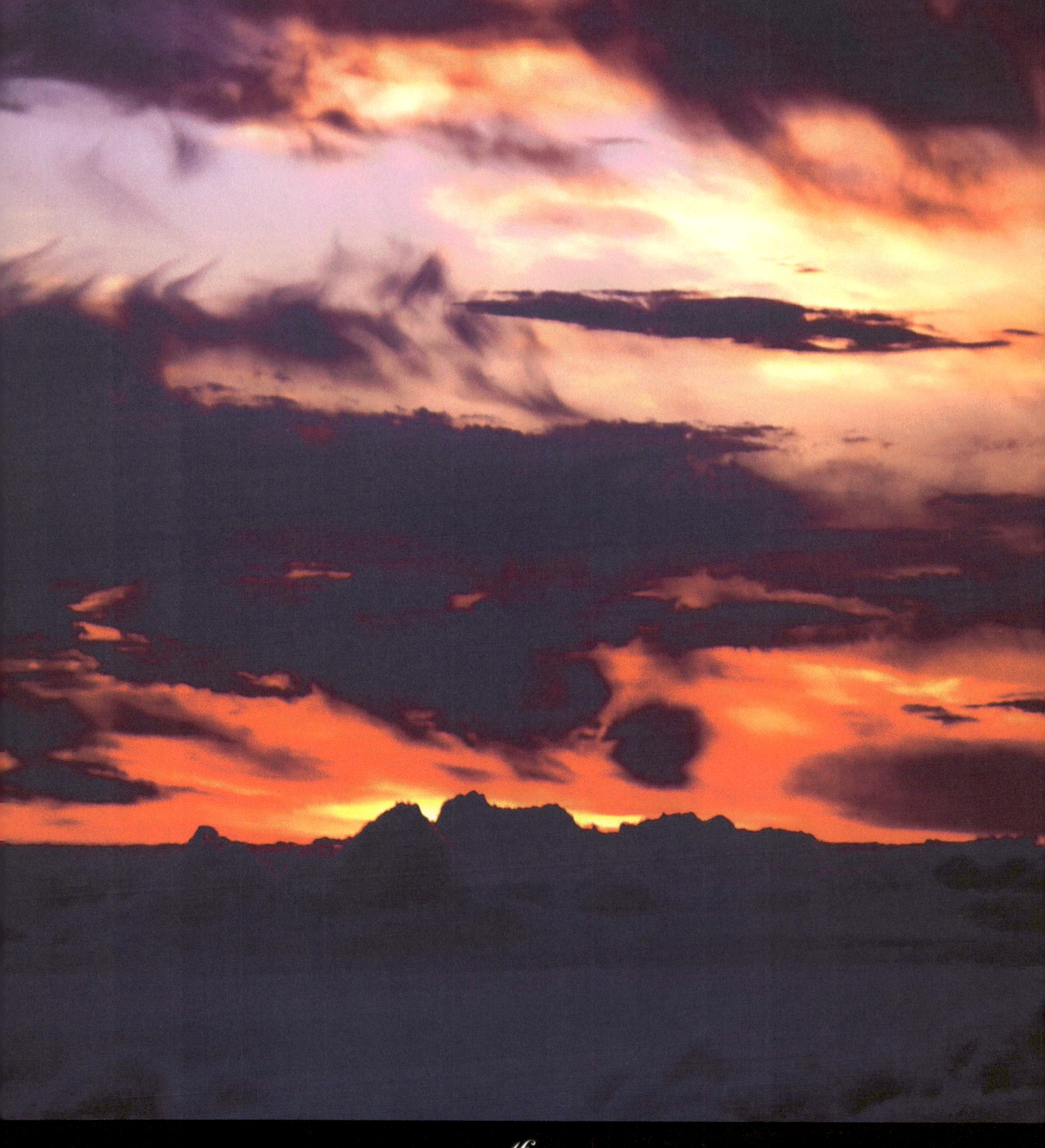

Sunrise at Haleakala State Park - Maui Hawai'i

I love me enough to accept my shortcomings as well as my greatest attributes.
I am truly a worthy human being and I am worthy of all good things,
not because I am perfect, but because I am loved by the Holy Divine.

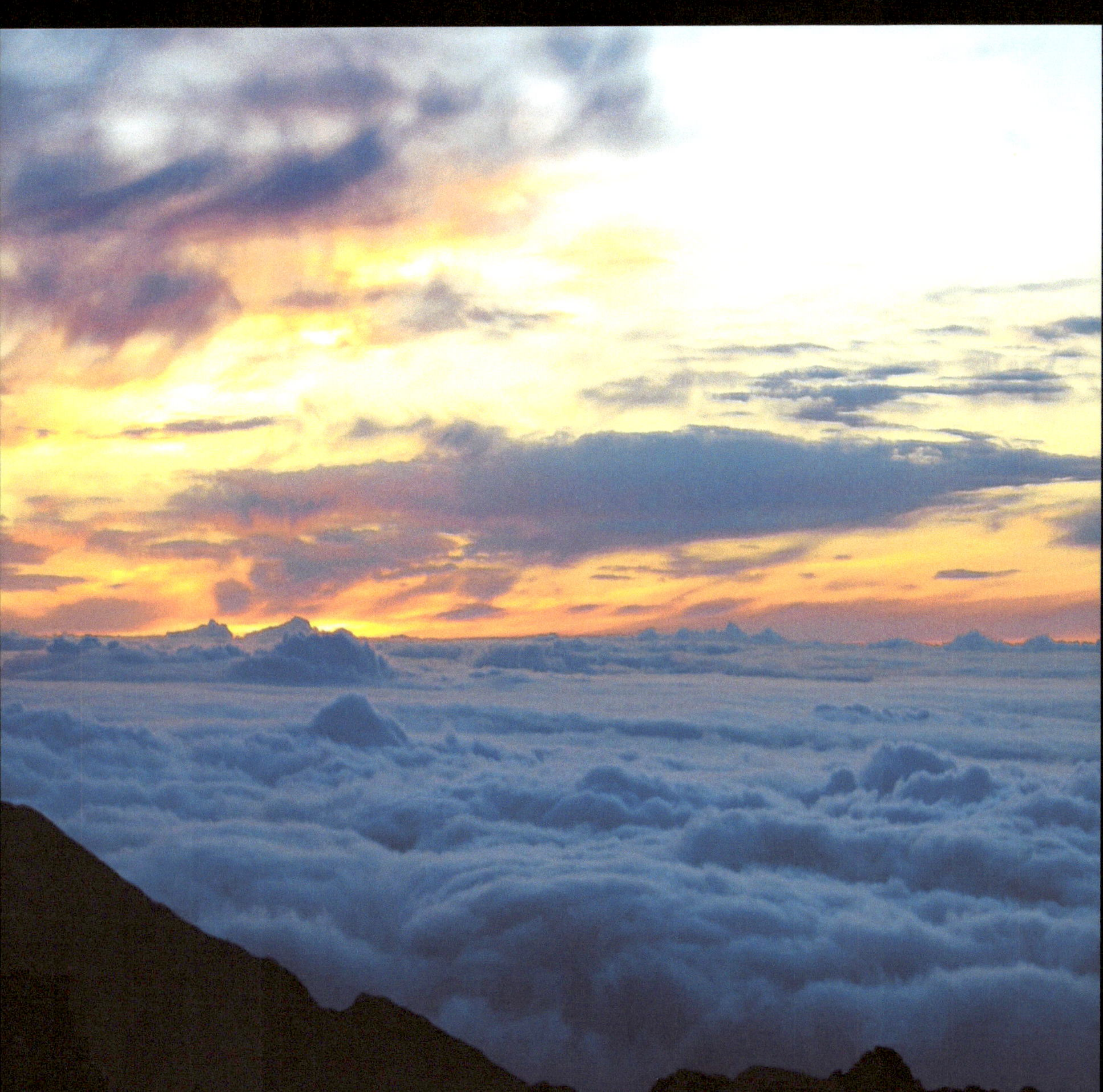

I will live my life according to what is right for me.

I am determined to be happy, to be prosperous, generous, loving, and kind.

I am determined to be me.

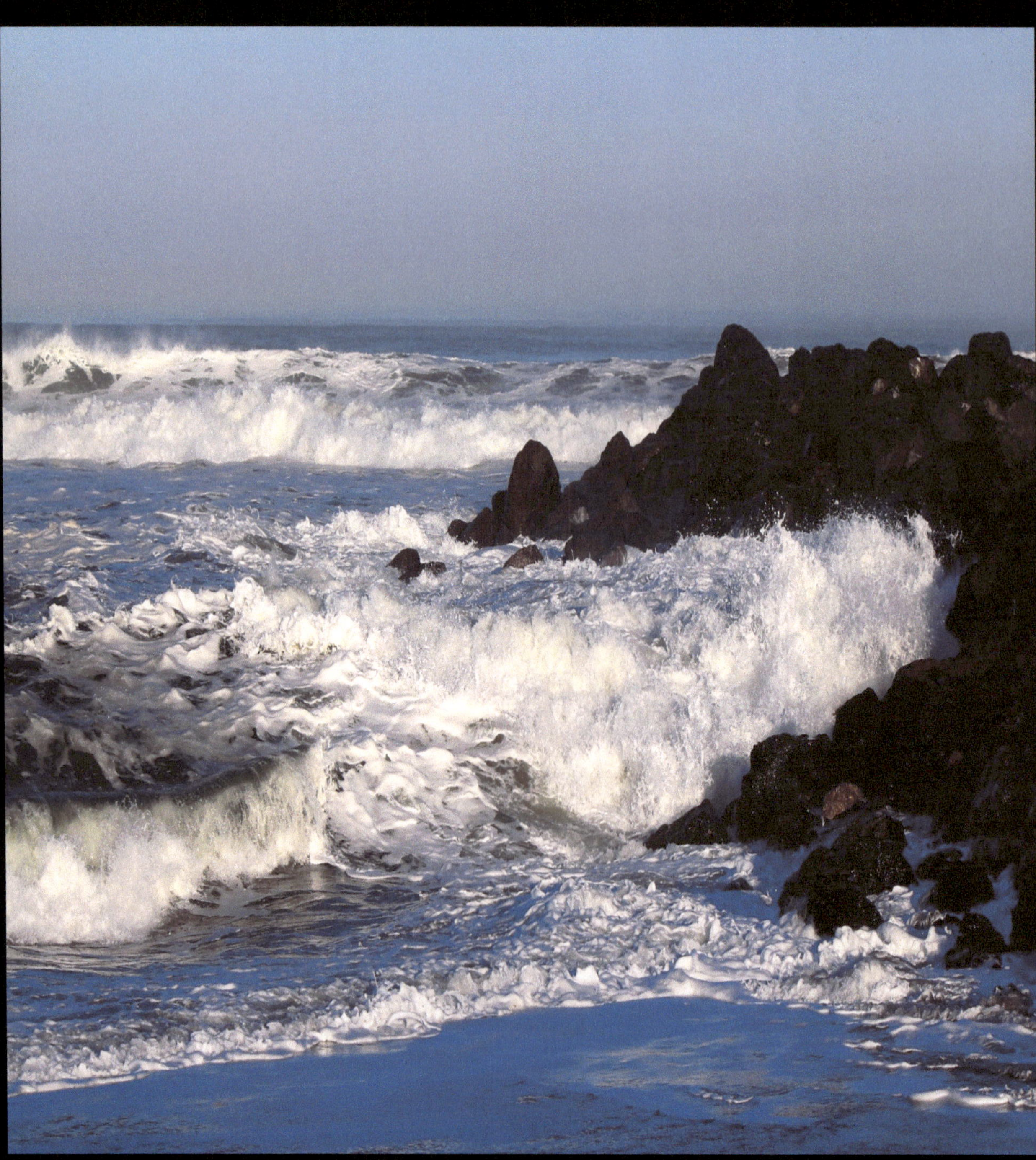

Chambre d'Amour - Anglet, France

I claim victory over everything
that prevents me from having a happy life.

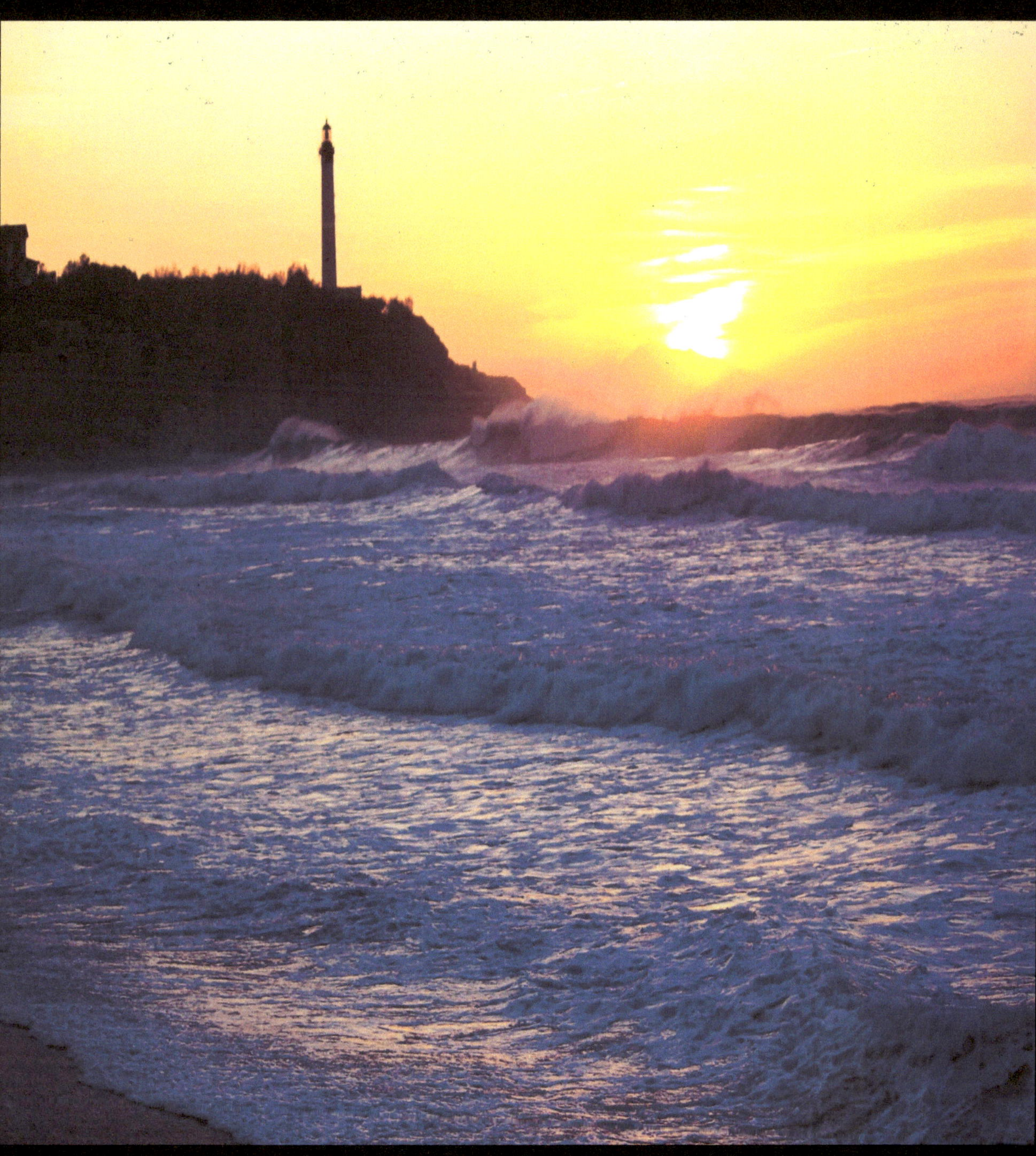

Chambre d'Amour - Anglet, France

I attract all things I need to my life and release all I do not.

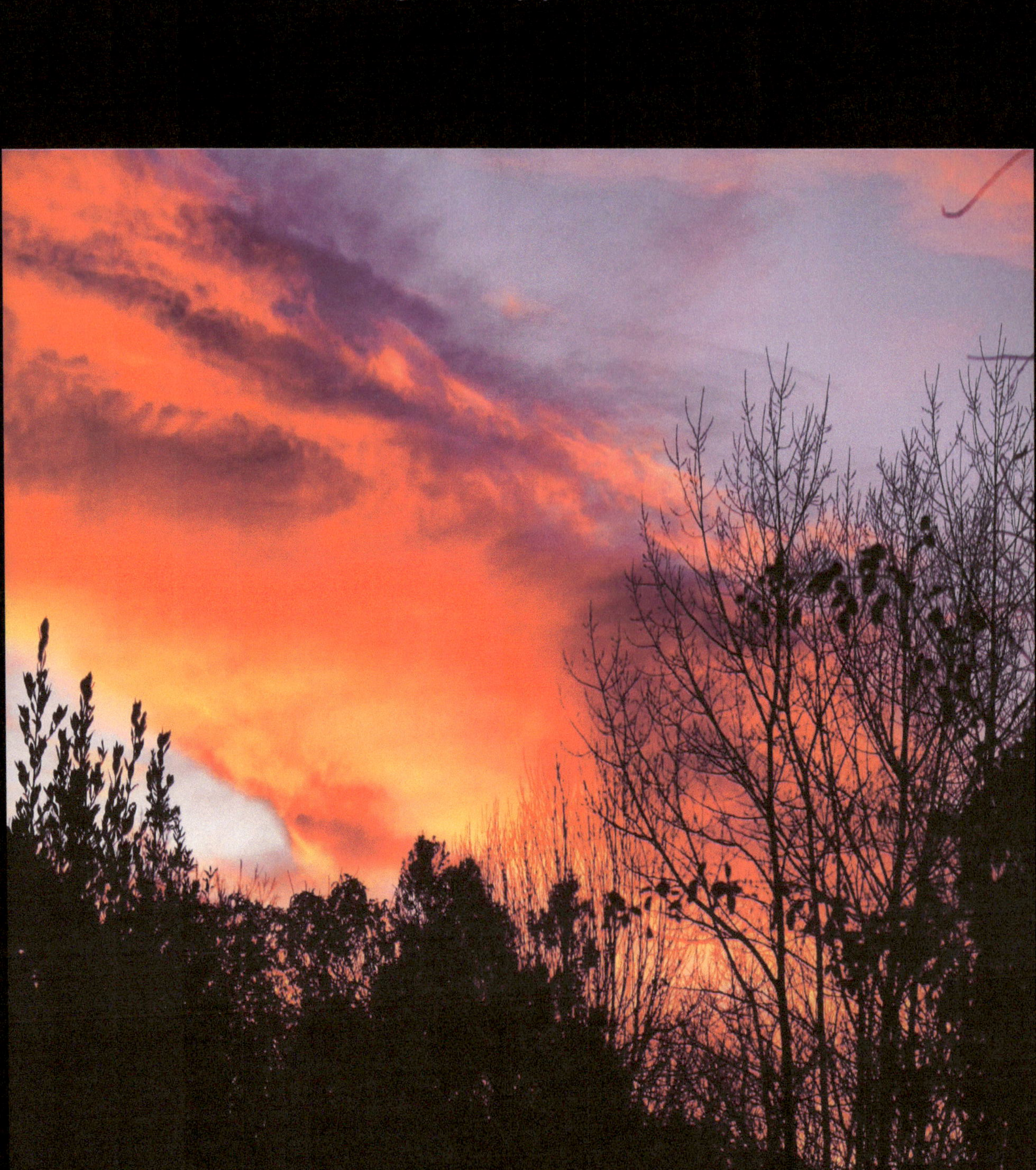

I put my mind on things that give me strength and the hopes that comfort me.

The past can no longer hurt me because I do not live there anymore.

I have moved on to my new home, and it is a place of peace.

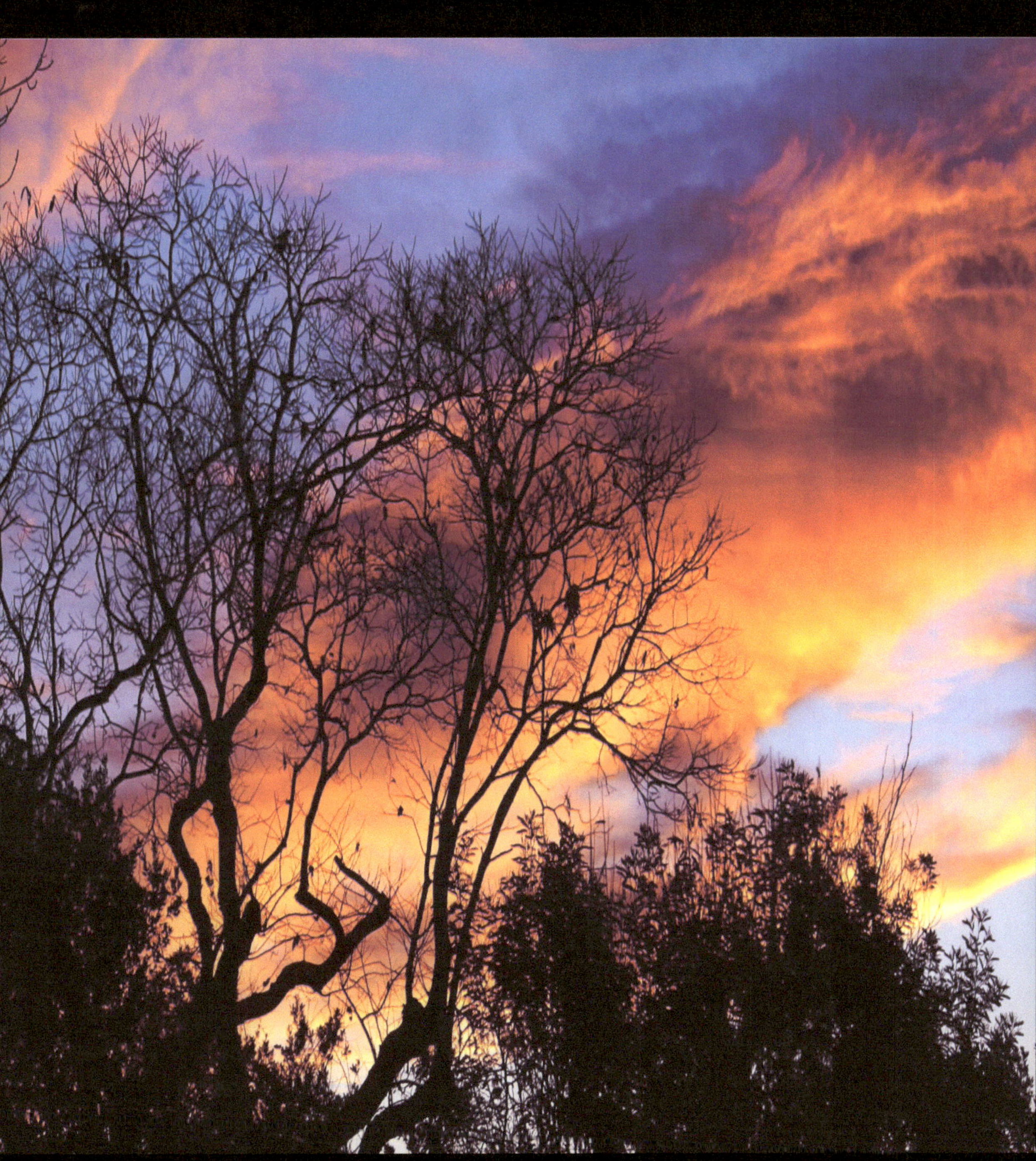

Morning Sky Cinq Cantons - Anglet , France

I invest in my possibility.
All I need to be already exists within me.

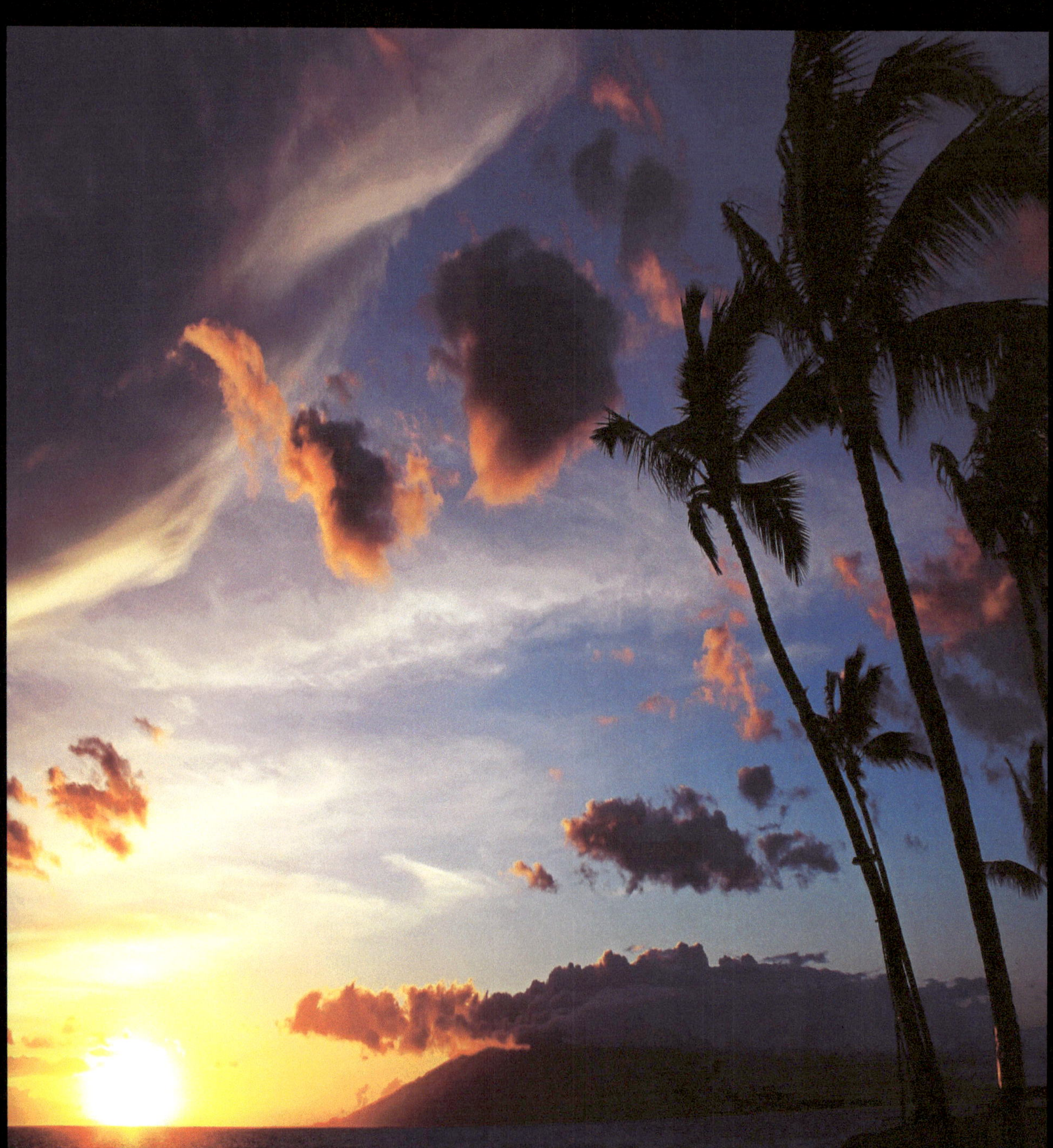

Kamaole Beach III - Maui, Hawai'i

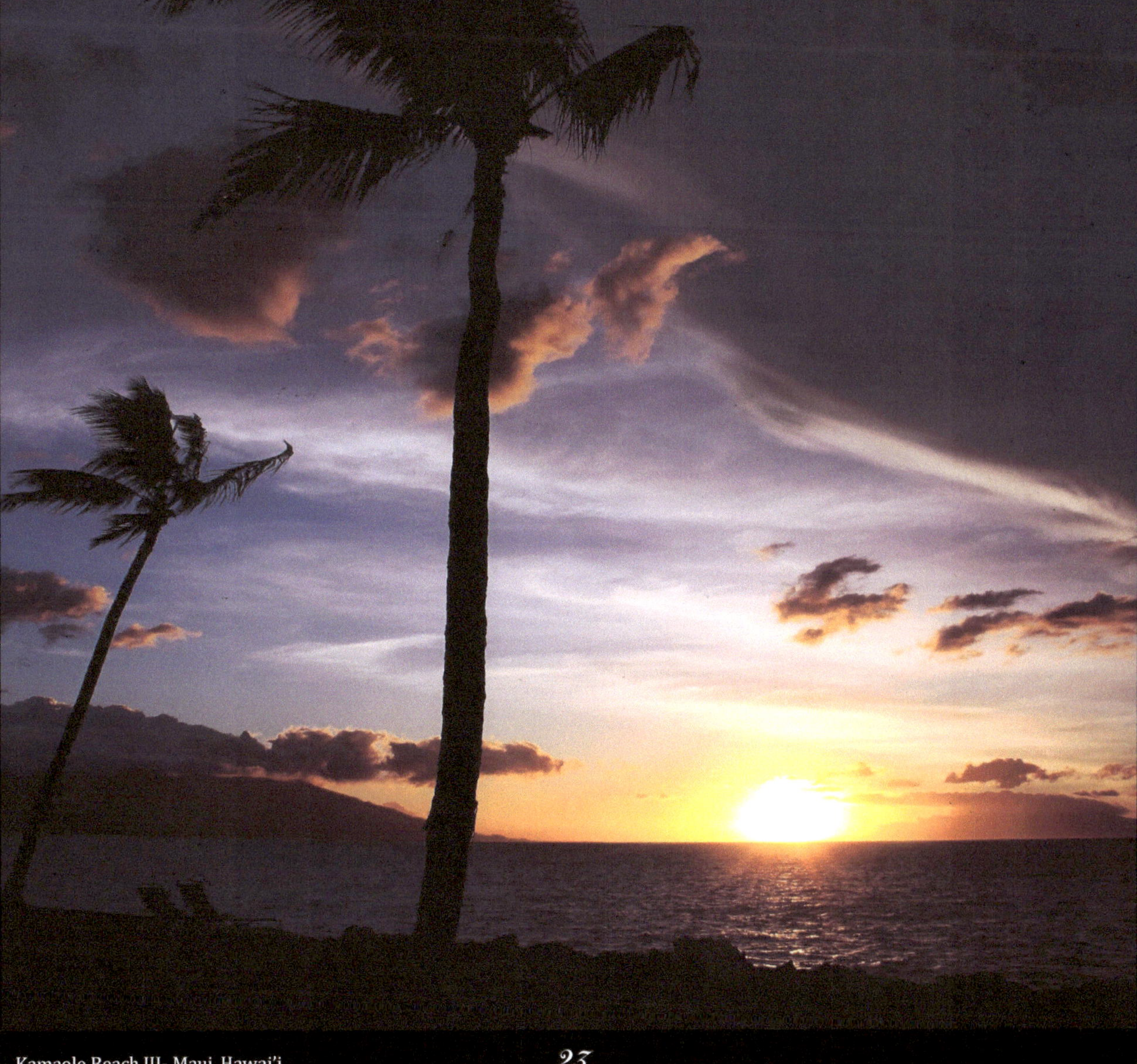

Kamaole Beach III- Maui, Hawai'i

I am made from love. And true love surrounds me in every way.

I am never without love, because love dwells within me.

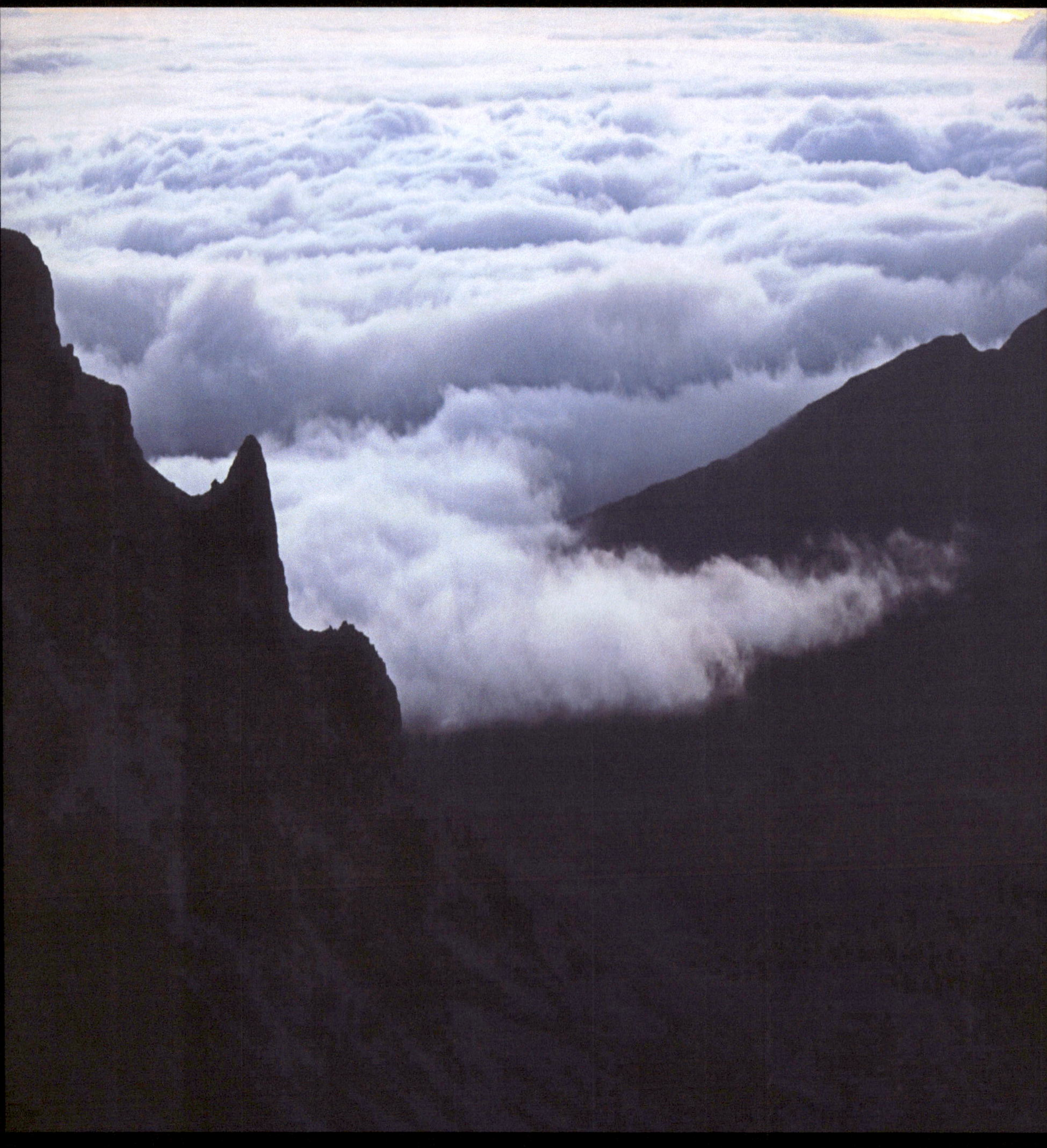

Haleakala National Park- Maui, Hawai'i

I will endure the shifts of the seasons and tremors of the land. I am deeply rooted in Divine wisdom, power, and love.. I will not be made to fall down in the face of adversity.

I am strong, courageous, and believing.

I shall not be moved.

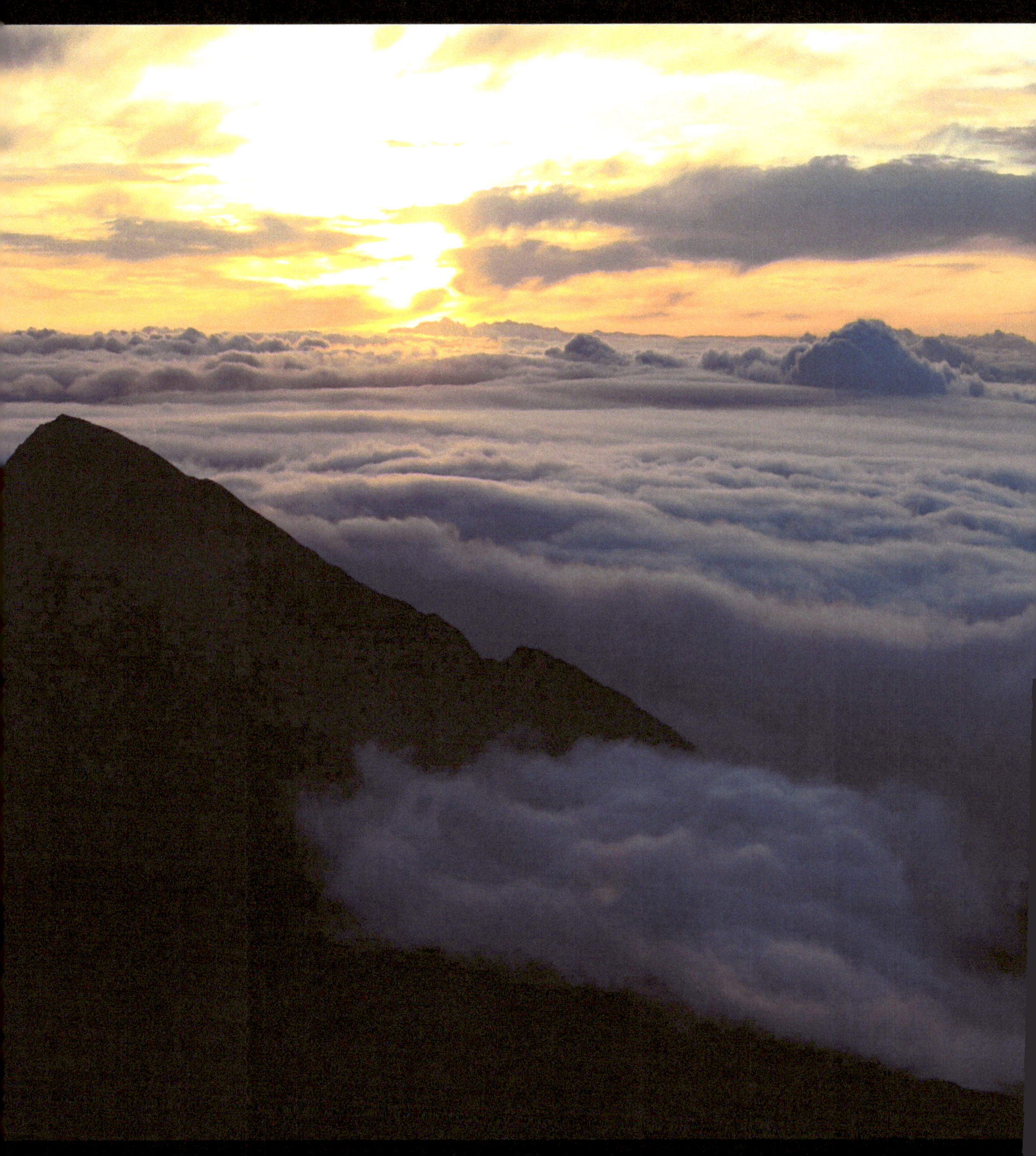

Sunrise - Haleakala State Park - Maui, Hawai'i

I am no one's victim. I take full responsibility for my life and I rise to the occasion to rebuild it if necessary.

I may bend, but I will not break. I will hold on to my faith and will endure.

I am like a tree deeply rooted in faith. I am strong, and I am not afraid.

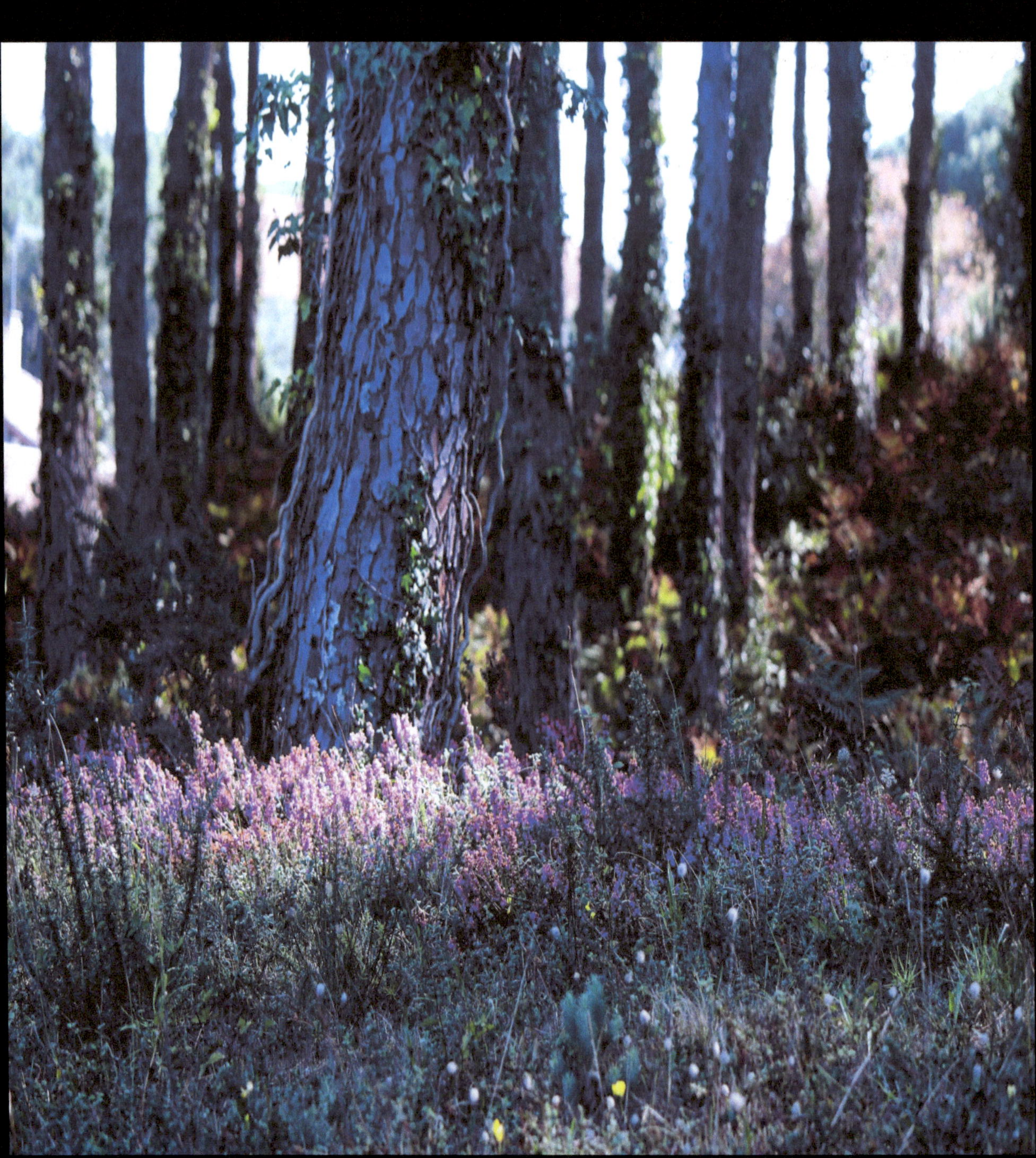

Forêt de Chiberta - Anglet, France

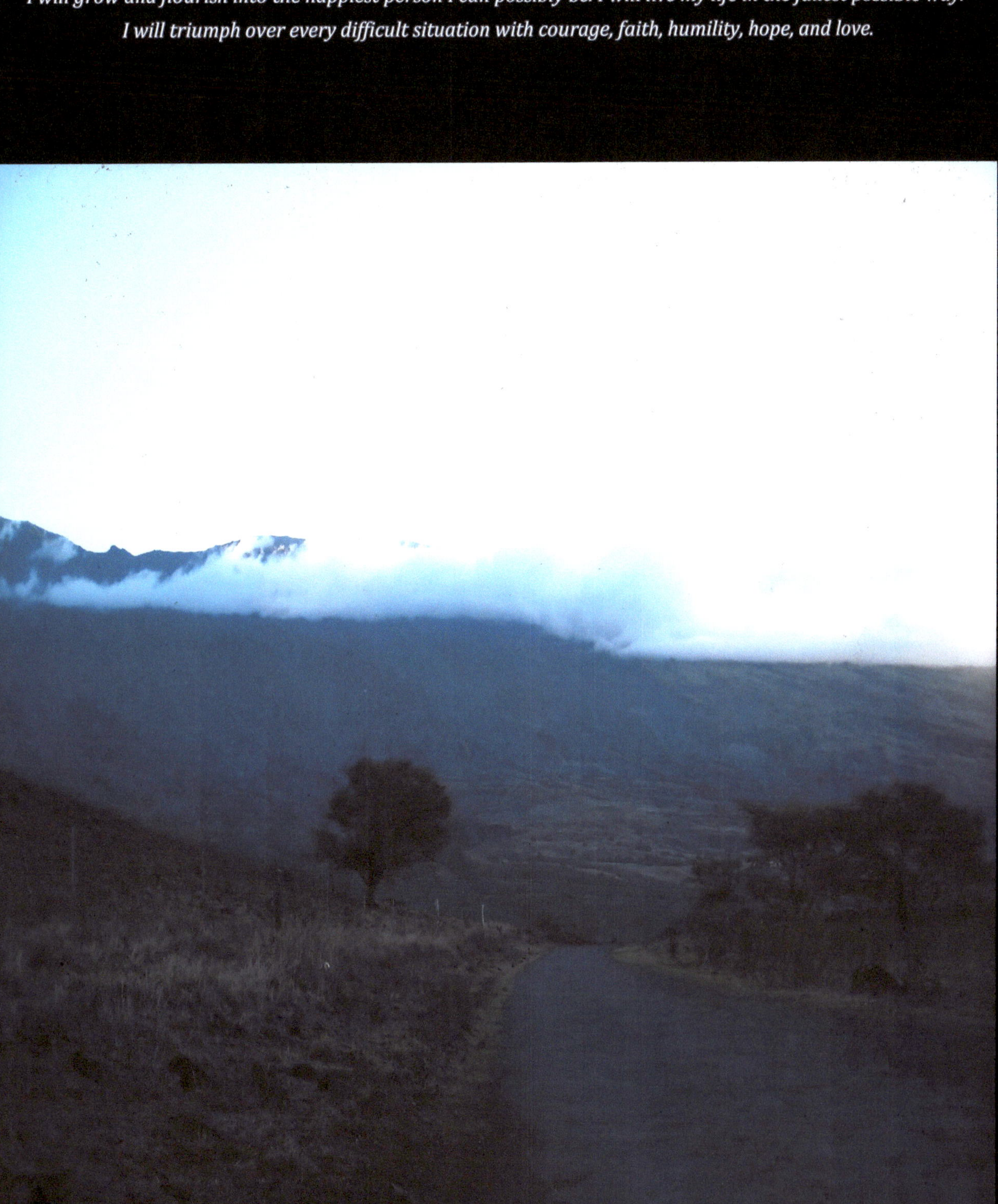
I will grow and flourish into the happiest person I can possibly be. I will live my life in the fullest possible way.
I will triumph over every difficult situation with courage, faith, humility, hope, and love.

I have hope and hope has me.

I am holding on to what keeps me strong.

And even if I grow weary, I know that my problems will be overcome.

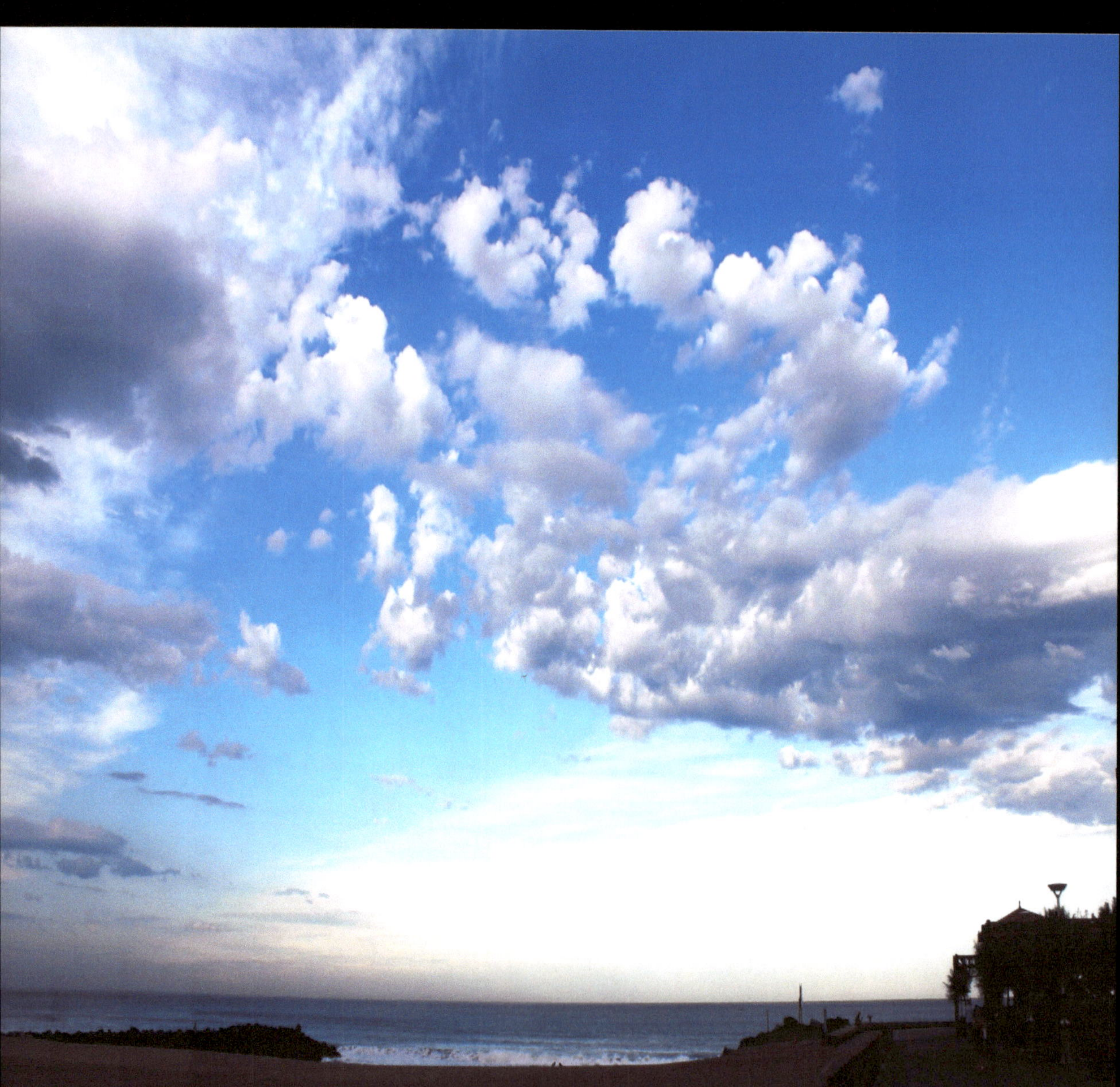

My worth is not determined by how much I own or I much I owe. Nor is it diminished by broken heart, a disappointment, or loss. My worth is completely Divinely given and cannot be taken away. I am as precious as life itself.

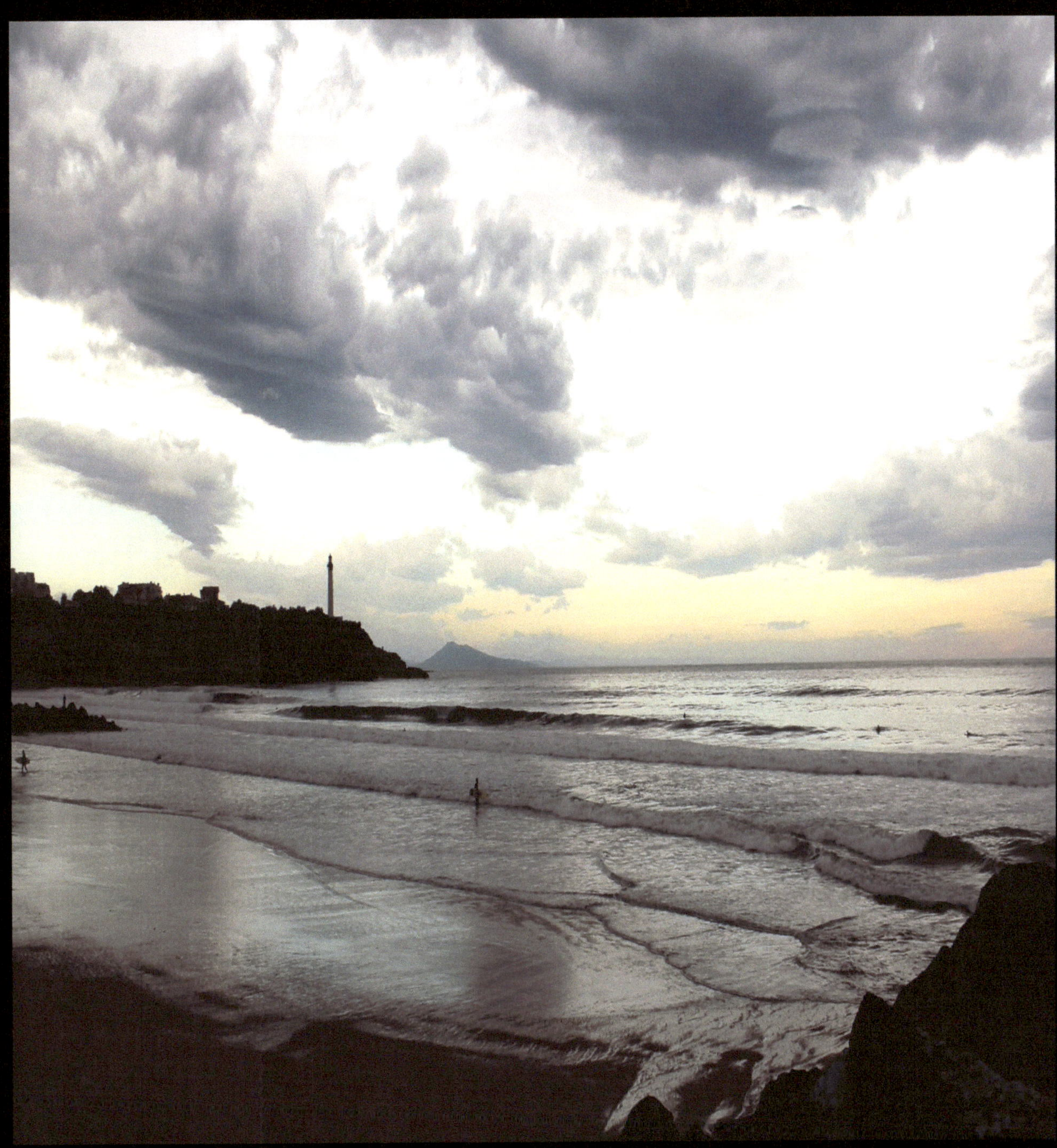

Chambre d'Amour - Anglet, France

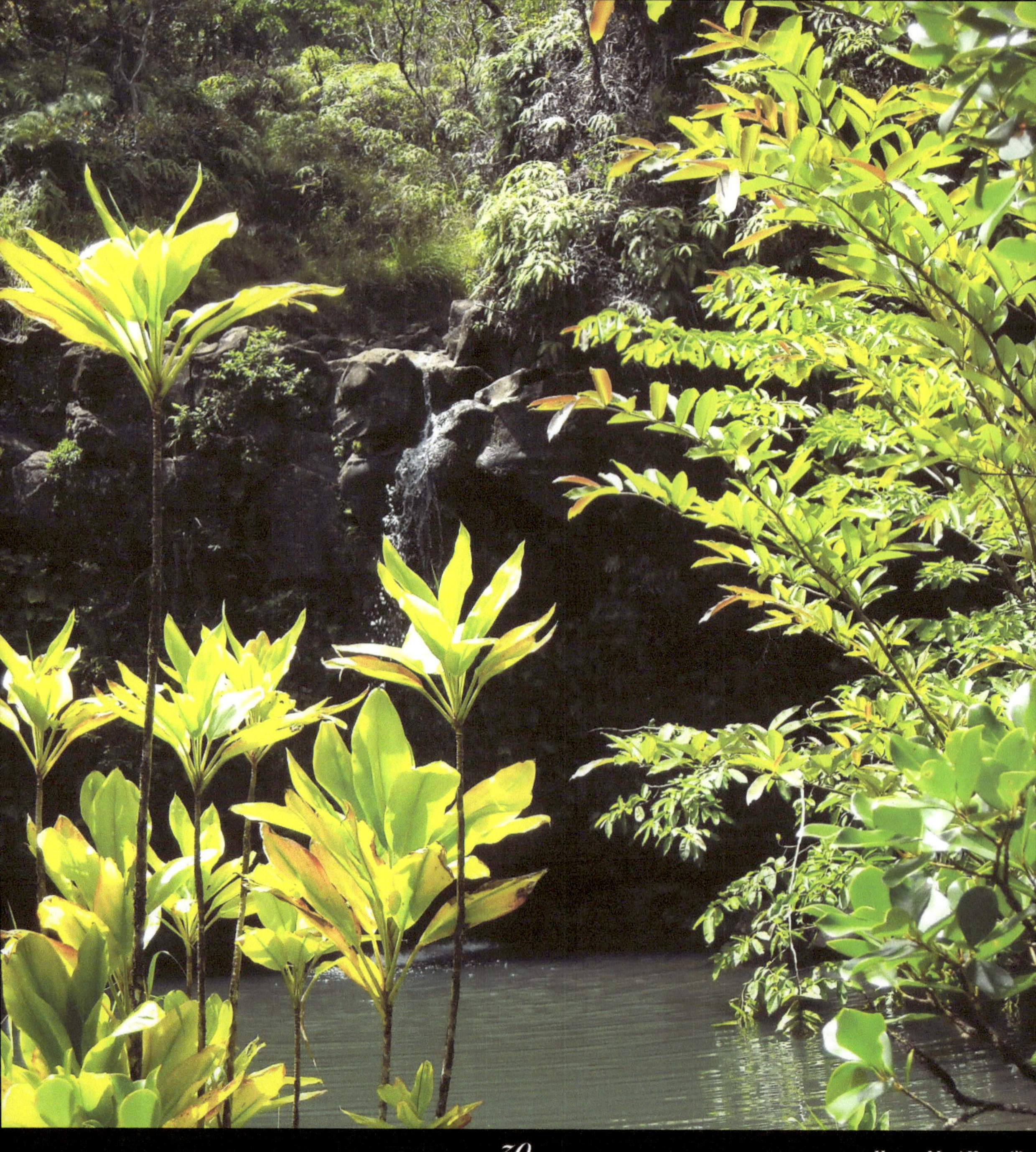

I choose to invest in my possibility.
I will not deny my gifts, talents, or abilities.
I believe in me; because I believe in GOD.

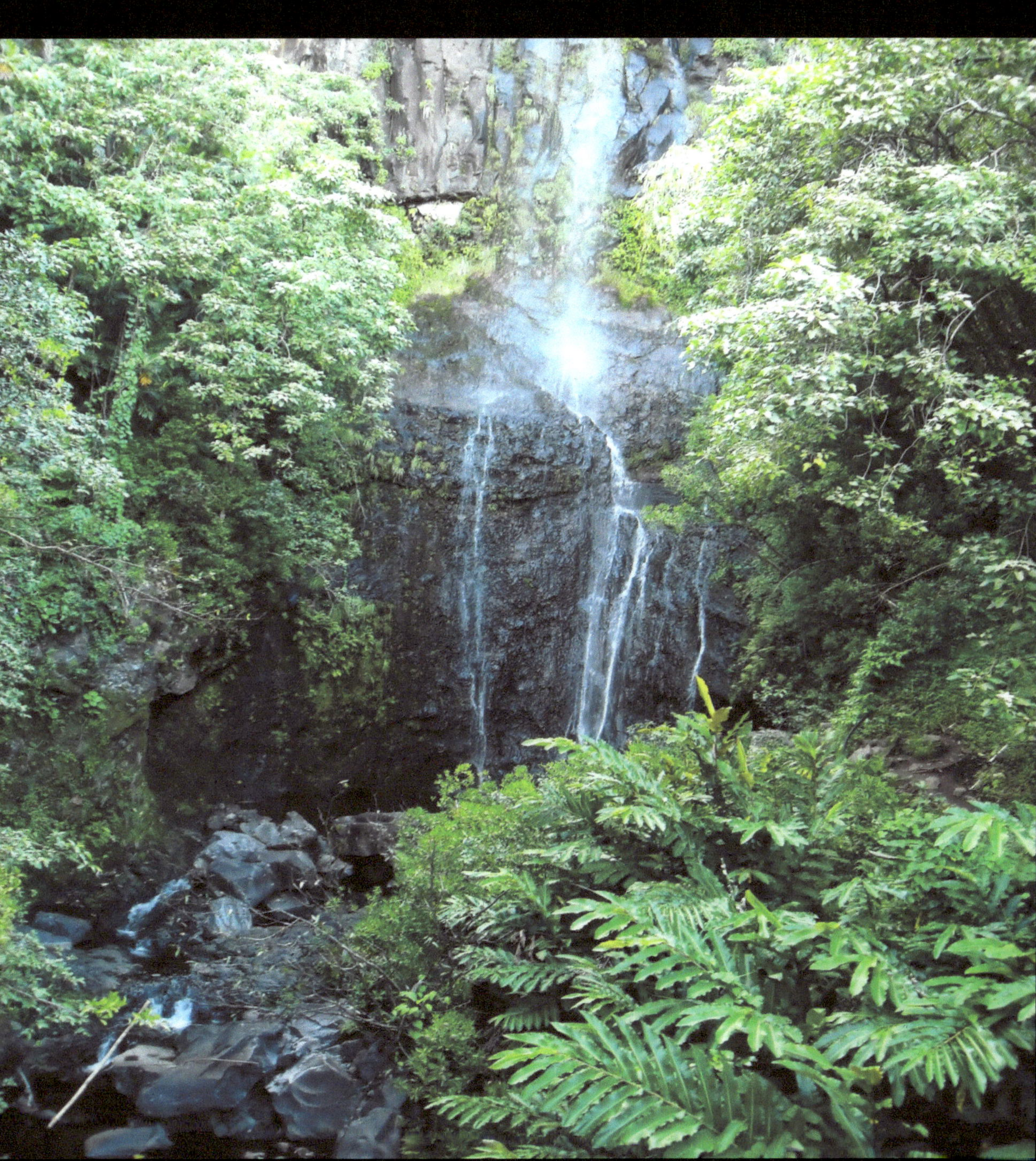

Road to Hana - Maui Hawai'i

I am never lost. I am following a Divine plan.

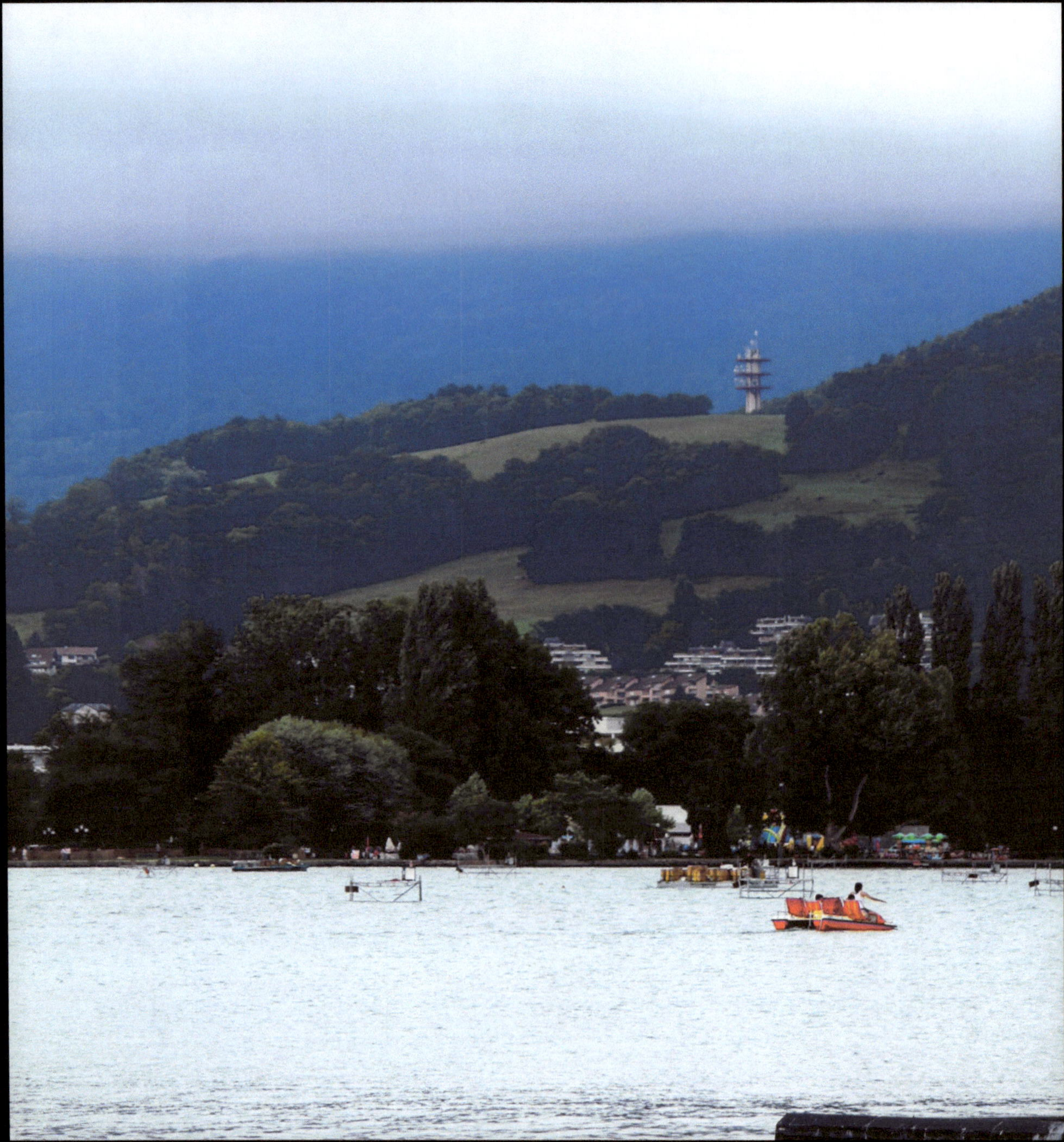

Lac Annecy - Annecy, France

I release my worries to the Divine, so that I am free.

I will do what needs to be done and focus on the now and not the why.

I will rise above all my circumstances.

And I believe in my heart that I shall prevail.

I hope, I act, and I pray.

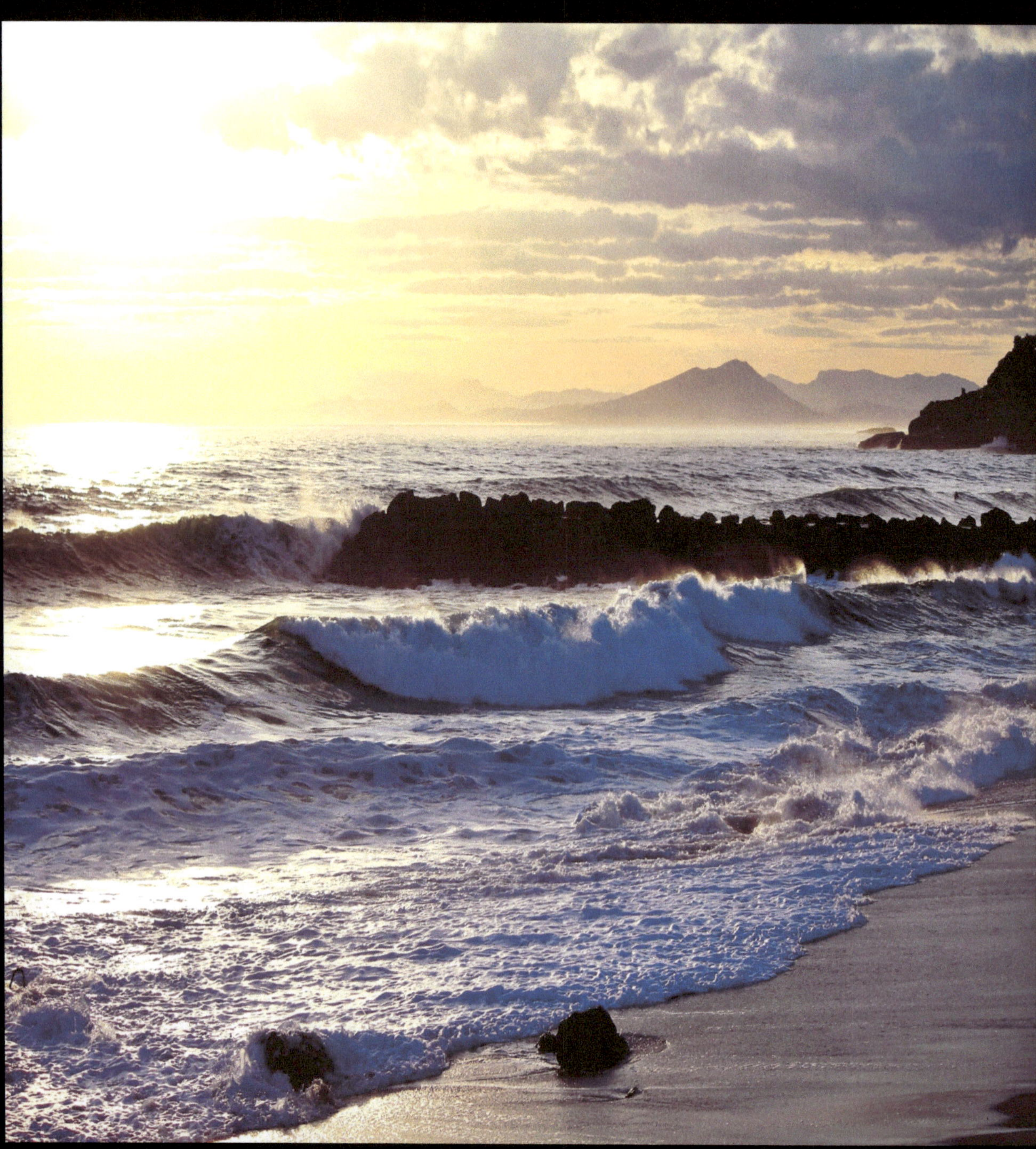

Chambre d'Amour - Anglet, France

I thank GOD for everything I have; every moment I ever laughed and every second I ever loved. For every hug and comfort I have received, and for every kind word or affection shown my way, I am forever grateful.

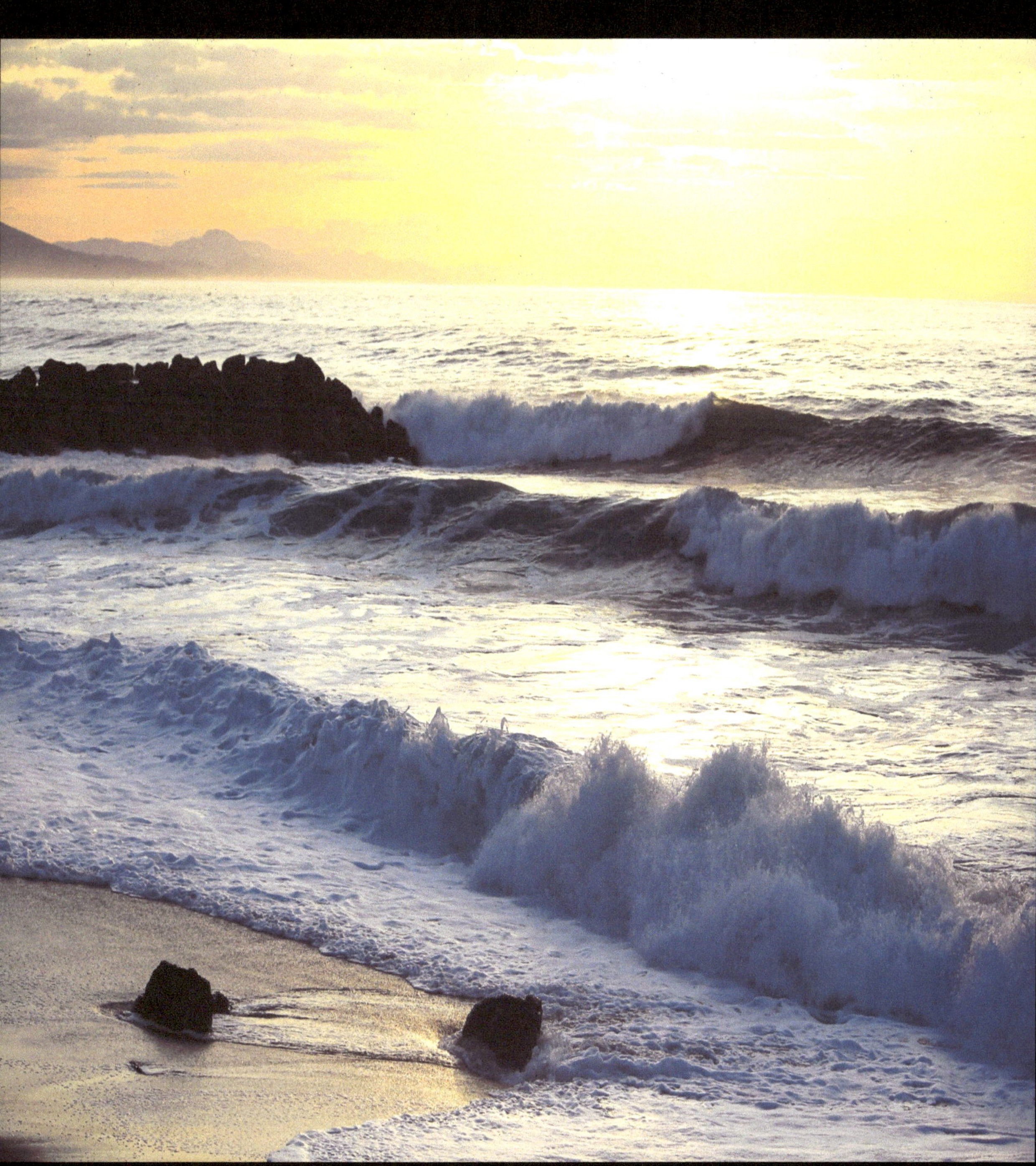

Chambre d'Amour - Anglet, France

If they speak to me with unkind words, or accuse me to break my heart. I will not listen.
There is nothing they can say to me that will bring me down.
I stand tall in the face of adversity for I know who I am.
And I am worthy of love.

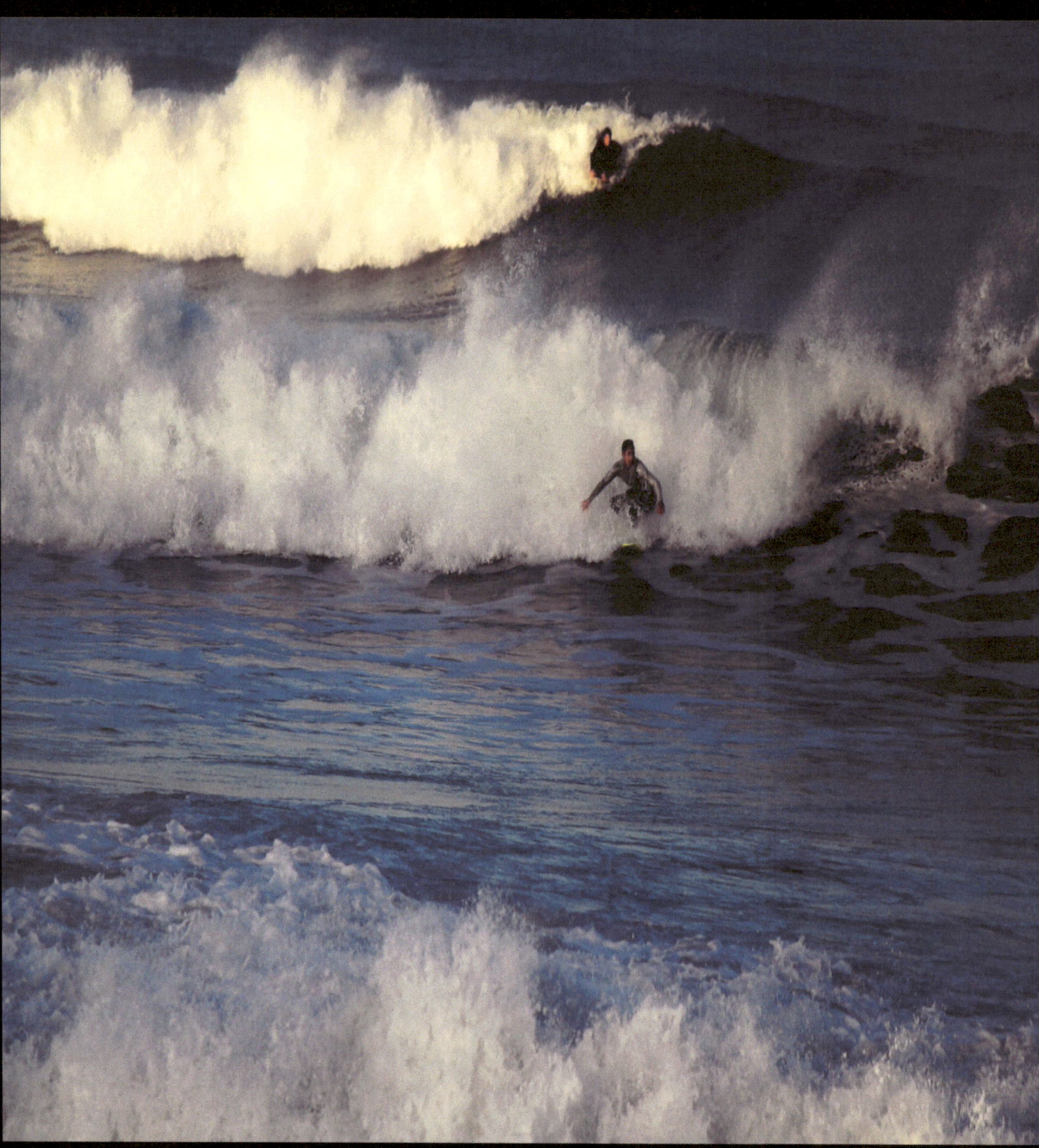

Chambre d'Amour - Anglet, France

Every adversity I face is a testimony to my courage and strength.

And every hardship I endure only makes me stronger.

I am holding on to the hand of GOD, and faith shall guide me and give me the courage to stand.

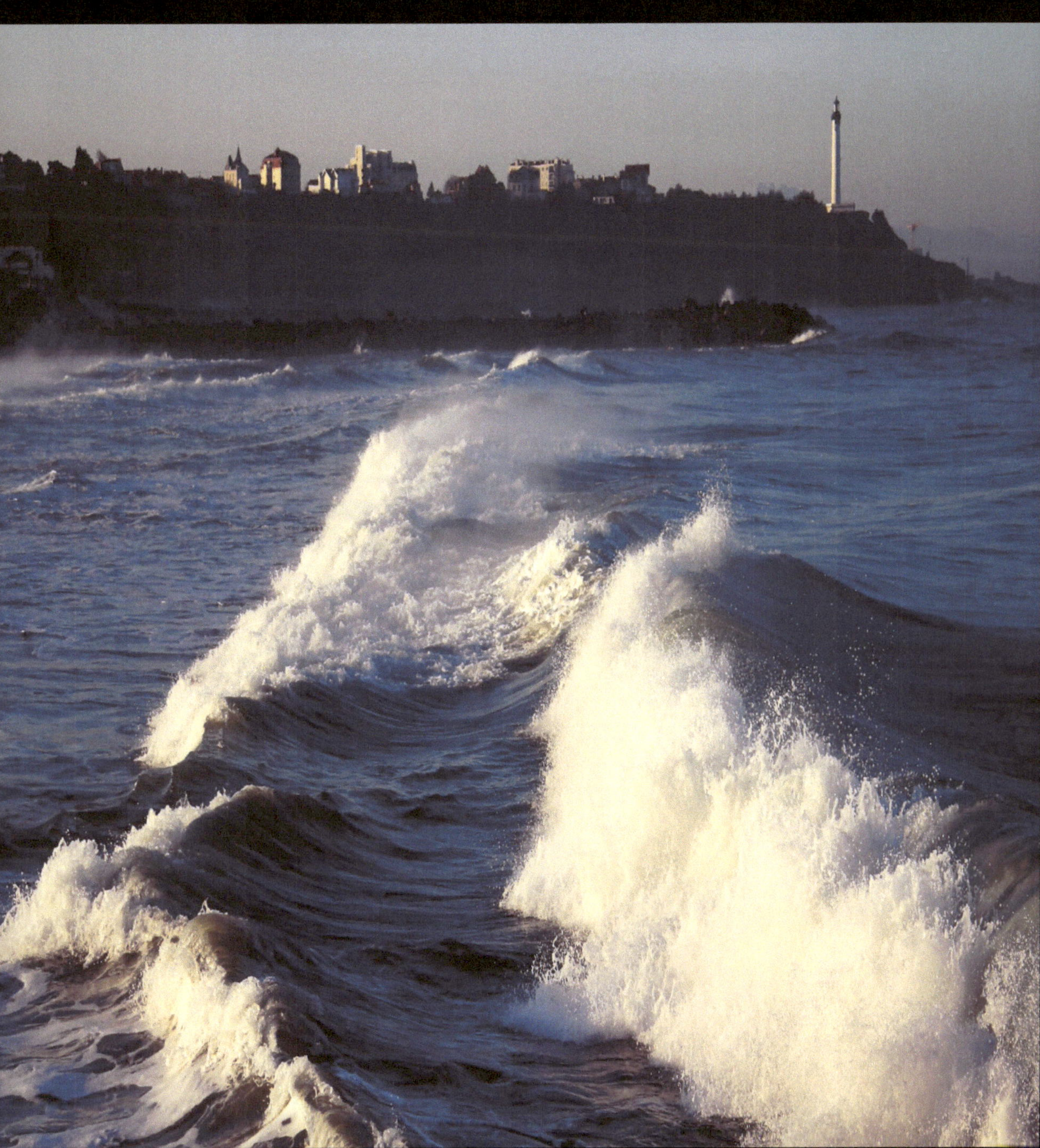

Chambre d'Amour - Anglet, France

I choose to focus on what is good, what is loving, what is prosperous, and what brings me joy. I will no longer allow worry to enter my mind.

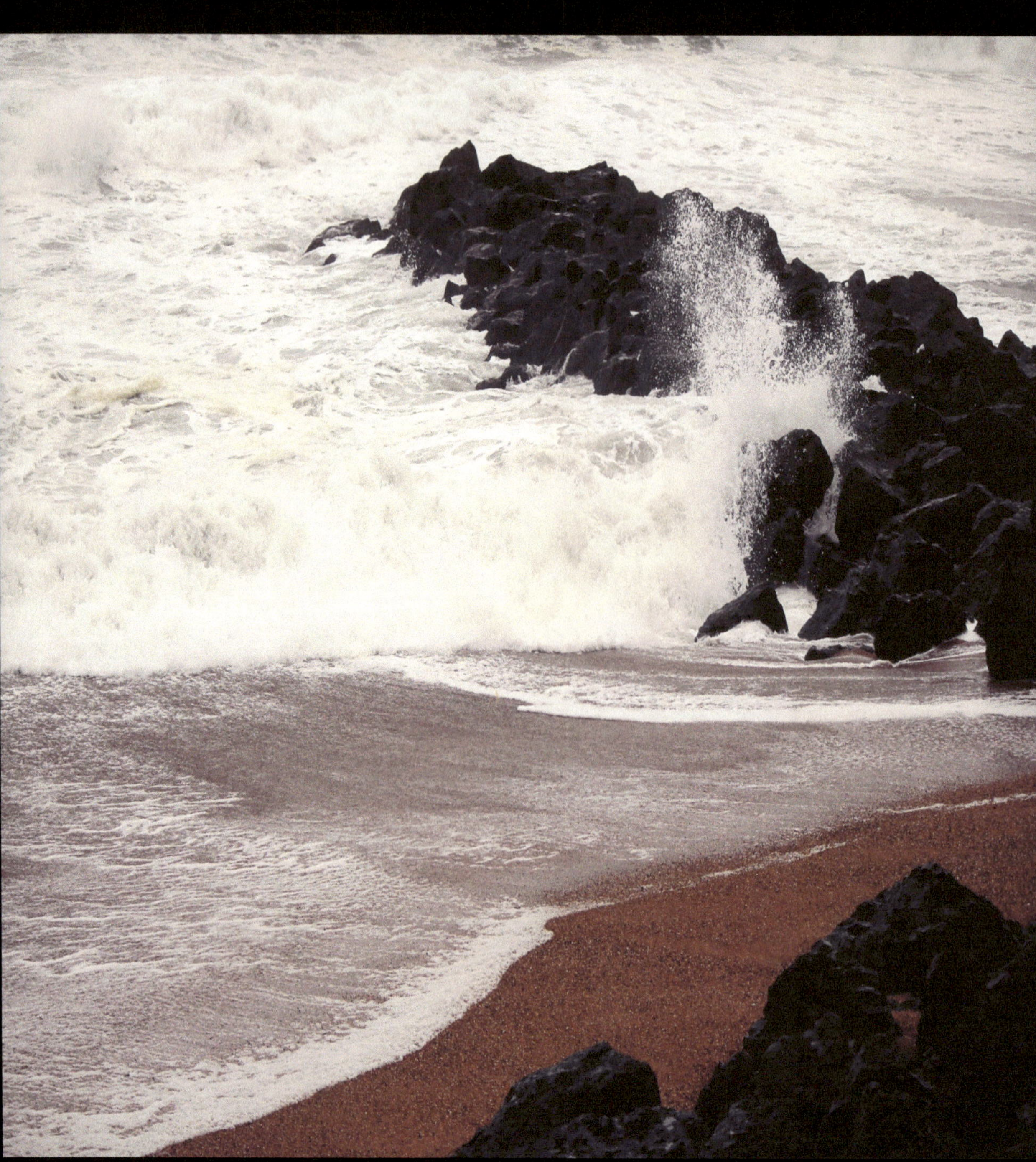

Pays Basque - Anglet, France

I Am Prosperous. I Am Wise. I Am Faithful. I Am Courageous. I Am Strong. I Am Confident. I am Intelligent. I am Fearless. I am Positive. I am Determined. I am Capable. I am Generous. I am Giving. I am Trustworthy. I am Patient. I am Decisive. I am Talented. I Am Secure. I Am Kind. I Am Loving. I am Happy. I am Powerful. I am Complete. I am Focused. I am Free. I am Loved. I am Me.

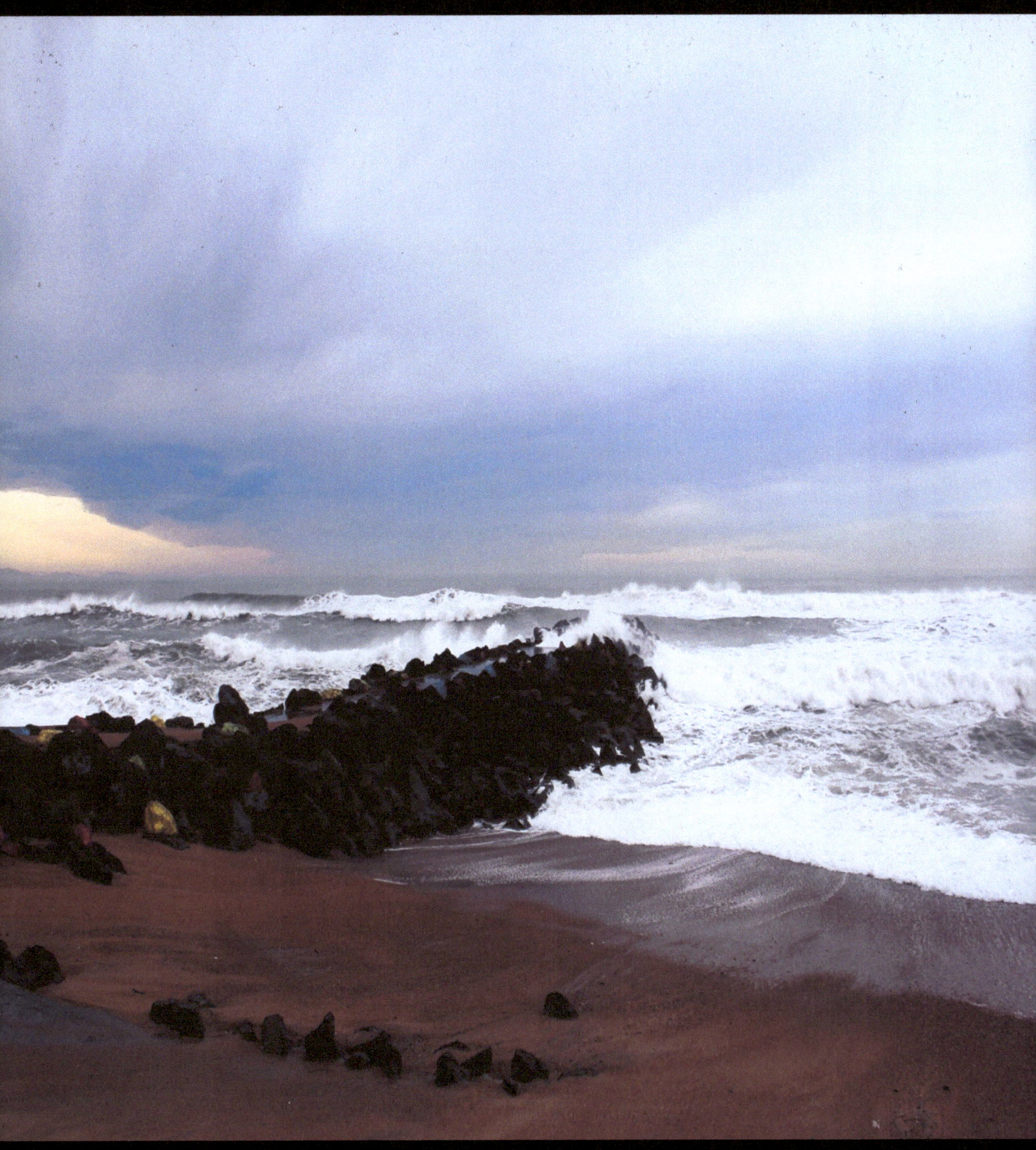

Chambre d'Amour – Anglet, France

The power to manifest is within me…
I was given the power to make it the day I was born.
I claim it. I believe it. I have it. It is done.

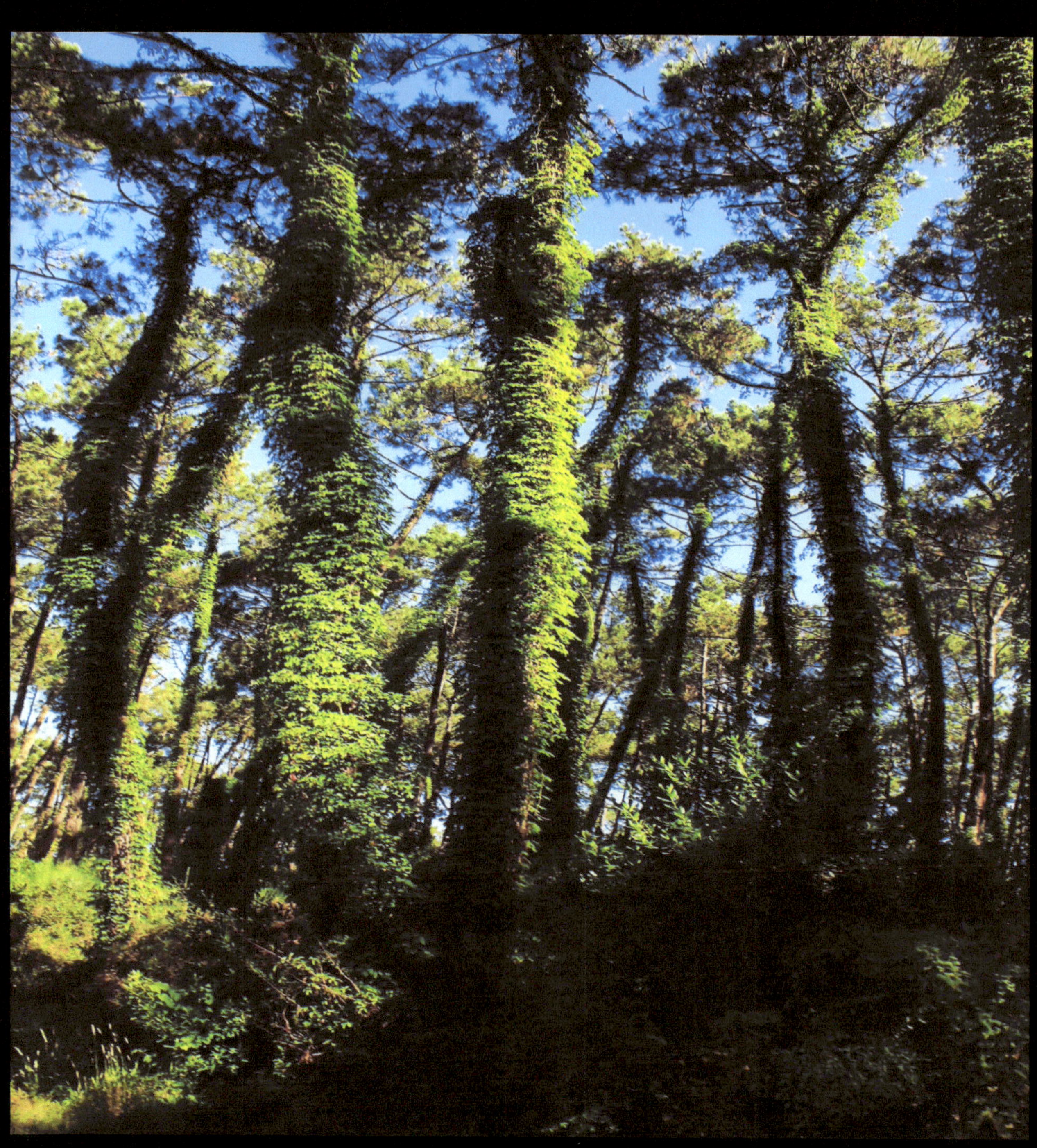

Forêt de Chiberta - Anglet, France

*Everything that I have lived, I have already overcome. There is nothing that I have done that the Divine has not already forgiven me for because I am deeply loved. And because of this,
I will not be defeated,nor will I grieve. I will be strong.*

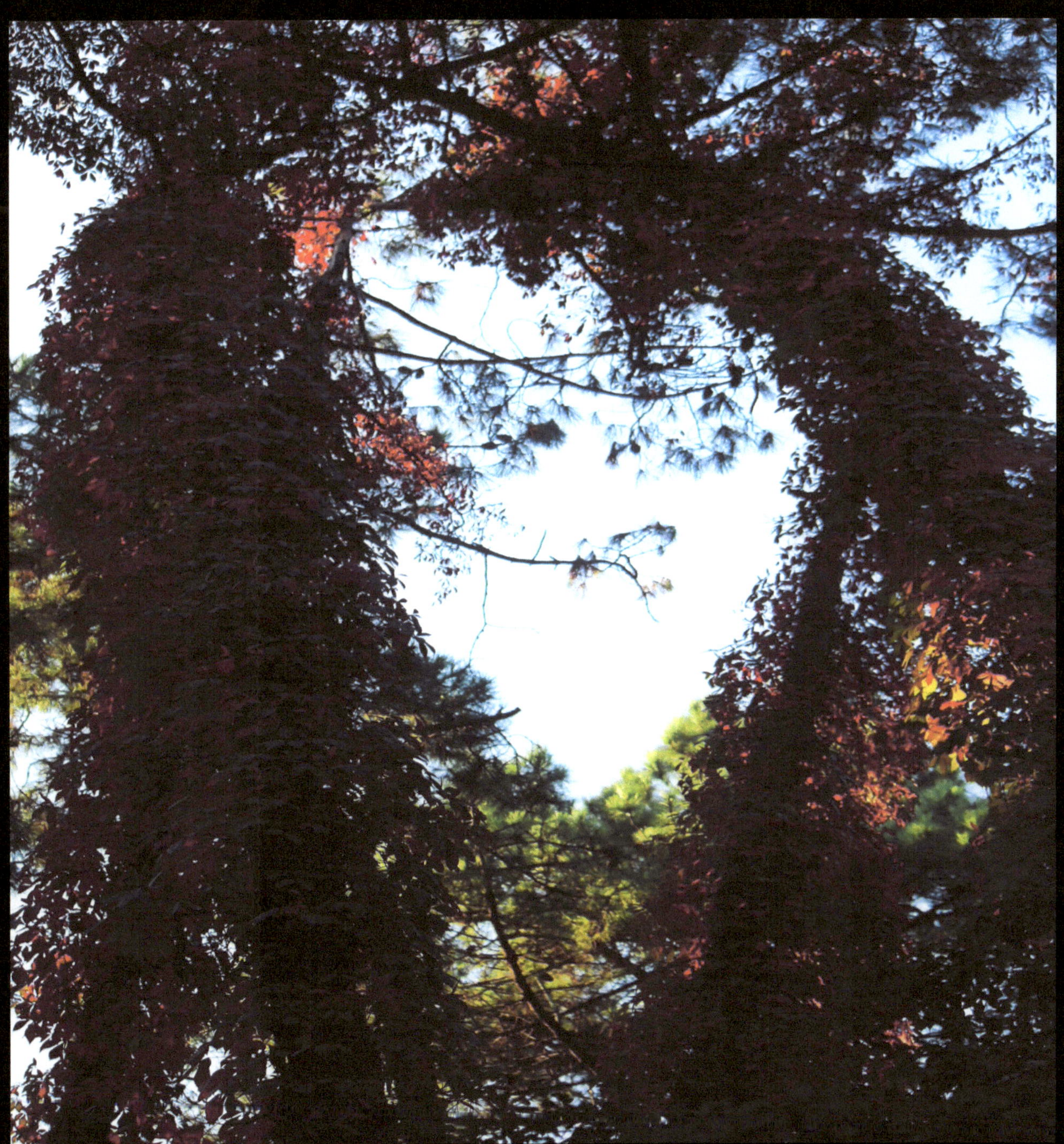

Forêt de Chiberta - Anglet, France

I trust myself, because I trust in GOD.
I have been taught right from wrong and will judge my road accordingly.
I will follow the signs left before me, and above all, I will be wise.

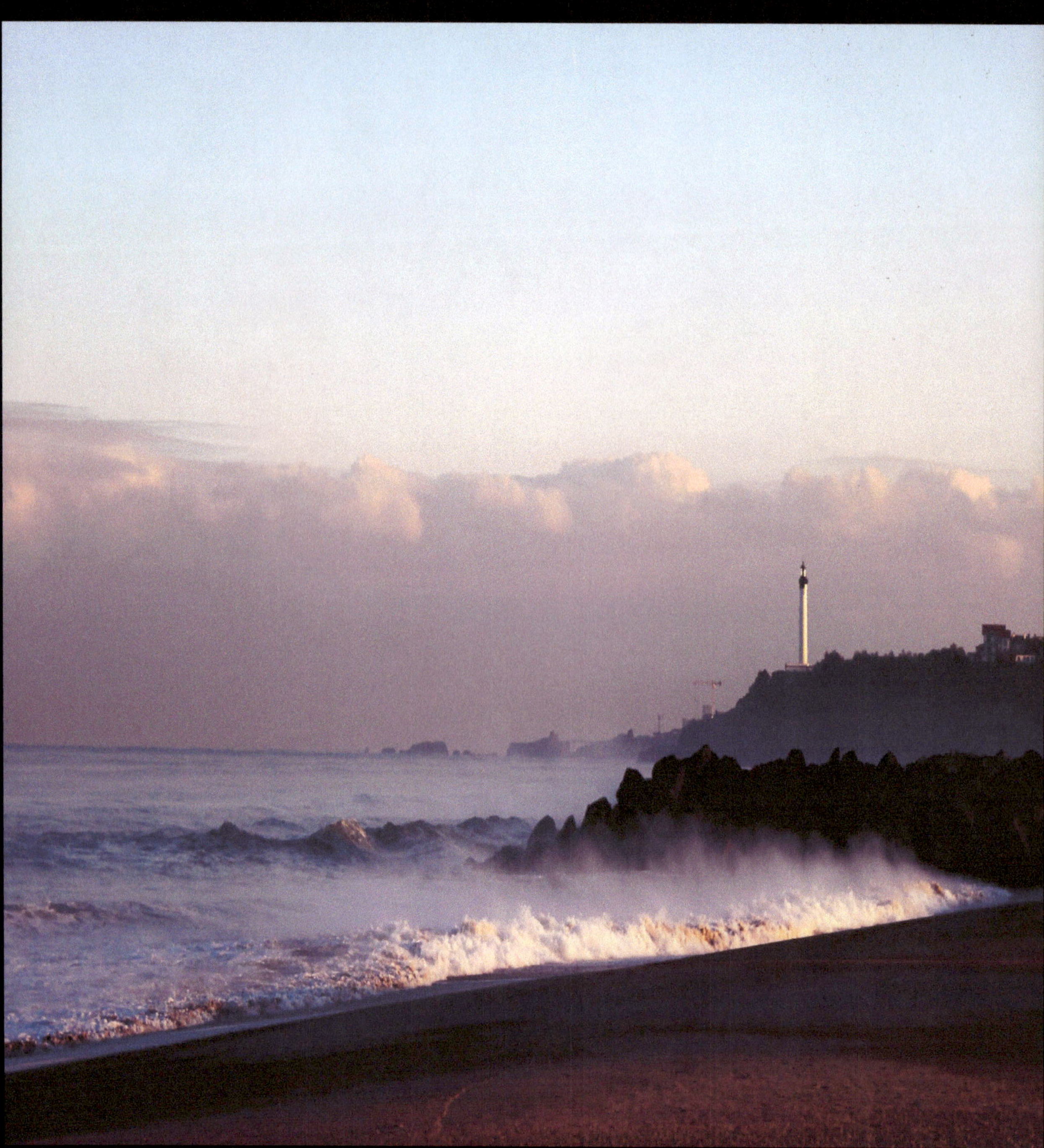

I will lift my head and live and my faith shall not be shaken
for the Lord GOD is with me and I am very much alive.

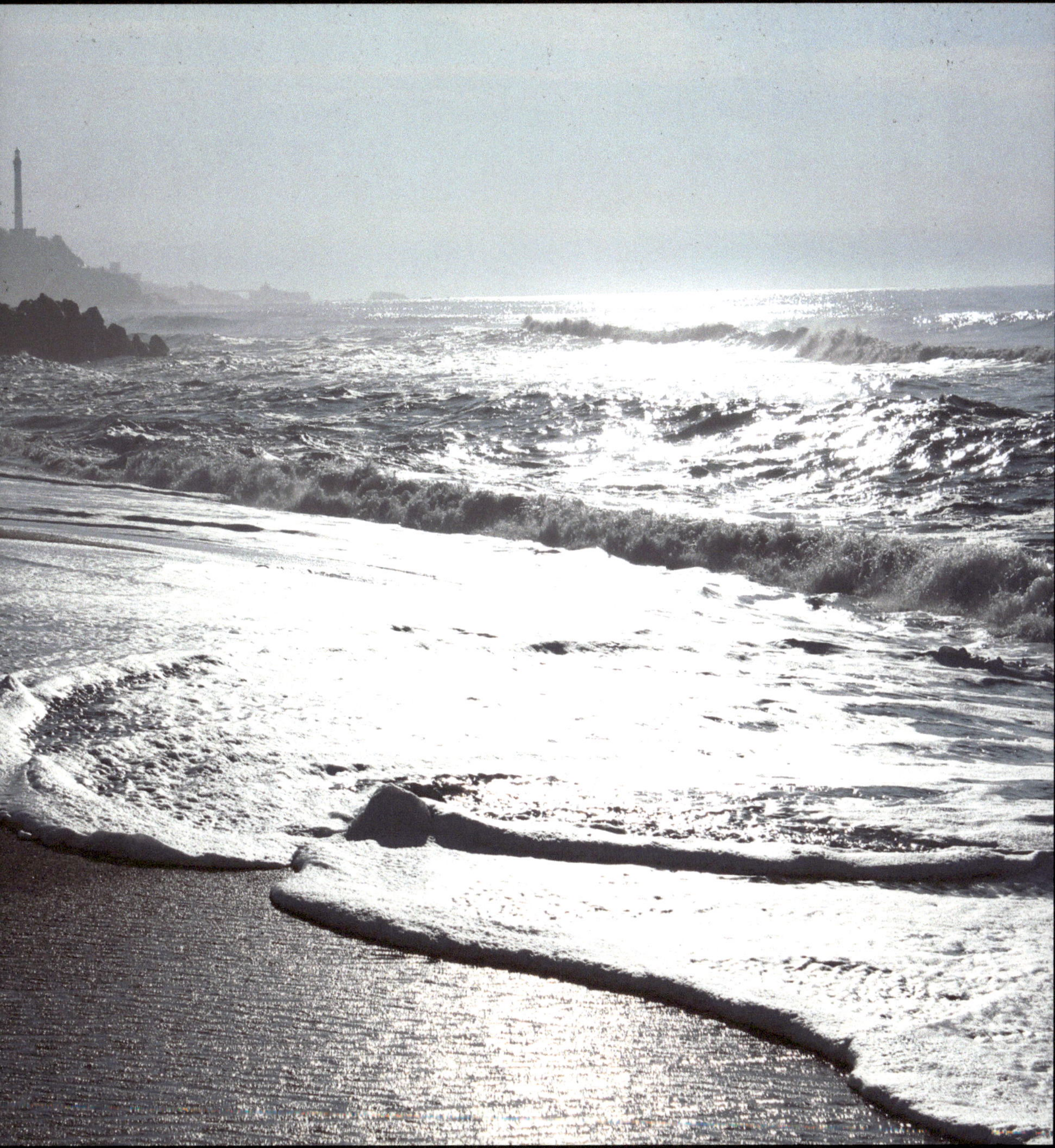

Chambre d'Amour - Anglet, France

I choose to embrace all the joy that is possible for me.
I do not look back towards regrets nor forward with any doubt.
Life stands before me and I rejoice.

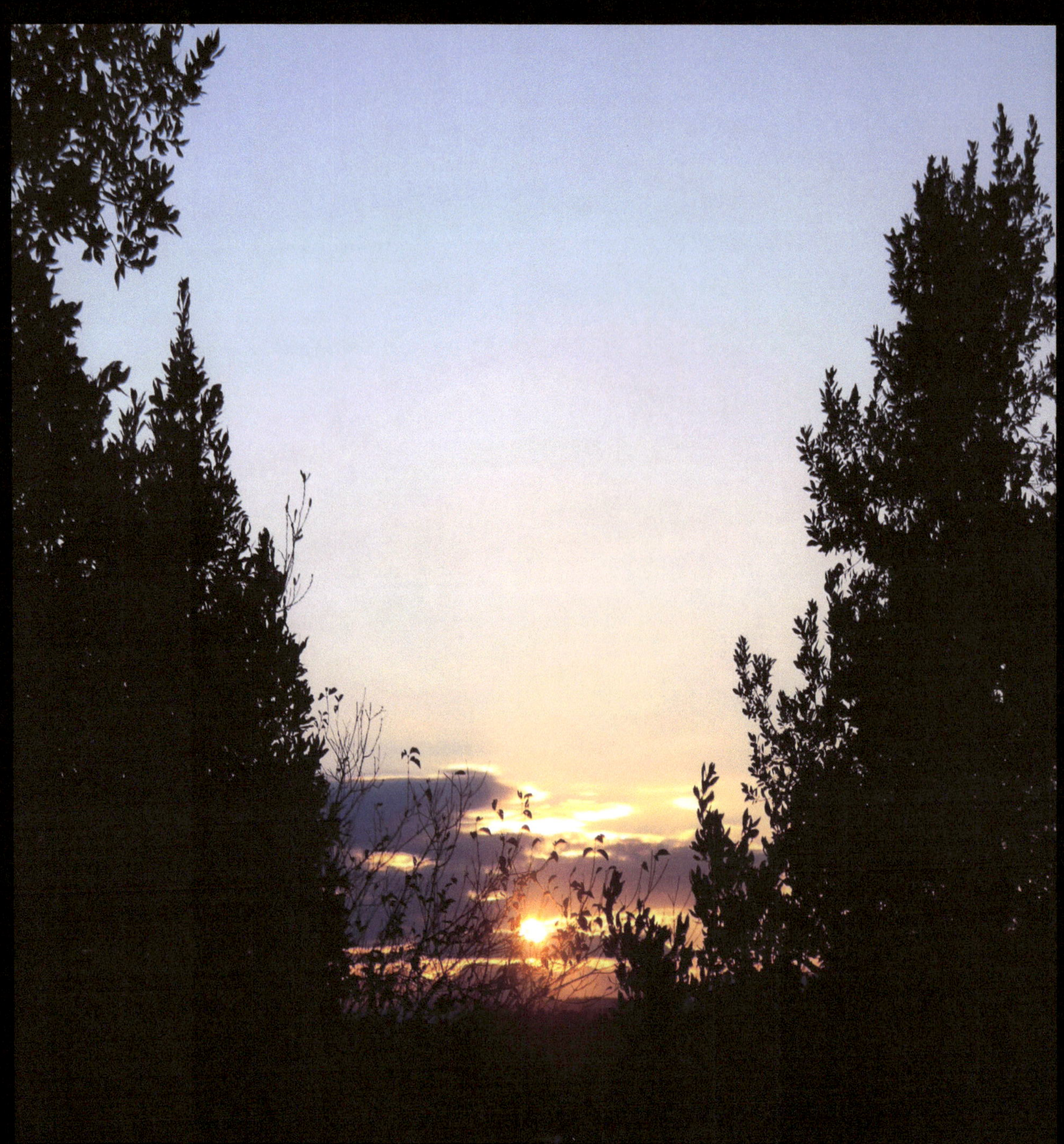

Sunrise over Cinq Cantons - Anglet, France

WHEN YOU NEED A MIRACLE PRAY

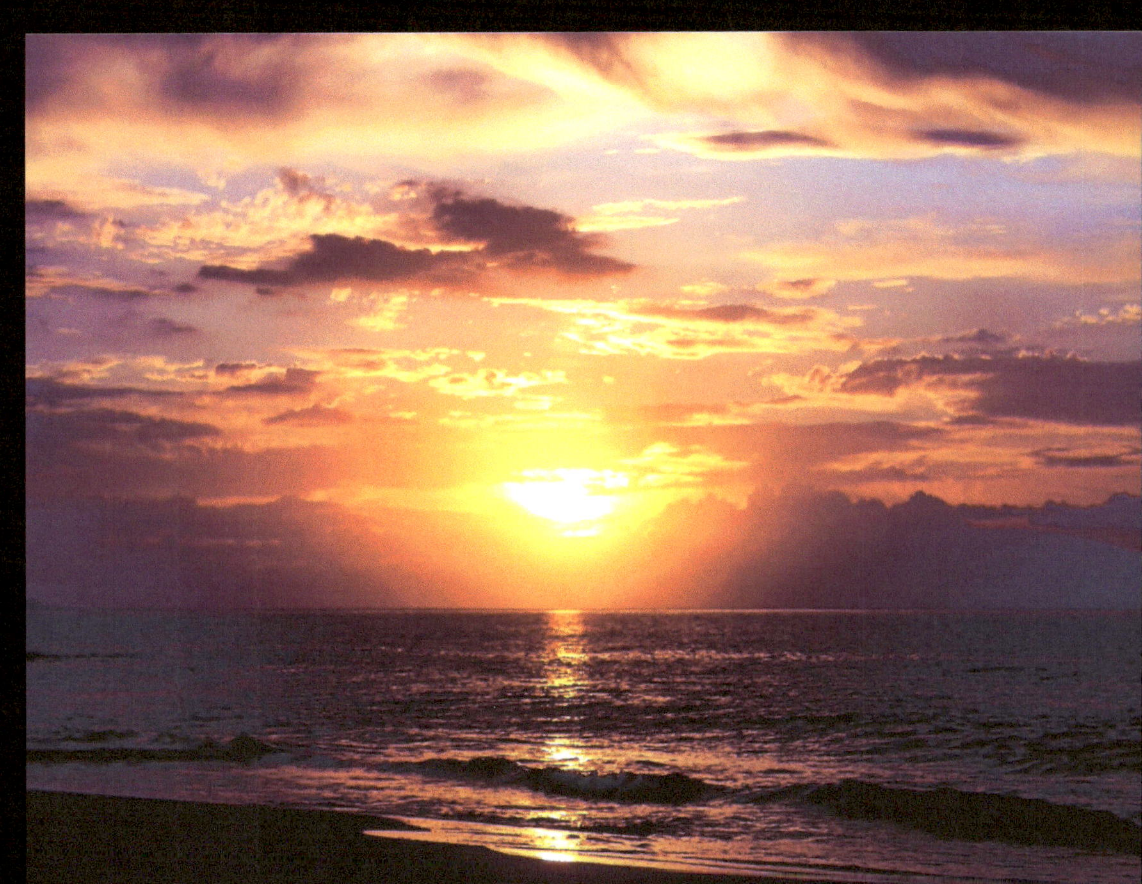

Thank you,Lord, for watching over me. You have been my refuge in every moment of my life. When the darkness overtake me and I can't seem to escape its doom, your grace falls on me. You are my shelter by day and you shield me and in my hour of need. I lay down every problem of my life before you. Every worry in my heart, and every fear that plagues my soul, I place in your hands. I rest in you, for you are peace. Amen.

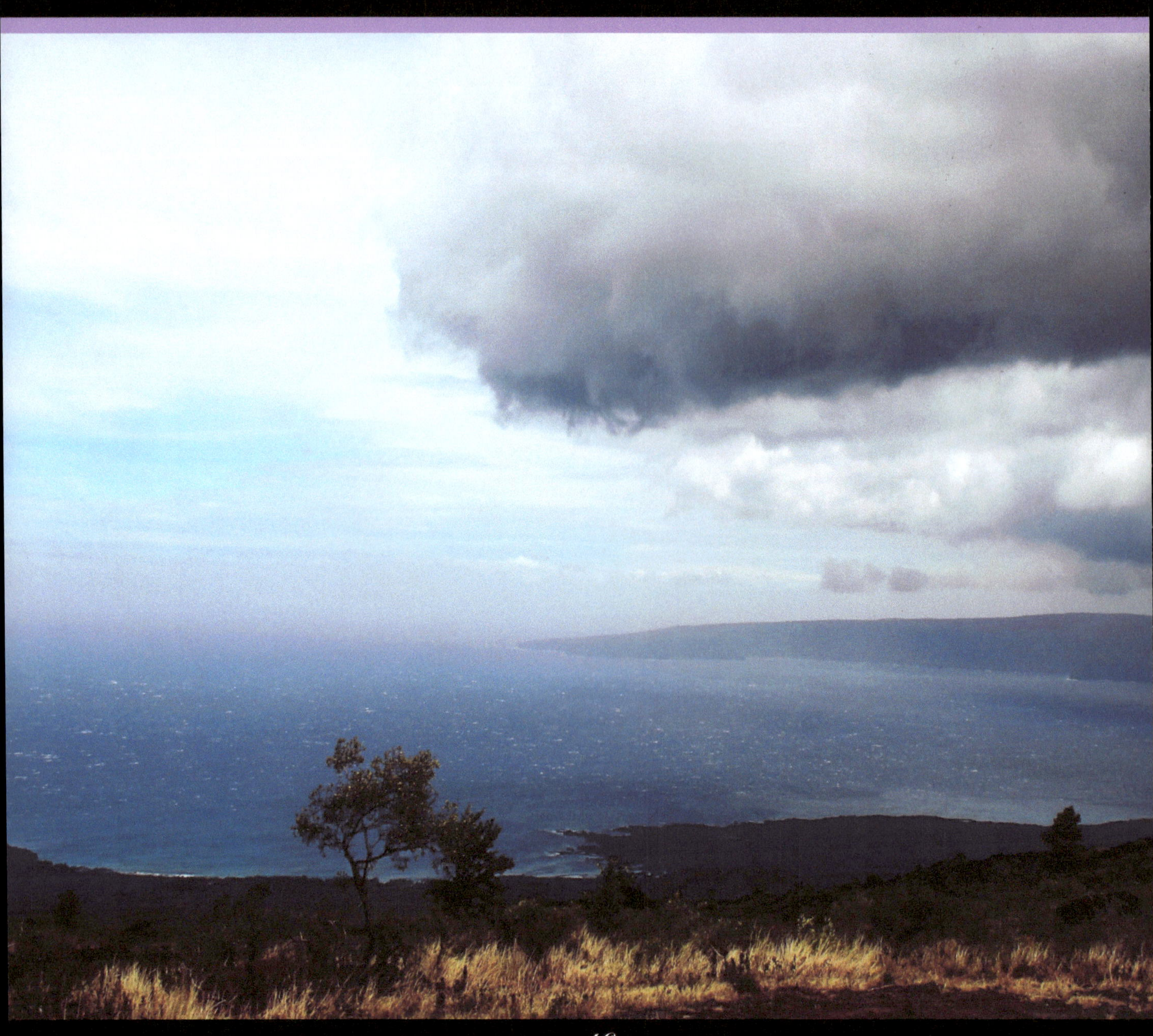

Maui, Hawaii - Kula

Help me, Father God... I need your guidance. Grant me wisdom in my decisions and give me your vision so that I know what I must do. And when I am lost in confusion, Lord, help me to see my way clear. When I am lost in the darkness, I pray that your hand will guide me. You, oh, Lord, you have a solution to every problem and for my every need. Help me to be more loving and wise, and keep me in your tender care. Amen.

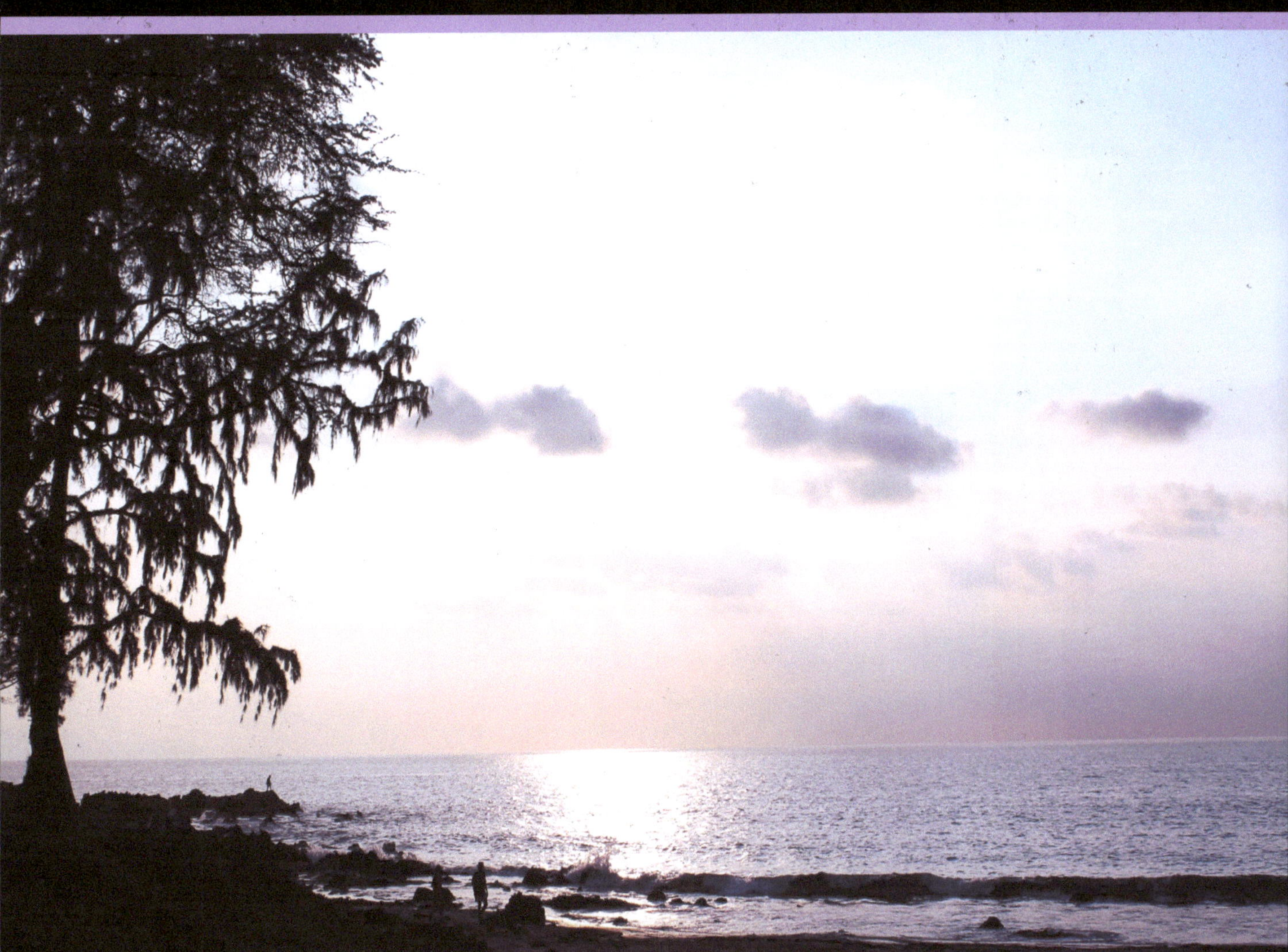

Holy Father, please deliver me from trouble. Descend upon my life and bless me with your gift of faith. I need you, Lord. I raise my voice to praise you, for only you provide for me. Only you can deliver me. Grant me courage, faith and hope, for through your might I draw my strength. You are Holy and your presence is Divine. You are my God and I wait on you. Lift my head and deliver me to your heavenly peace. Amen.

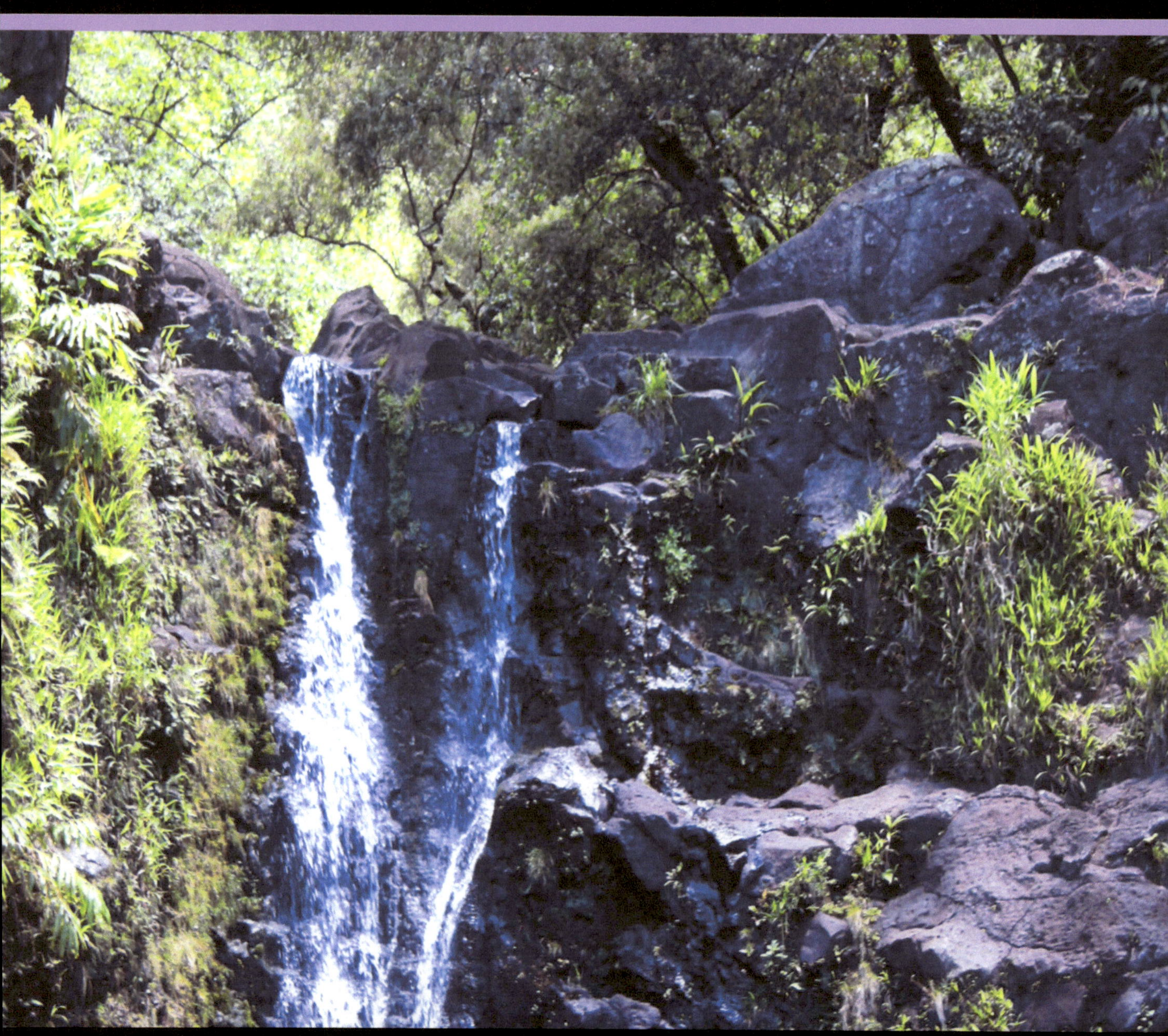

Maui, Hawaii - Hana

Healing to Survive

Father, you alone keep me from falling when the whole world is falling apart. Lord, when I am sad, you comfort me. When I am weak, you raise me up. You are my way tout of no way. On your strength alone I stand. You are the wall between me and poverty, illness, and disease; only your grace can heal. Have mercy on me, Lord, for I cannot make it alone. I need you desperately. Heal me in the name of Jesus Christ. Amen.

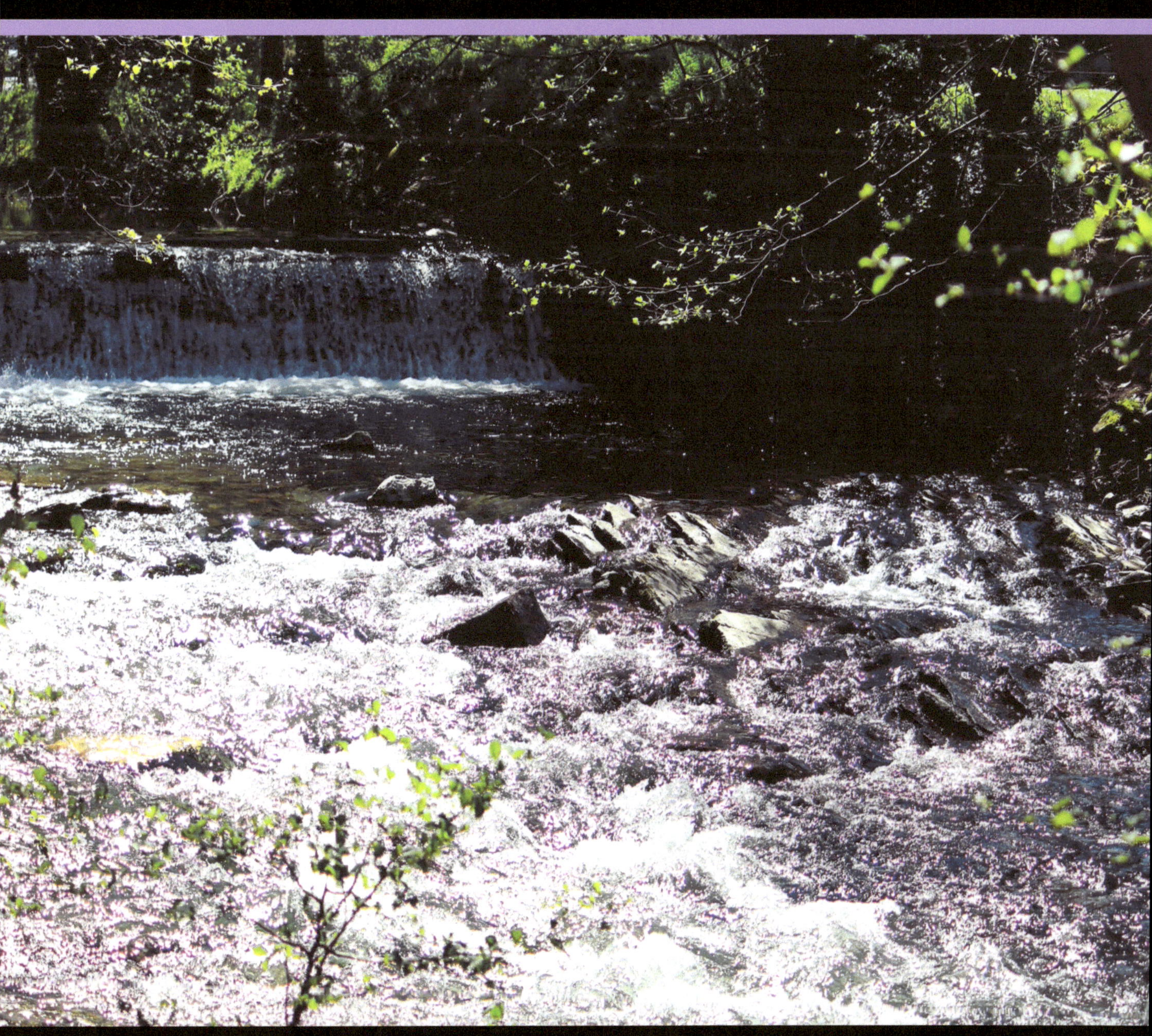

Guéthary, France - Pays Basque

Lord, please forgive me for everything I've done wrong. Empty me of all that is unclean and make my life acceptable to you. Fill me with your mercy and Holy love. Take me and make me what I should be. Cleanse me and heal me of all that is not pleasing to you. Pardon the words I've spoken in anger, and the hurt I've caused to others. I am asking for your forgiveness. Pardon me. Let me stand in your presence today. Amen.

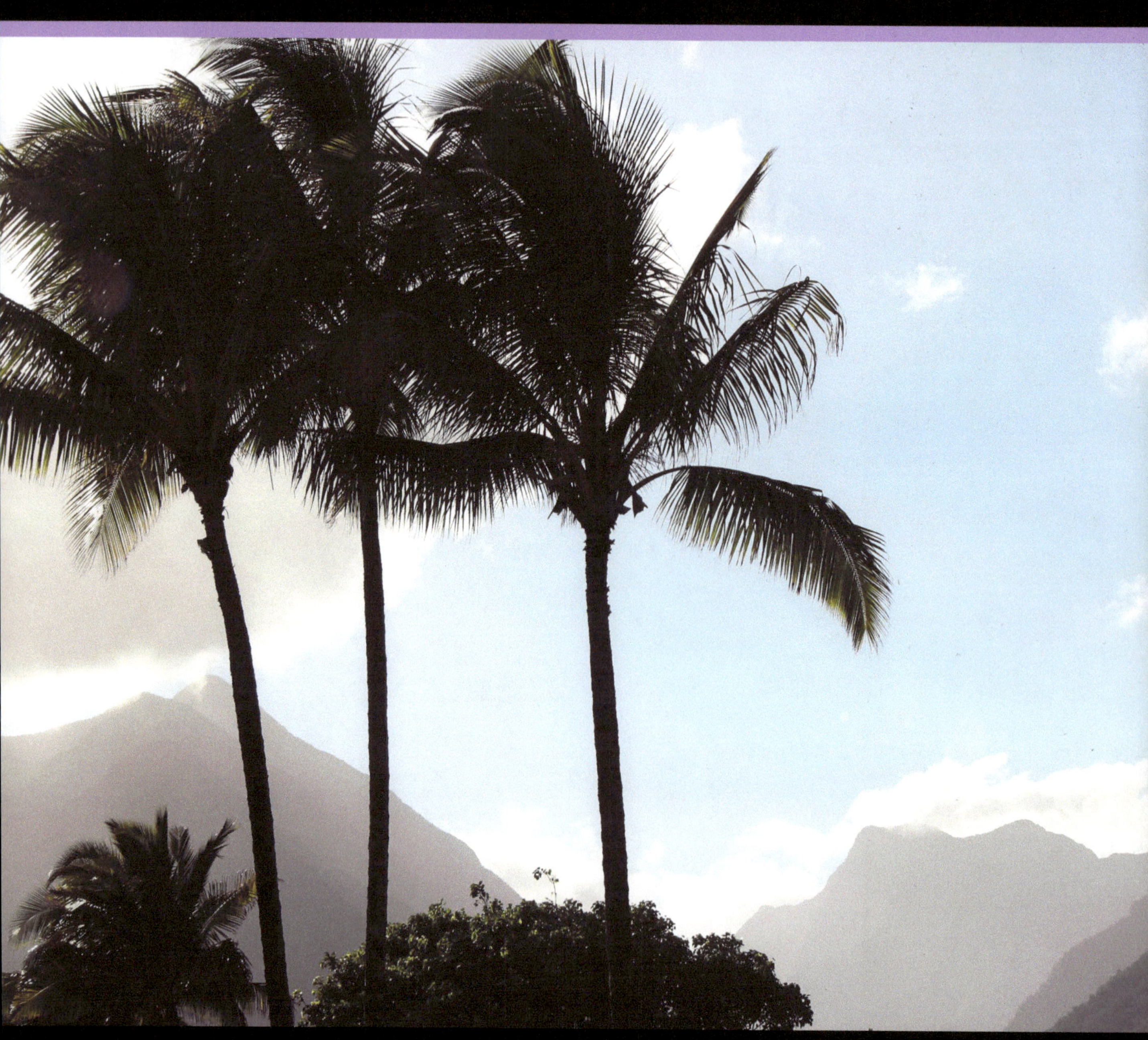

Maui, Hawaii - Kahalui

Lord God, I need a miracle in my life. Please lift me out of sorrow and show me the way to rise above my circumstances. Your wisdom is mighty and your compassion is great. If there is a door that I can't open, open it for me. If there is a window that leads to my destruction, please bar it from me. Guide me to your everlasting peace, and allow me to live in dignity. Provide for all of my needs. I praise you forever. Amen.

Bless me, oh Lord, for I need you now. Protect me with your healing hand and lead me to a place of peace. Troubles bring me down and anger rises up, but oh, Holy Divine, you wipe away my fears. The worry and pain, anger and distress all disappear when I place my mind on you. Hurtful things have no place in me because they do not come from you. Grant me peace and healing this very hour. I praise you, Lord, forever...

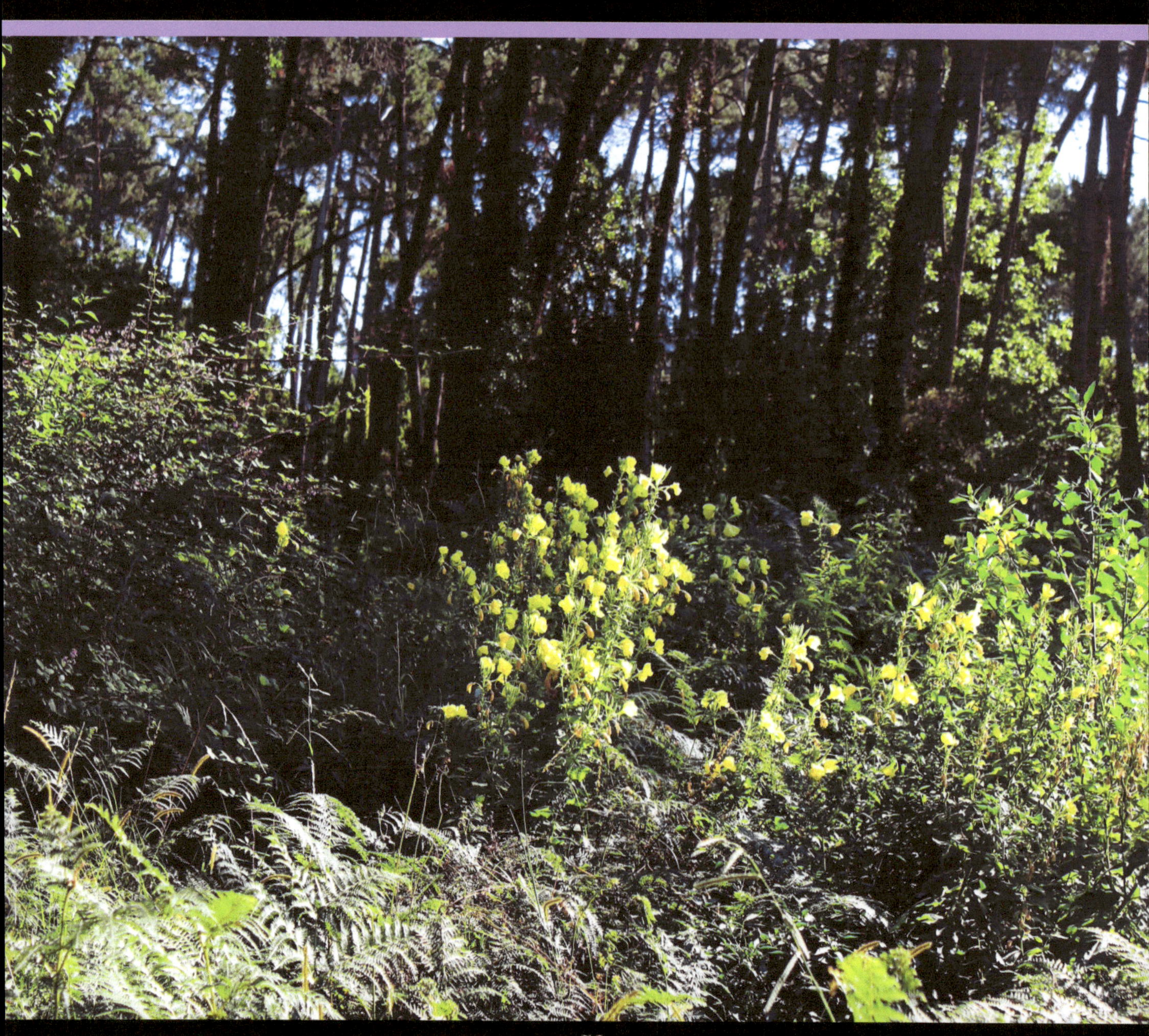

Anglet, France - Forêt de Chiberta

You are the keeper of my soul. You are my God; my sweet deliverer. Only good is found in you. And though I stumble and fall, your grace saves me. Even though I am bitter-sweet and salty to the taste, you look at me through eyes of love. You comfort me like honey and care for me, yet I am imperfect in every way. Bless me with your Holy presence and send your angels to watch over me. Lord, bless me this day... Amen.

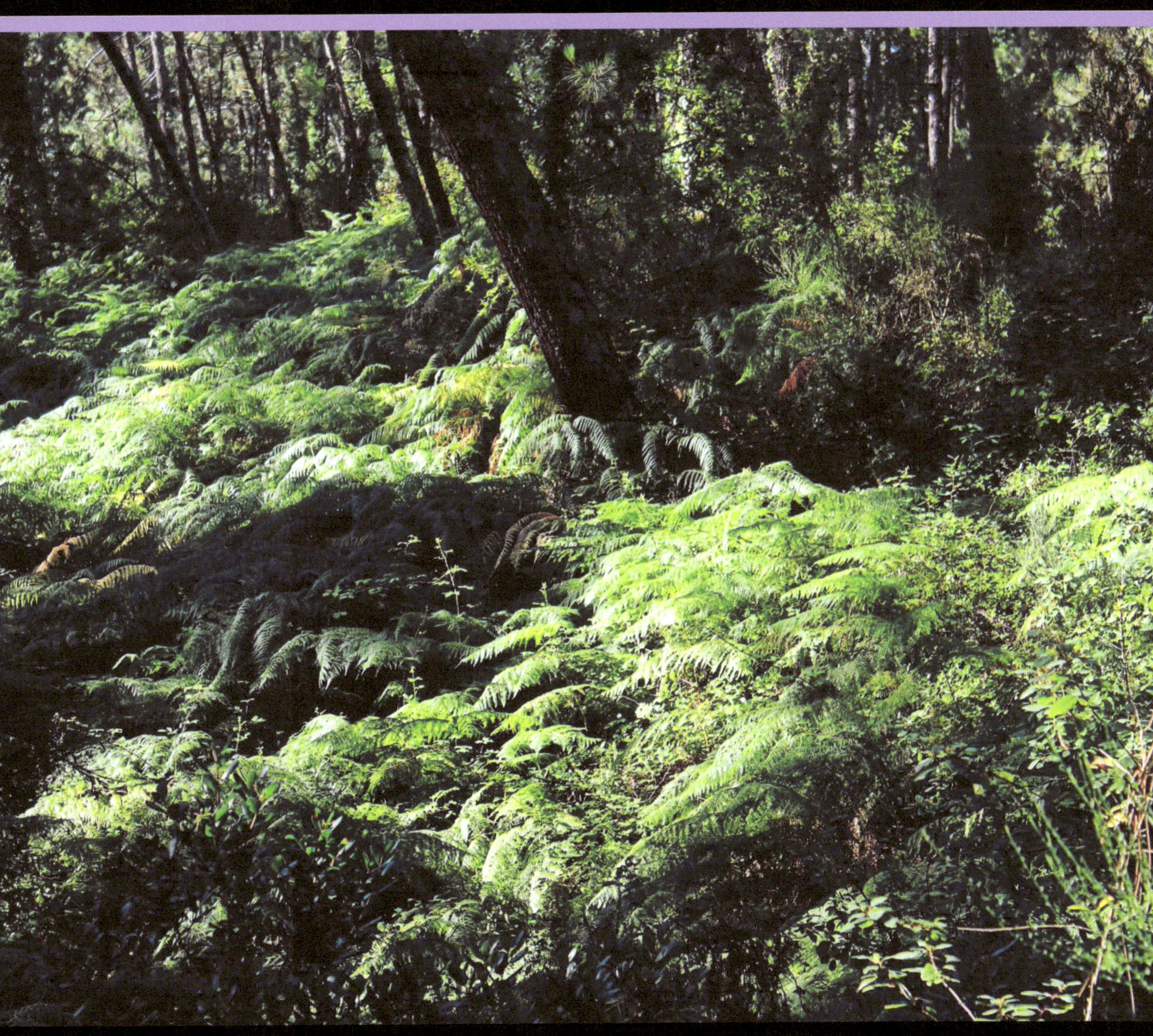

Anglet, France - Forêt de Chiberta

Lift me, oh Lord, for I am down on my knees. I lay my head upon your feet and cry out your Holy name. This life is not easy, fill me your precious peace. Heal me, Savior, for only you can deliver me. Thank you for your mercy though I've done things for which I am ashamed. But you, Father, forgive my faults and my past, and love me unconditionally. Through your perfect love, I am healed. Have mercy; I'm calling on you...

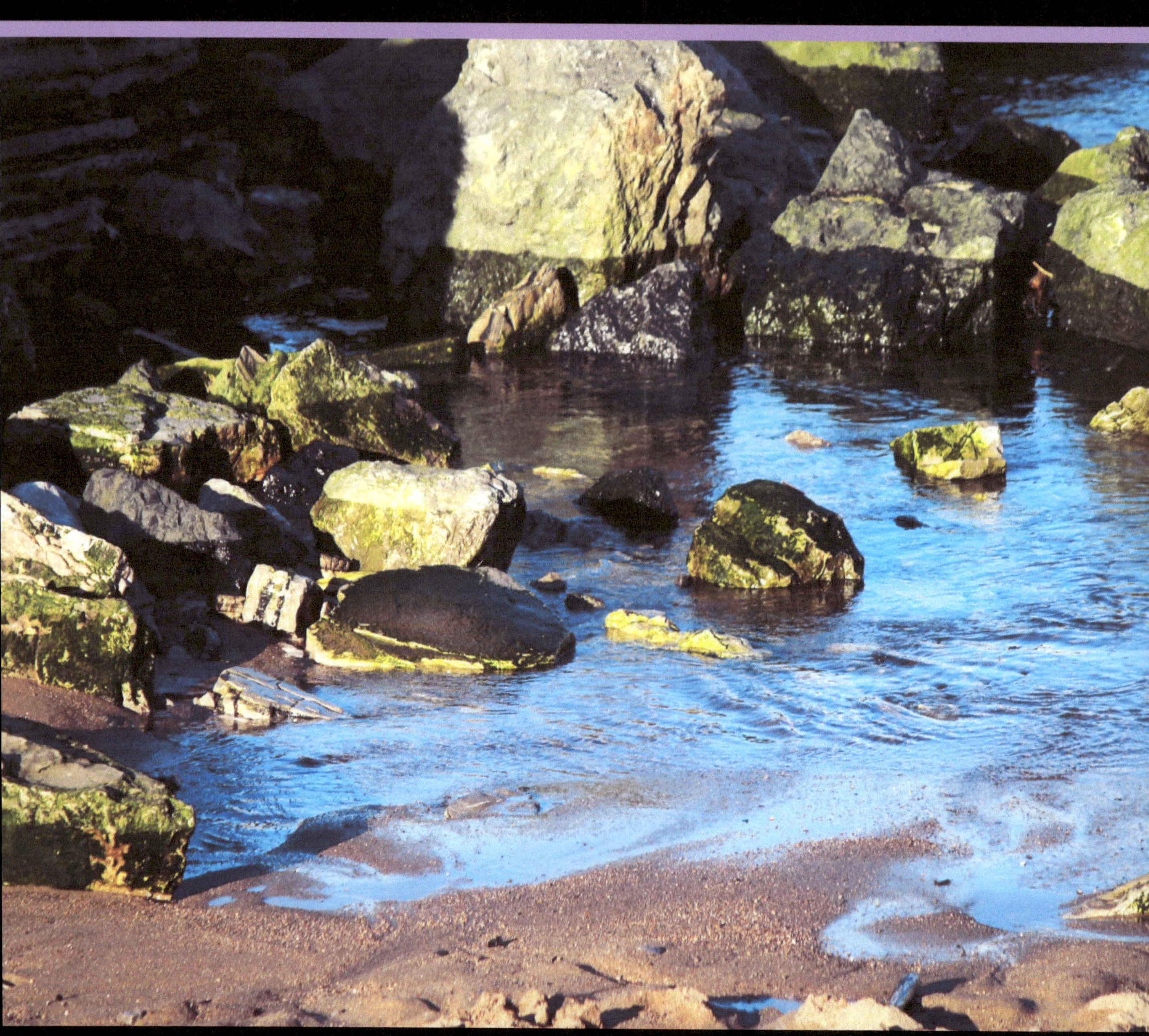

Guéthary, France - Pays Basque

You are my Heavenly Father, my blessed sacred hope. Touch my life with love and fill me up with mercy. Lord, I am so thankful for my life. You have taken away my pain and replaced it with faith. You have kept my mind and soul and have given me Divine peace. You are my Lord and Savior, my hope in times of trouble. You are my strength and my deliverer. I praise your name for all you have done for me. You are my God...

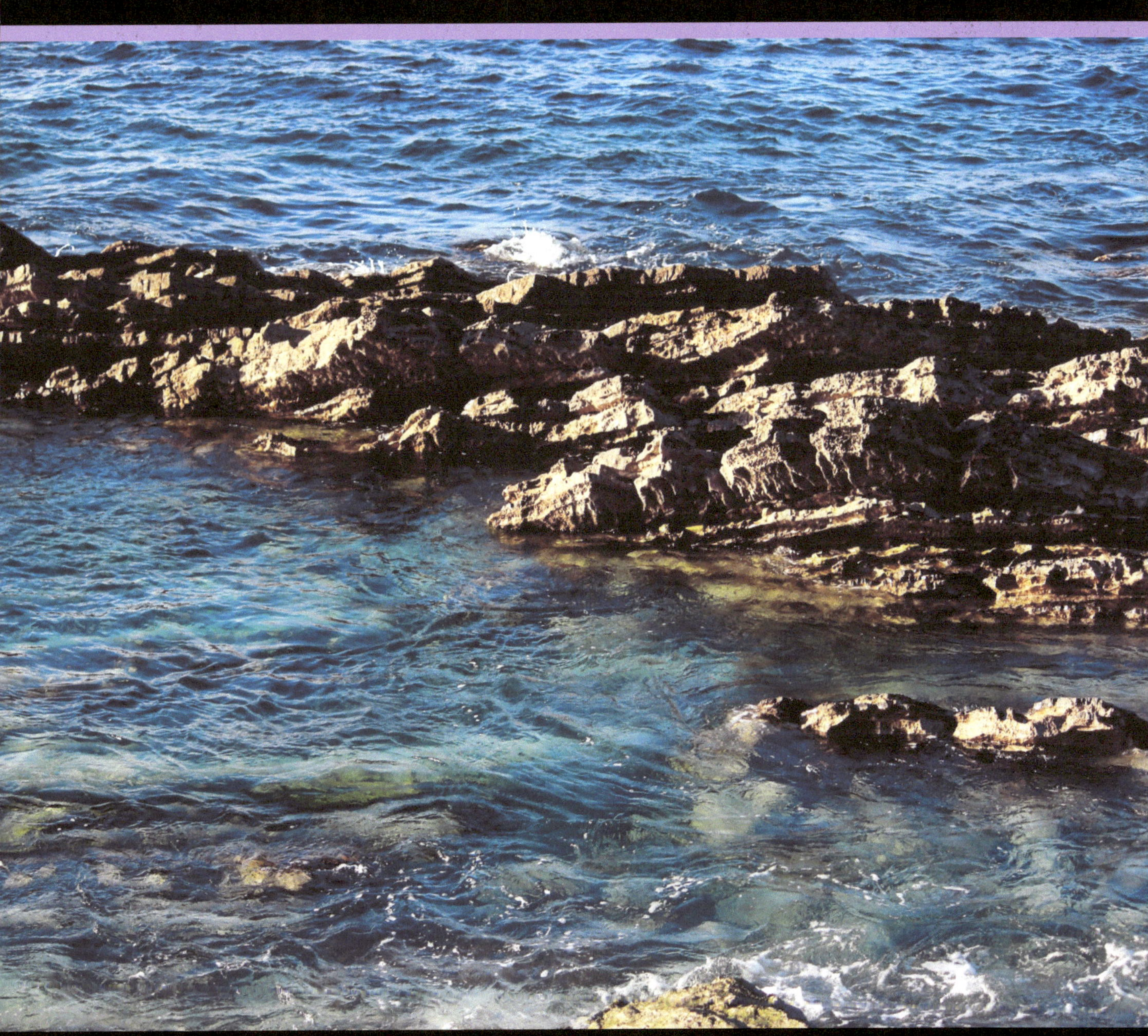

Guéthary, France - Pays Basque

Precious Lord, where would I be if you were not in my life?Through every storm, though I was afraid, you comforted me and kept me safe. You forgave my faults and teach me your ways. Through your grace, I survived, for you provide all my needs. You give me sustenance and give me peace. You guide me when I'm awake and protect me when I am asleep. You deliver me from my troubles, and I thank you for my life. Amen.

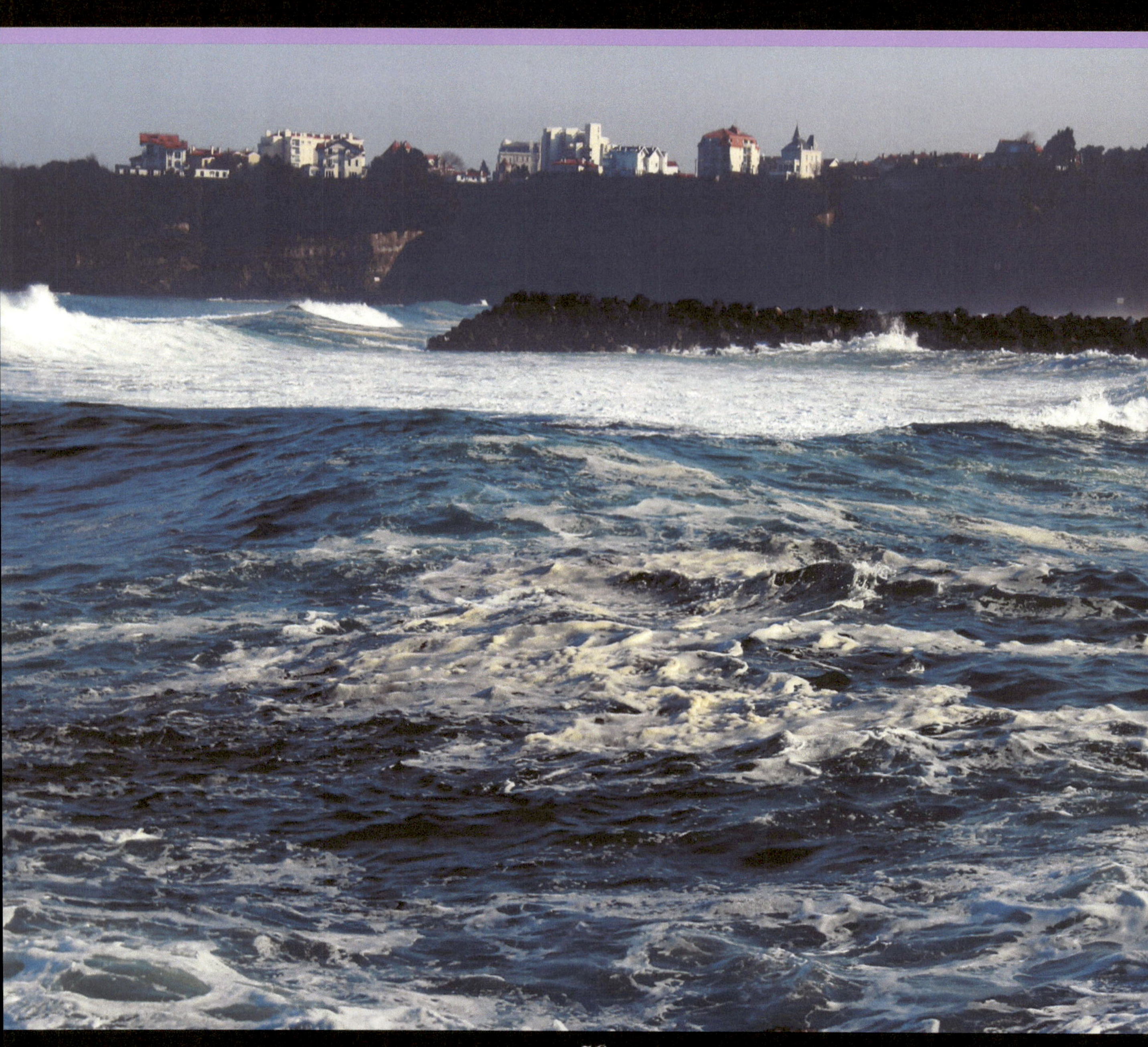

Anglet, France - Chambre d'Amour

Heavenly Father, my heart is aching and I don't know where to turn. Sorrow has overtaken me; I am worn and feel so alone. Lord, I look to you... I need your presence close to me. Help me climb my mountain. I need your strength to make it through. Please deliver my feigning spirit and turn my darkest days into joyful morns. Come, Holy Spirit, and grant me peace through the eye of the storm. Strengthen me, oh Lord. Amen.

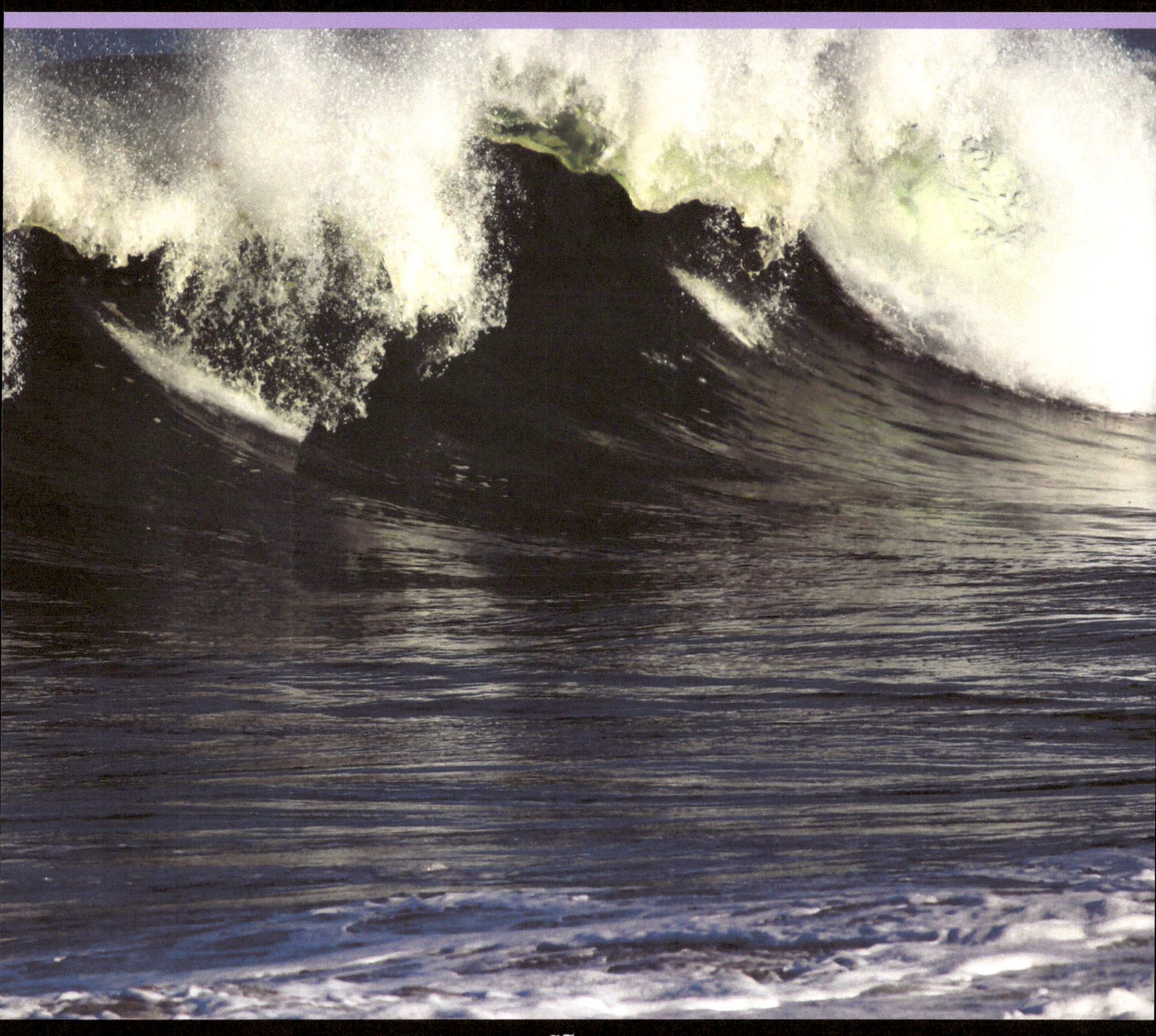

Anglet, France - Chambre d'Amour

Oh, Holy One, please hear my cry. I am on my knees and need you now. My enemies are set against me, and those whom I trusted are corrupt. I cannot make it all alone. Lord, you are my only hope. Father, you know what I am going through. I lay my troubles before your feet. Master, I know you can deliver me. Change my situations; even change me. I need your help, my Heavenly Father. I need you Lord, today. Amen.

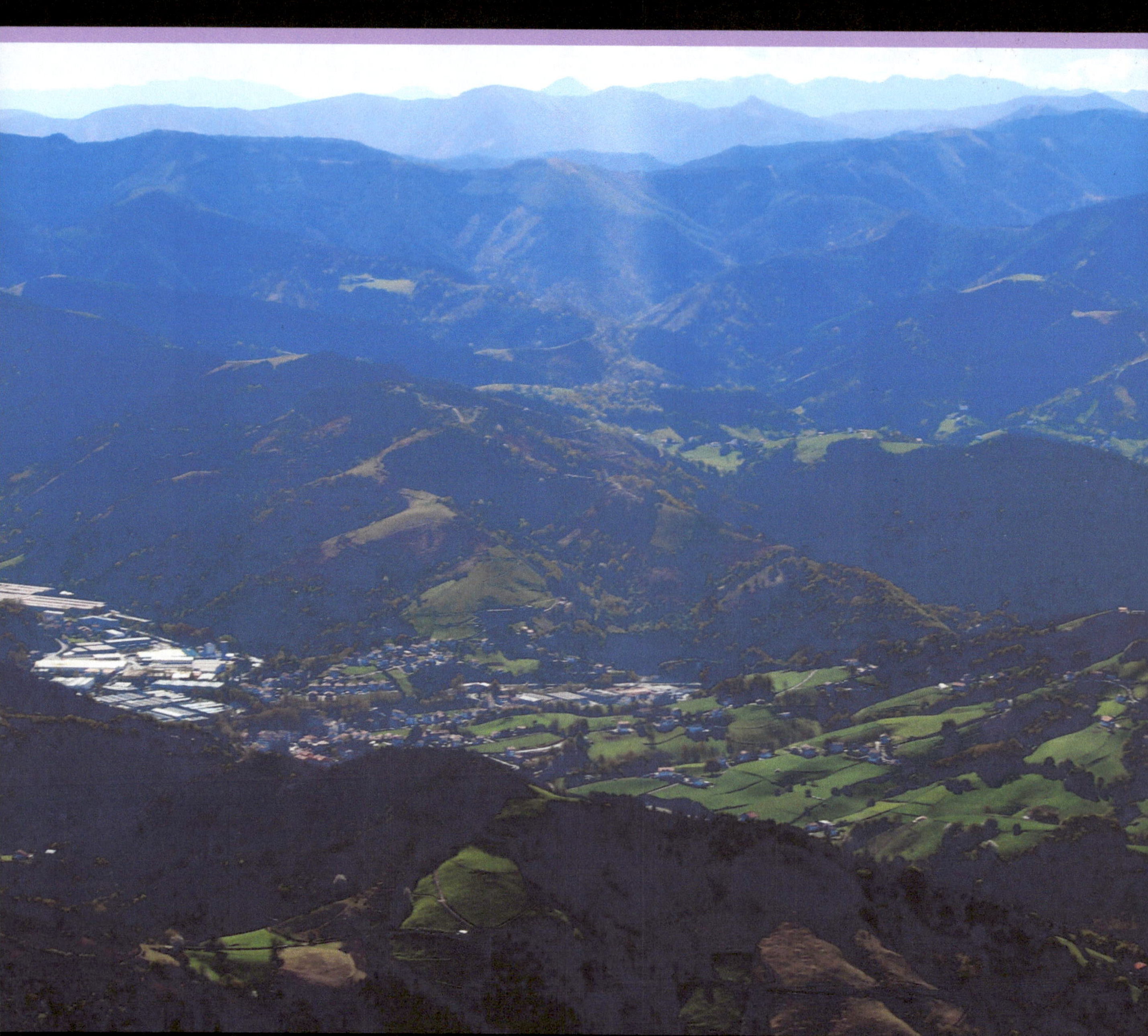

Take my hand, Lord, and lead me as I walk this road. I place all my trust in you. Thank you for letting me see another day and thank you for the grace you've given me. Thank you for keeping for me and my loved ones safe. Lord, you are my Everlasting Father and my deliverer. Master without you I would never make it through this life. Thank you for giving me your eternal peace. I praise your glorious name, forever. Amen.

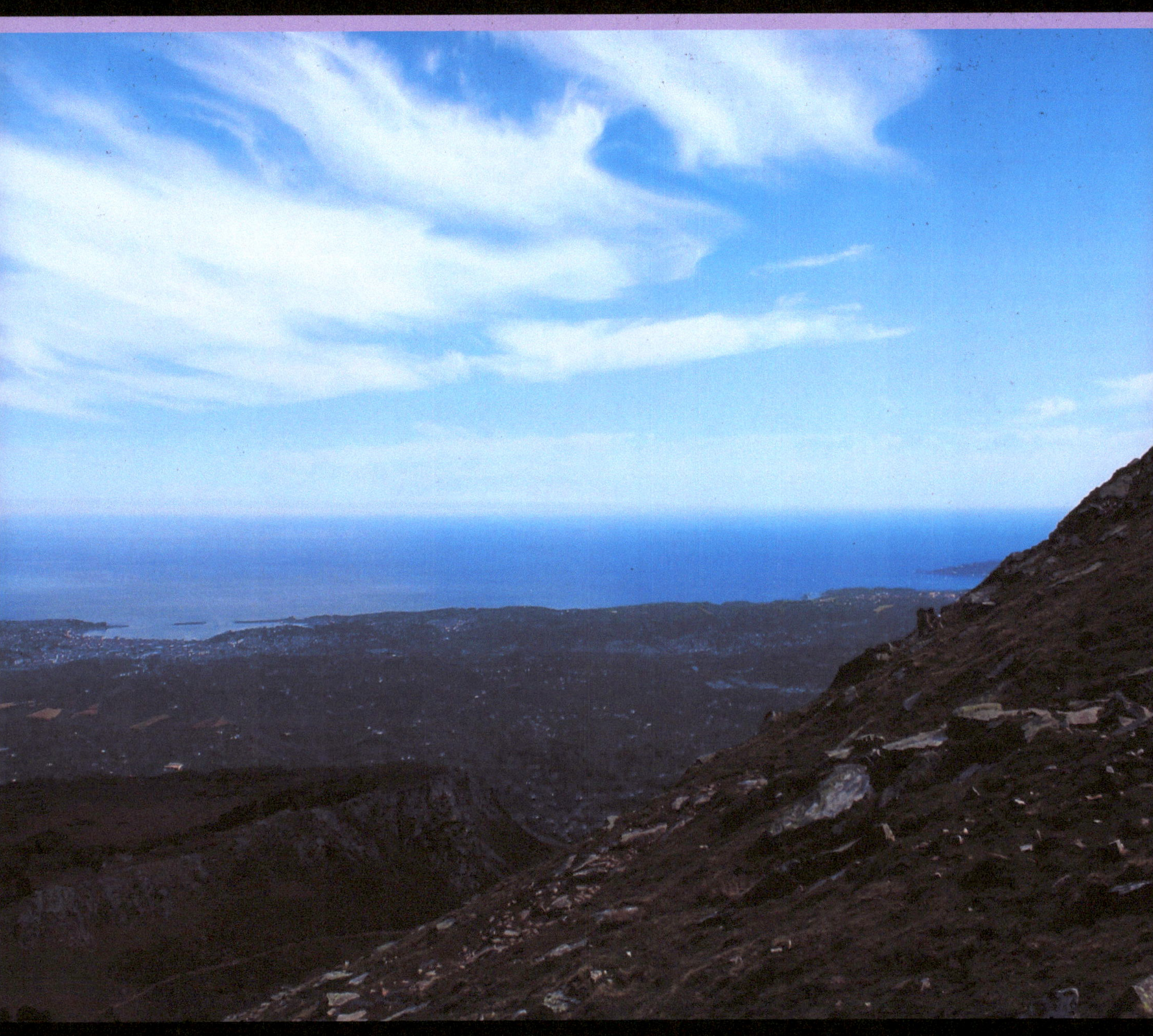

La Rhune, France - Pays Basque

Lord, thank you so much for all you have done for me. You have kept me through the good times and protected me through the bad. And because of your grace, I have enough to eat and a place to lay my head. And though the days are long and my nights have been filled with tears, I wake with my heart filled with hope for I have triumphed over the night. You were with me and kept me, and I thank you, Lord. Amen.

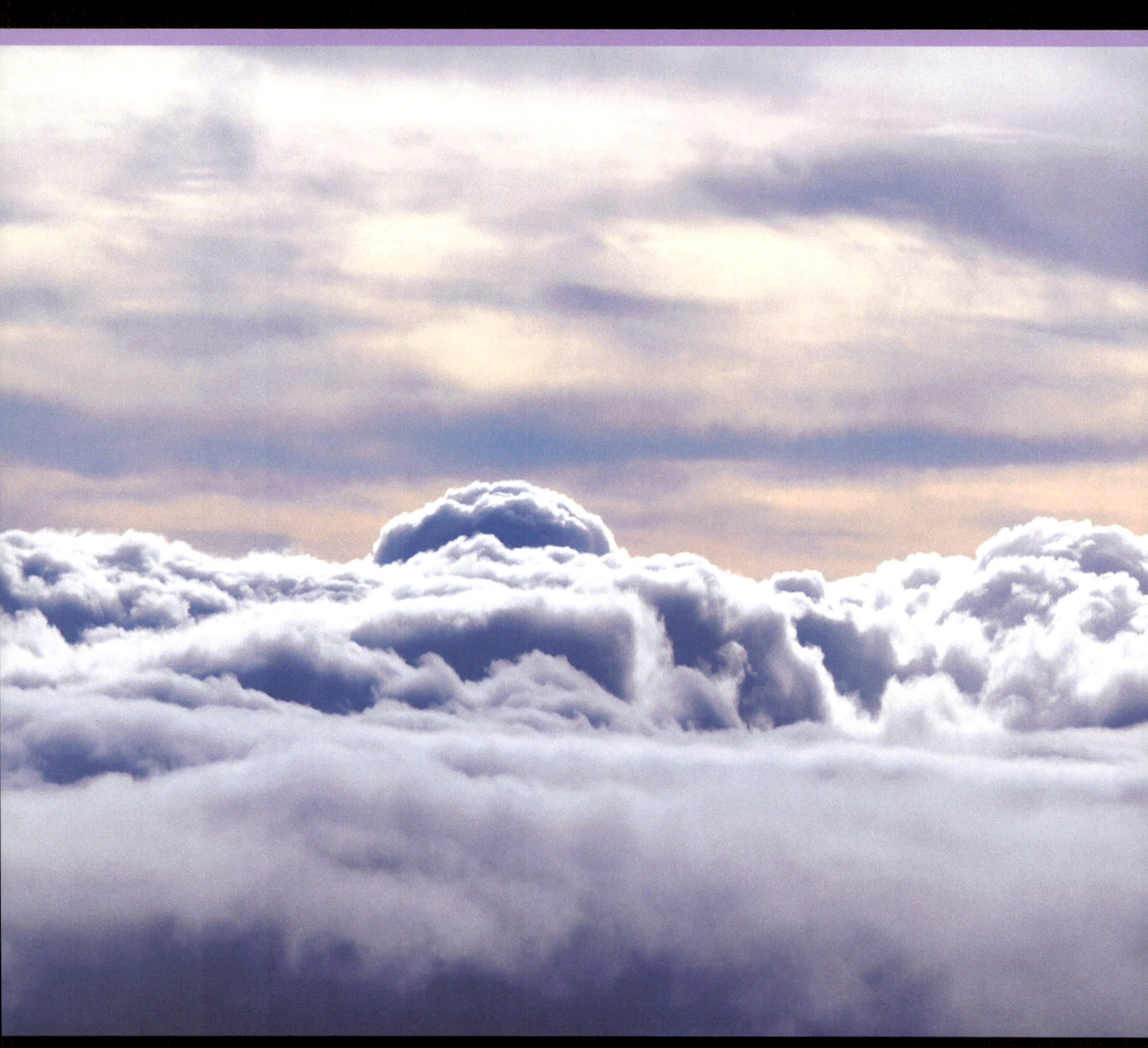

Maui, Hawaii

Oh, how I need you, Christ Jesus, when the world is set against me and tears are falling down my cheeks. You are the one I cling to when I feel trapped in misery. Lord, you to lift my soul so that I may feel joy in my heart. You take away my worries and ease my mind with faith. You guide all my footsteps that I may live my life in truth. Help me to be more loving, and give me your Holy strength. Lift me up in victory this day. Amen.

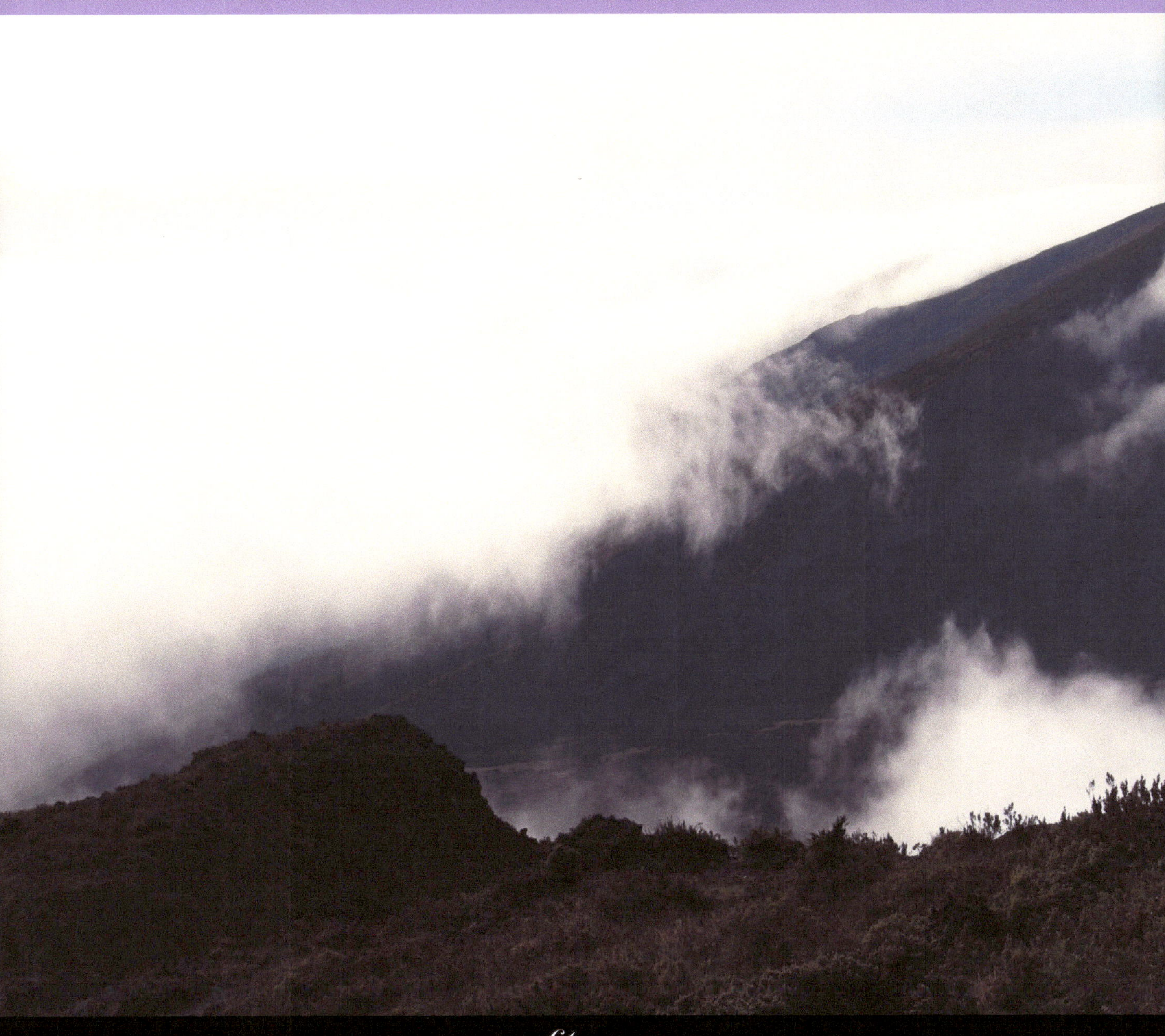

Maui, Hawaii - Haleakala

Oh, Lord, my God, heal me with your Divine love and make me whole again. I am bowed down low, breathe life into my soul and make me reborn. Take these shackles and free my spirit; heal me from the pain. Raise me up, free my mind, and deliver me from all shame. I come to you for I have no where else to go. I stand on the promises of faith and your everlasting hope. Please bring peace to my life. In Jesus name I pray. Amen.

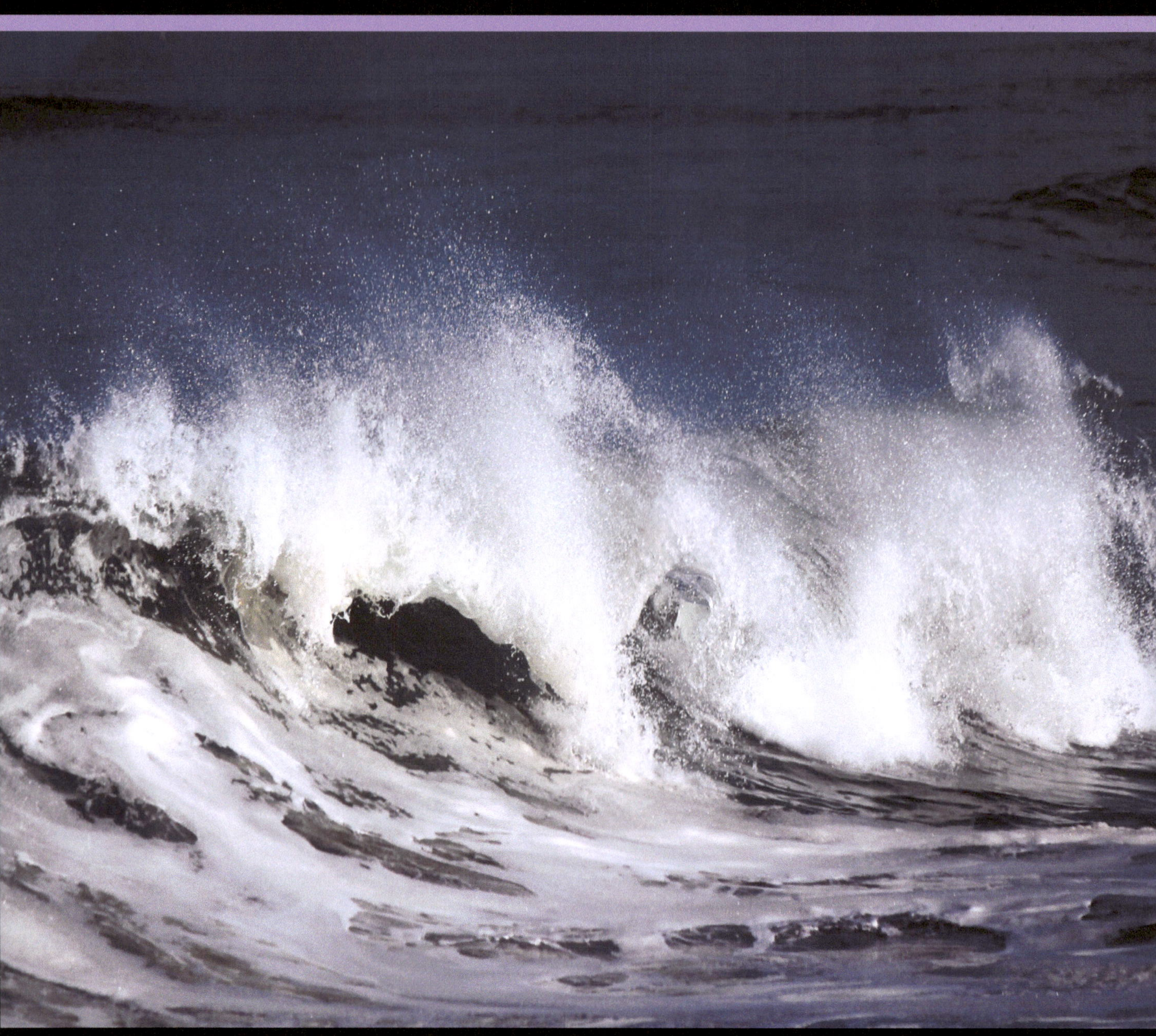

Anglet, France - Chambre d'Amour

Lord, please look inside my heart and change my ways. Help me to be more like you. I wish I could undo many of the things I have already done, but if you just wash away all the hurt and pain and take away all that is not of you, my life will be renewed. Free me of these burdens; I am tired of my imperfect ways. Lord, just lift me up and make me whole again. I want to live my life in peace. I want to be whole in you. Amen.

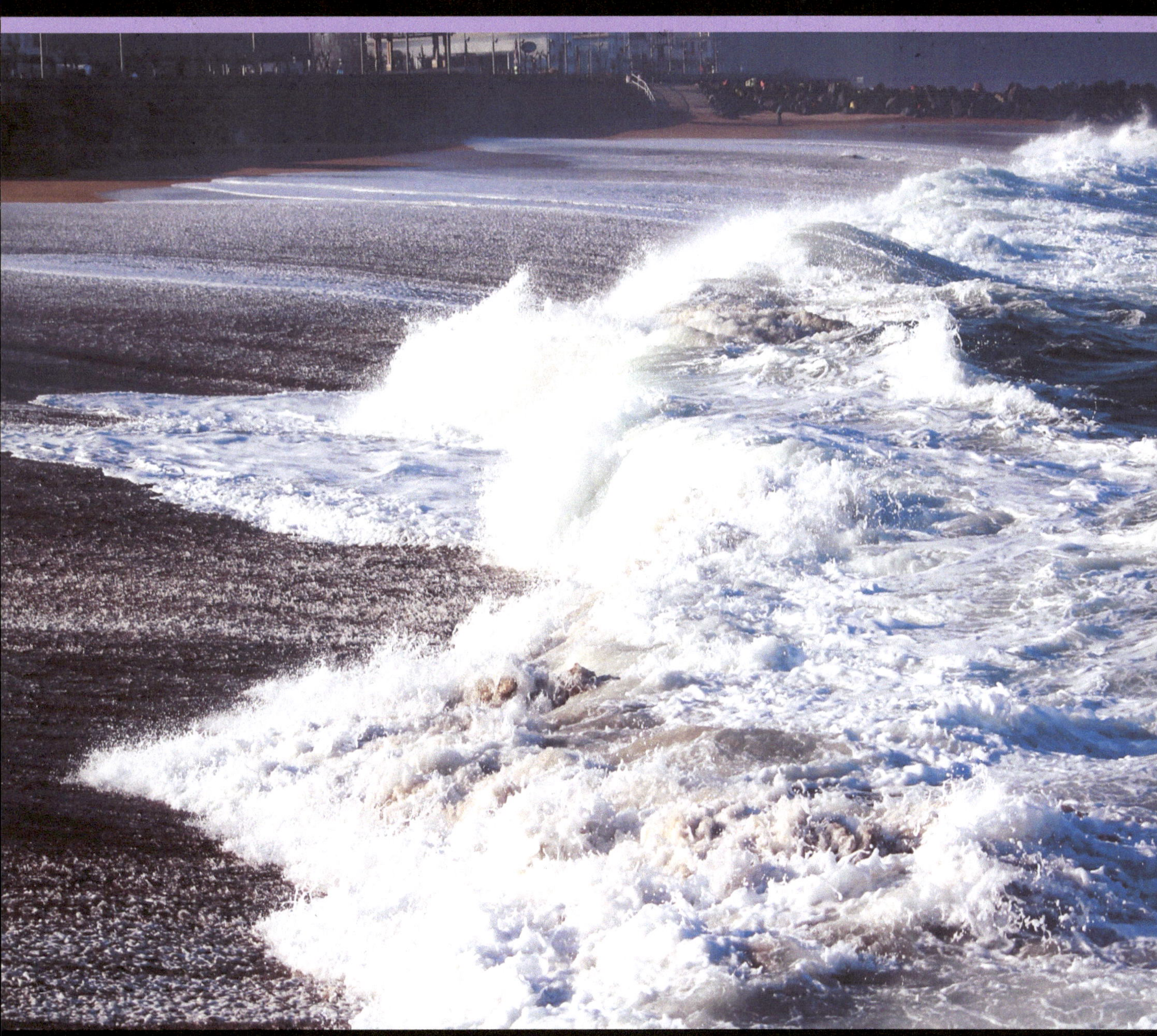

Anglet, France - Chambre d'Amour

Lord, help me to be the person that I need to be. Calm me and give me inner-peace. Grant me patience and help me to handle the stresses of my daily life. Lord, I want to be able to listen and not get angry, to speak and not be rude; to live and not regret. I want to be more loving; to treat others as you treat me. Please take away all within me that is not pleasing to you. I want to be more like you. In Jesus name I pray... Amen.

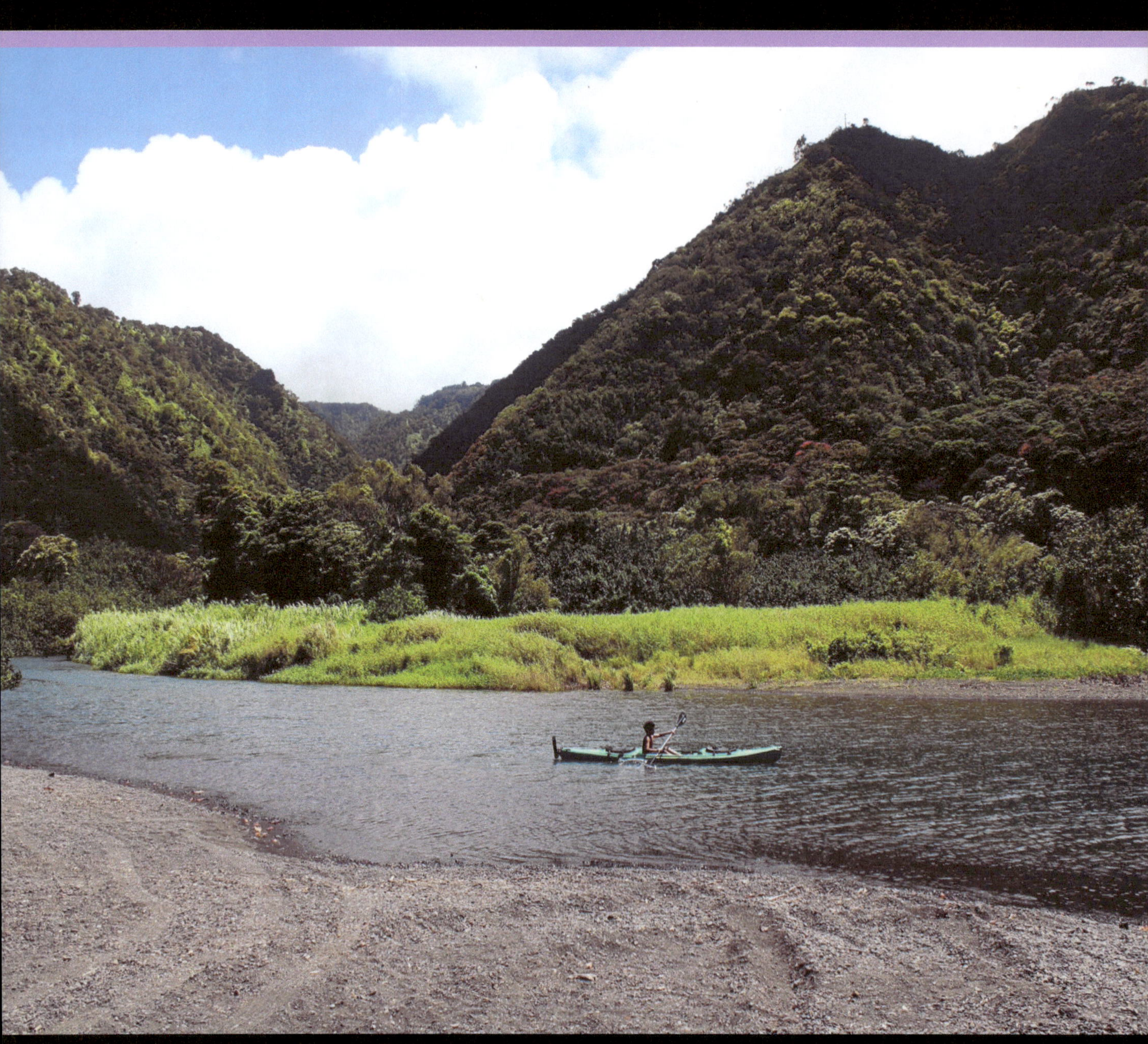

Maui, Hawaii

Lord, all blessings comes from you. Sometimes, I feel so alone, then you comfort me. I say the wrong things and make many mistakes, yet you love me. You pick me up when I am down. You gather me when I am falling apart. You hold me when I am in the cold. You bless me when life is cruel. Lord, I want to be forever in your presence. I never want to be without you. For all the blessings you have bestowed on my life, I thank you...

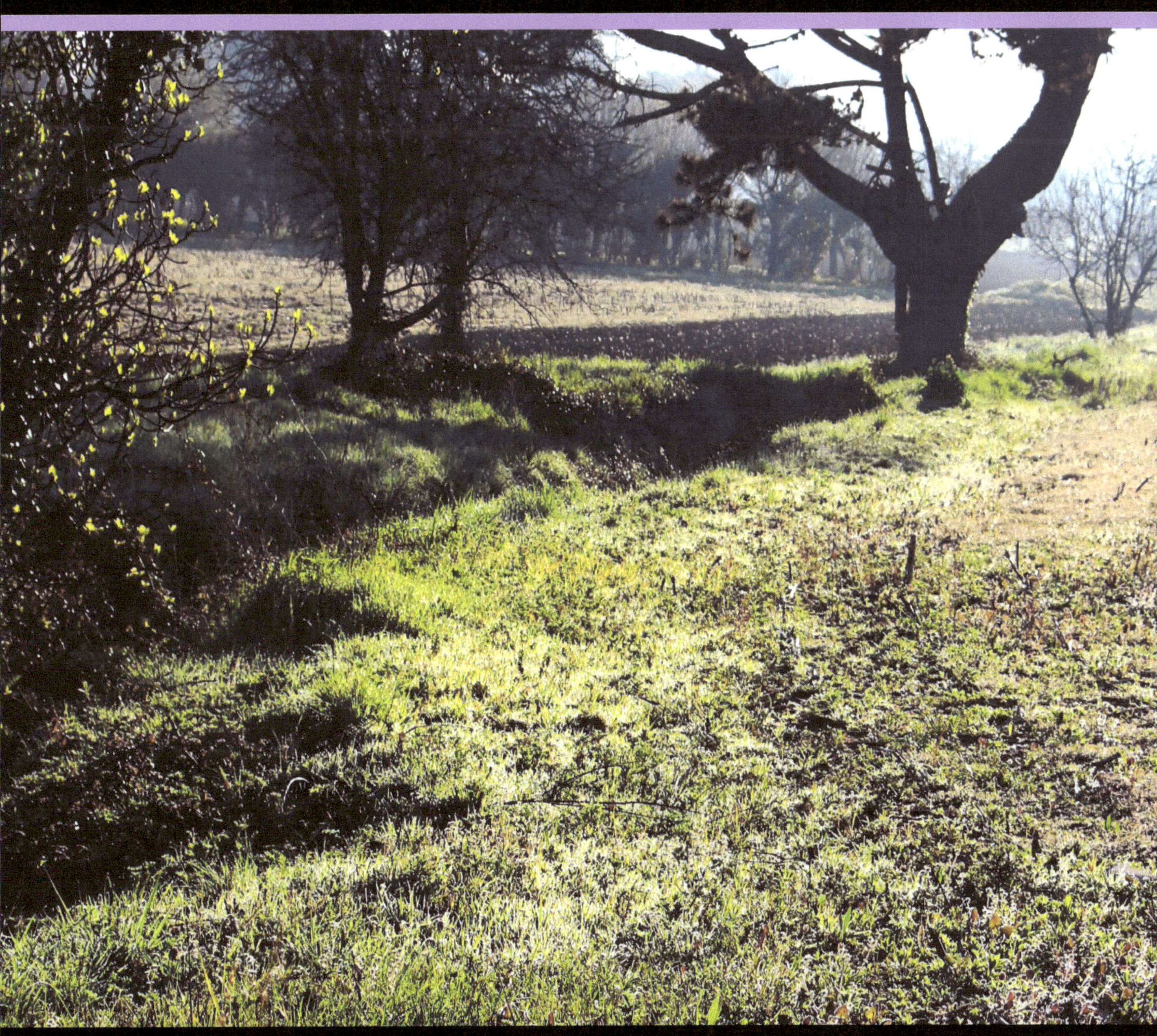

Guéthary, France - Pays Basque

Lord, let my mouth speak your wishes and my heart reflect your love. Let me be wise in my decisions, and forgiving in my heart. Let me choose the roads you have destined for me and avoid the ones where I will fall. Lord, in you I put my trust and release what separates me from your will. I glorify you and magnify your name with my small insignificant voice. You are my God and I believe in you. May your will be done. Amen.

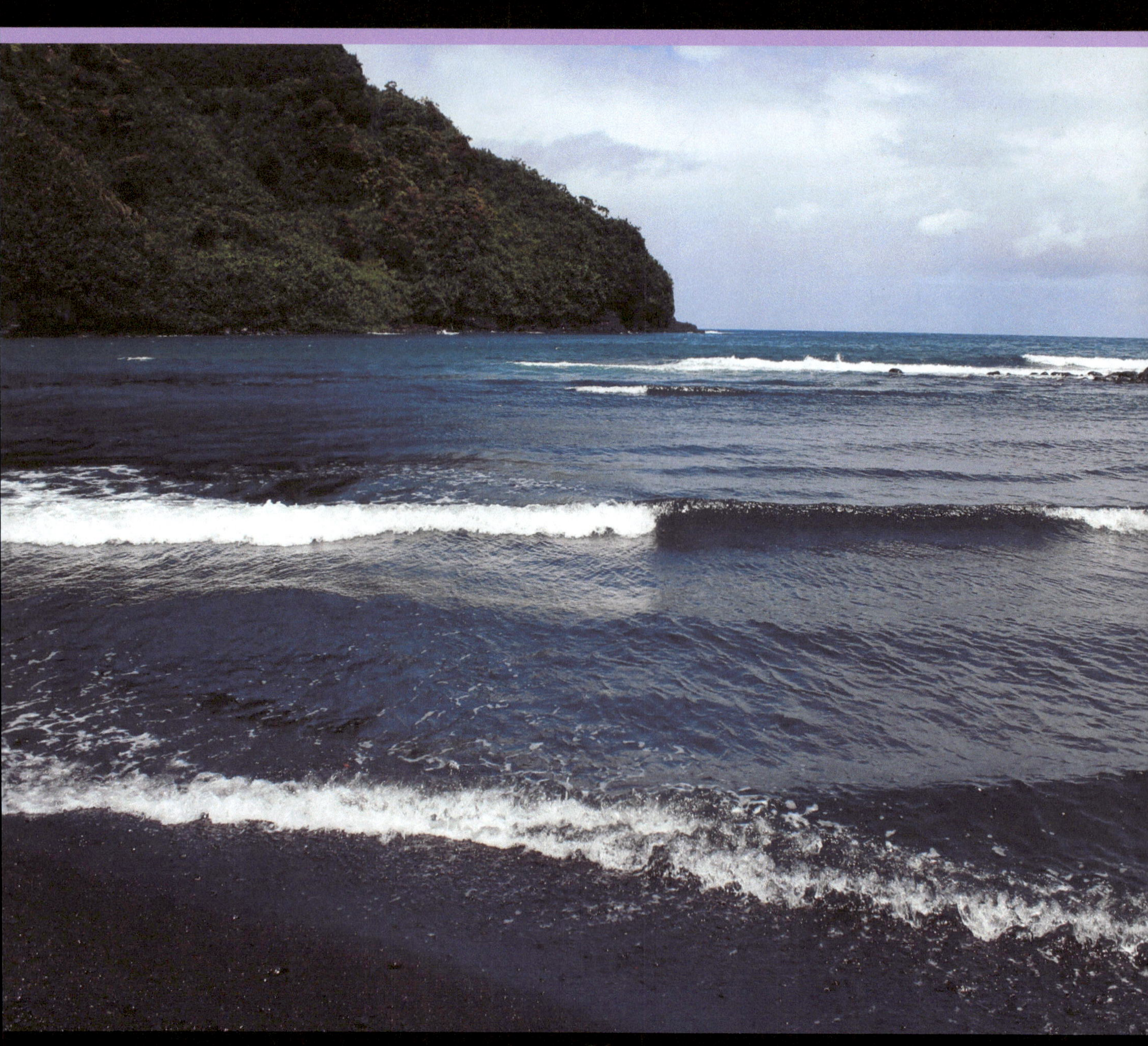

Maui, Hawaii - Hana

Heavenly Father, grant me clarity in my situation. Give me the right things to say and allow my spirit to be one of peace, wisdom, and competence. Let others see the good in me and treat me fairly and kind. Bring out the best in me, Lord. Let me possess your spirit of hope. Let me be the parent, friend, co-worker and family that is understanding, patient, loving, faithful, and kind. Help others to see your love in me. Amen.

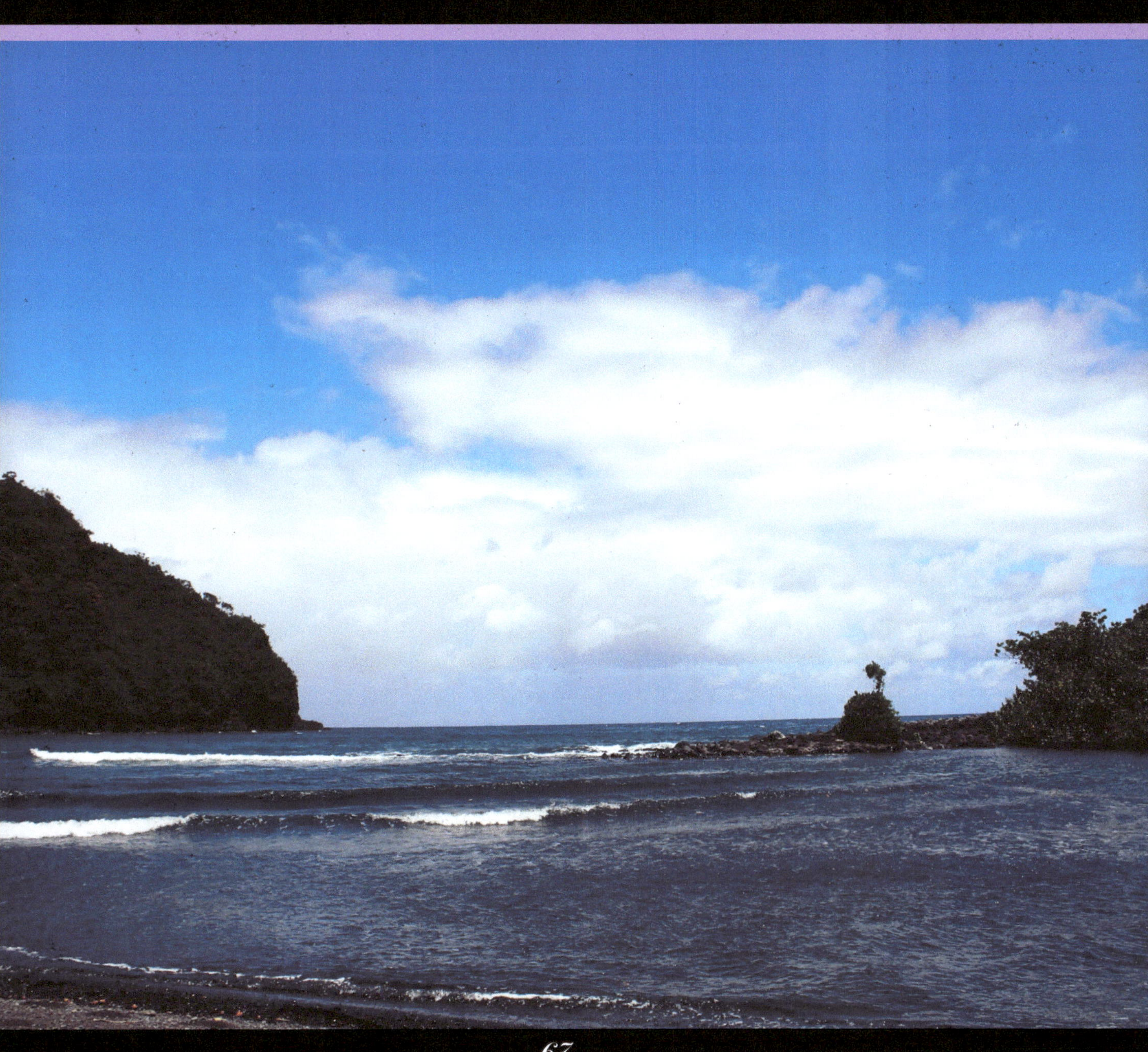

Maui, Hawaii

Thankfulness

When I was weak, you and made me strong. Lord, you've lifted me up and showed me the way. I've been alone in the darkness and you brought me into the light. You have helped me in so many ways. Lord, you have been my salvation. Without you where would I be? You found me lost in the wilderness without a dime to my name, and I lift my voice to praise you for your love is my sweet reward. I thank you for my life. Amen.

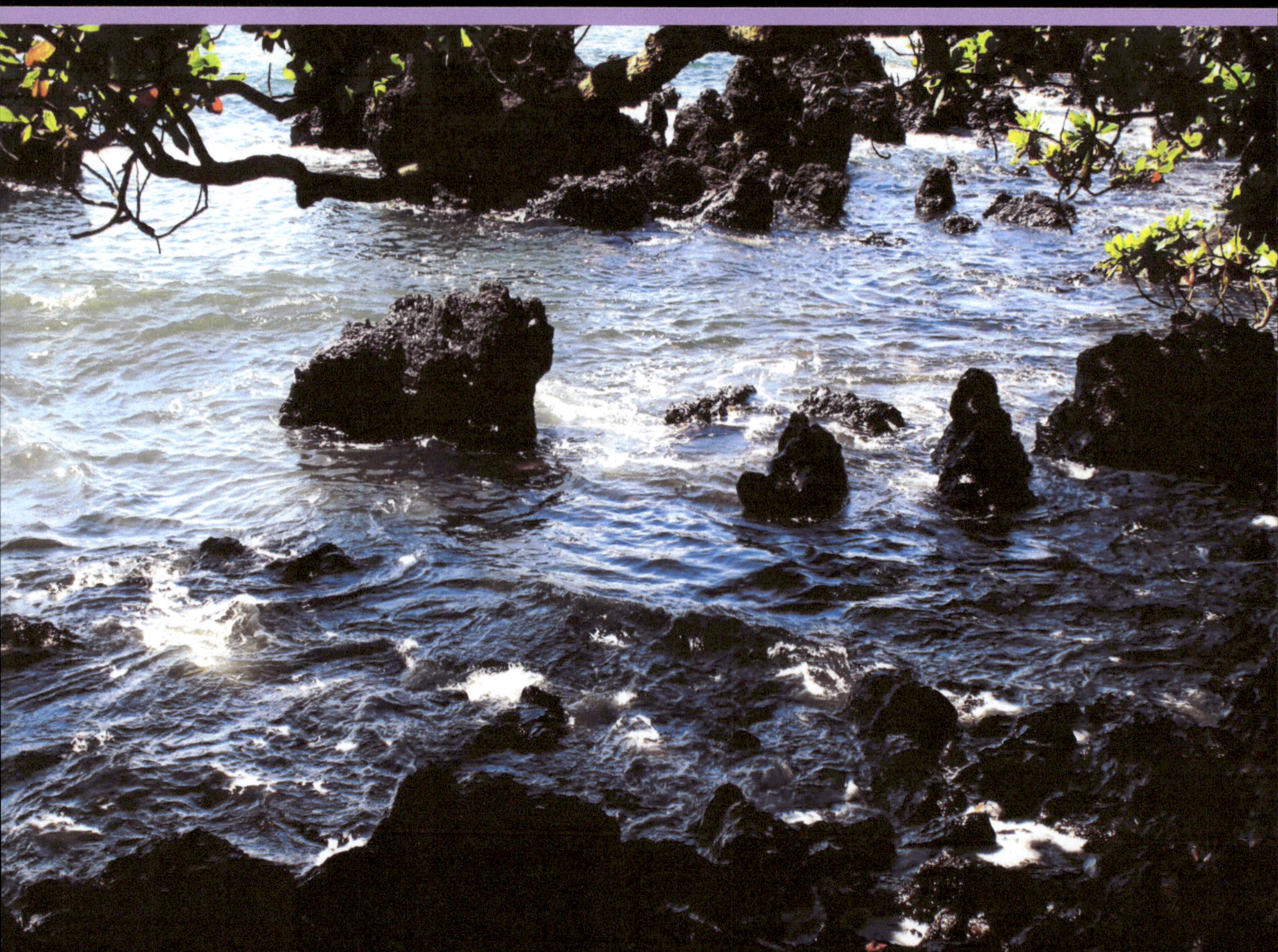

Lord, I'm going to keep praising you. I'm going to keep worshipping you. I'm going to keep magnifying your name for all you've done for me. I want to thank you for saving my life. I want to thank you for the blessings I couldn't do without. You saved me from myself and every one else. You've been so good I want to holler and shout. I thank you for all you've done for me. I'm going to praise you because you set me free...

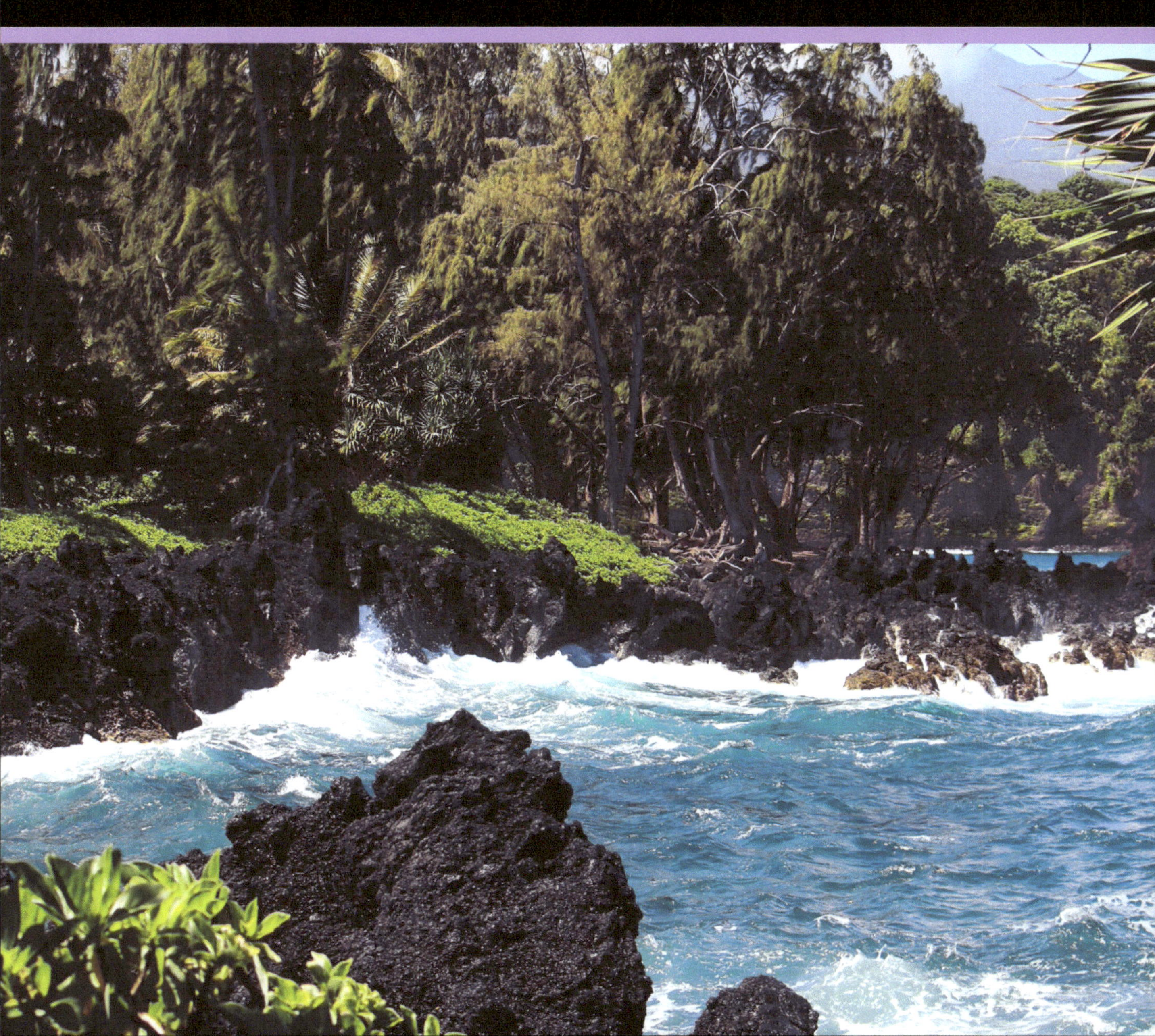

Maui, Hawaii

Thank you, Father, for this day. Help me to reach all my goals and not turn towards the wrong, but towards the righteous path. Help me to be free of my fear and walk in your light. Lord, I am your child, and I pray that you walk with me and shield me. I ask that my heart be delivered from trouble and my life made whole. I ask you to guide me and protect me, even from myself. Keep me safe and deliver me from harm. Amen.

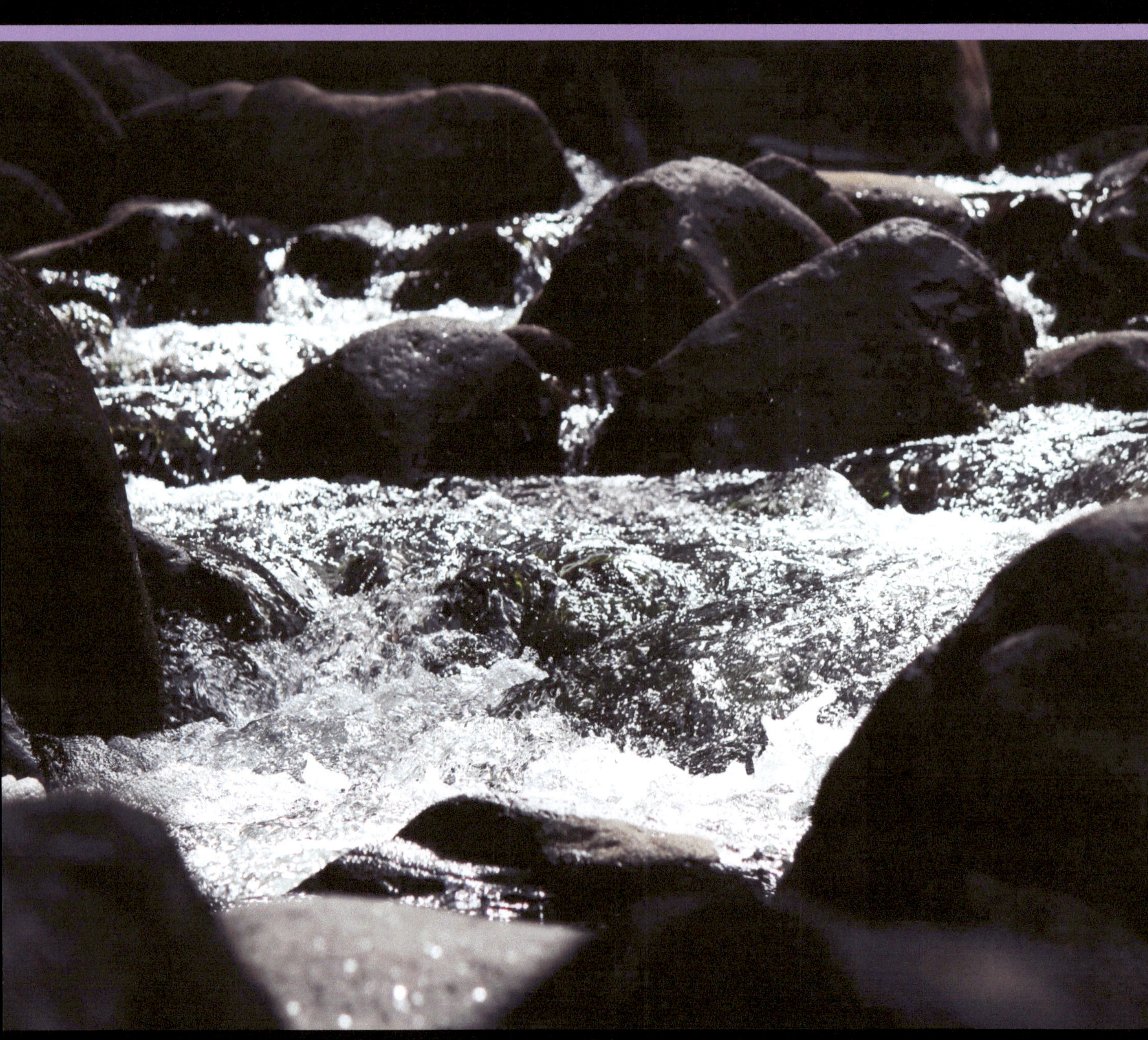

Maui, Hawaii - Wailuku

Comfort and Strength

Oh, Father, bless me this day. Please help me to overcome my trials. How I need your love right now. Father, please deliver me from circumstances; make me whole again. Take care of me. Stand with me and hold my hand. You are my hope; my only source of joy. You are my strength, Lord. Hold me in your arms. Father God, I need you. I need near me now. Let me lay in your arms of grace. Please take my tears away. Amen.

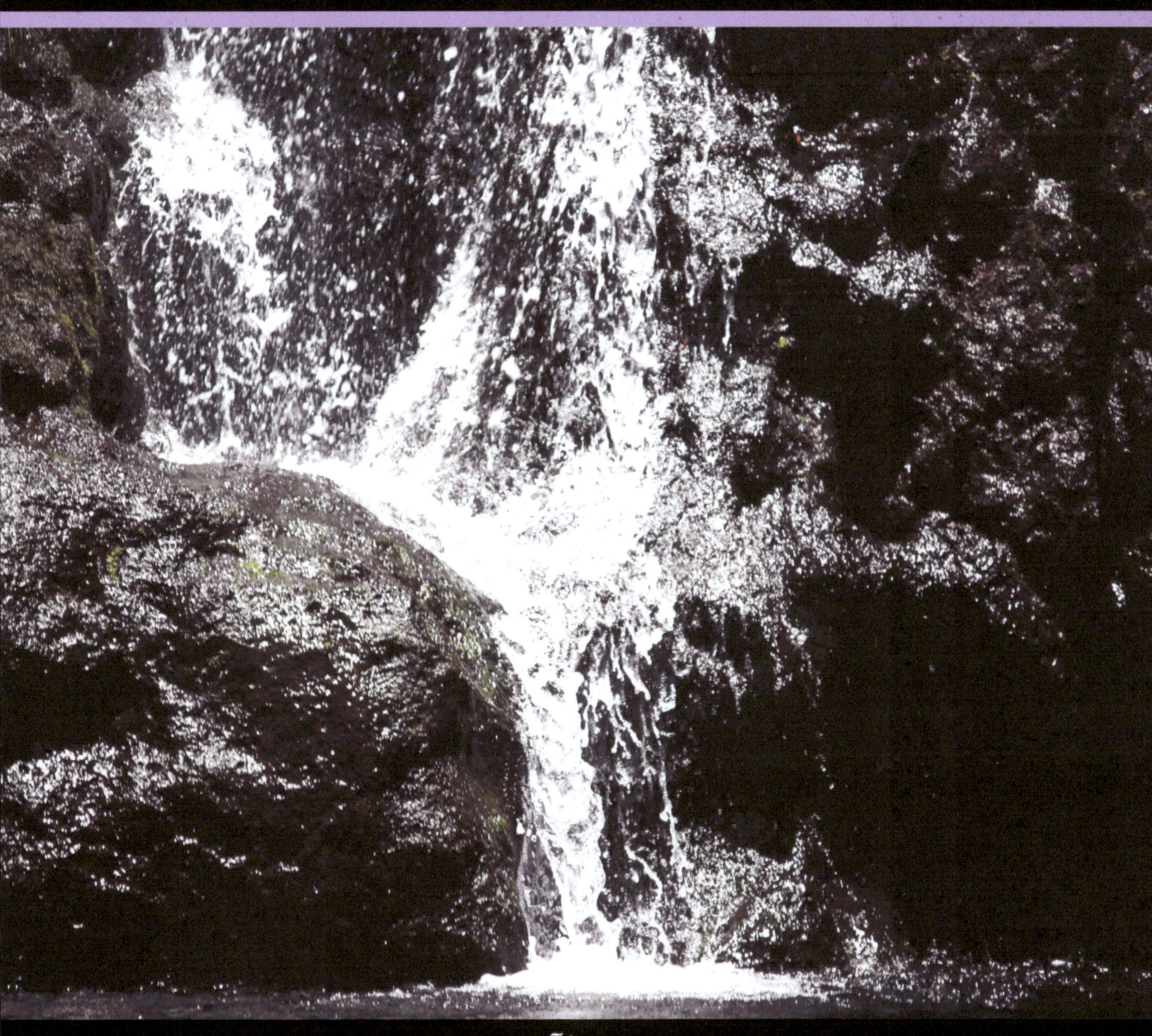

Maui, Hawaii - Hana

My heavenly Father, have mercy on me. I am lost in the wilderness, but when I call on you, you comfort me. In the blink of an eye I feel your presence near. When I feel so alone and my heart suffers in pain, I know, oh God, that you have never left me, for you have kept me time in and time out; sun up and sun down. Thank you for loving me. Thank you for bringing me peace and for sending your Holy Spirit to comfort me. Amen.

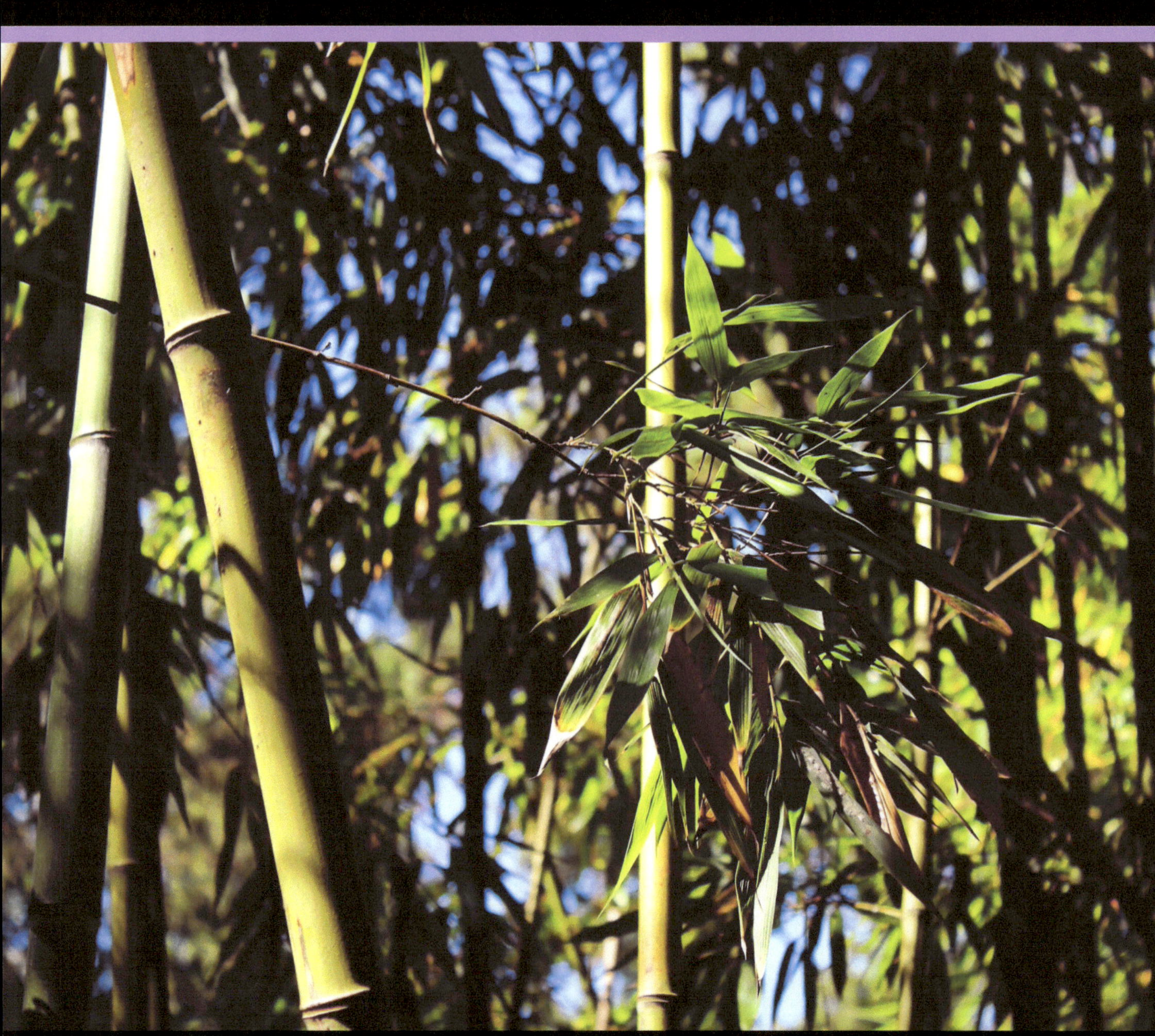

Anglet, France - Forêt de Chiberta

Father, let your love rain over me. Lord, I need your will in my life. Please calm my fears with your everlasting peace and fill my heart with compassion and understanding. Lord, help me to be all that I dream, and help me to attain my goals. On this day and every day of my life please walk with me, so that I may overcome this world. Lift me up. Keep me close... Lord, I need a miracle in my life, and that miracle is you... Amen.

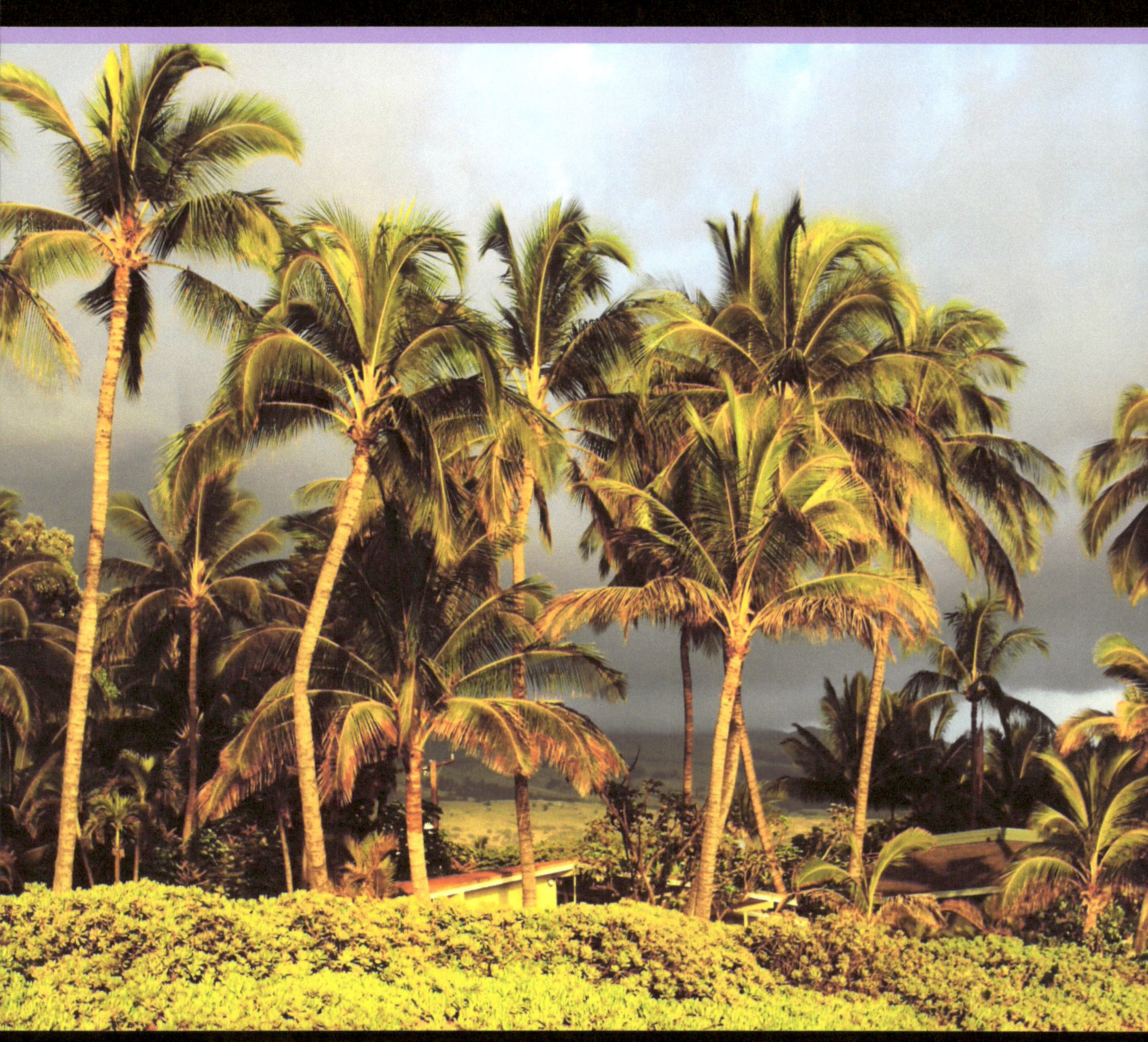

Maui, Hawaii - Kihei

Heal me Master, my sacred Lord. My body is weak, but you are strong. Grant my life your abiding peace. Send your love and comfort me. I thank you, Lord, for this day and for everything you have done for me. You are worthy of all praise. Where would I be if it weren't for your grace? You have kept me from falling and I thank you for your love. You are a generous and loving God. Bless my soul and heal me now. Amen.

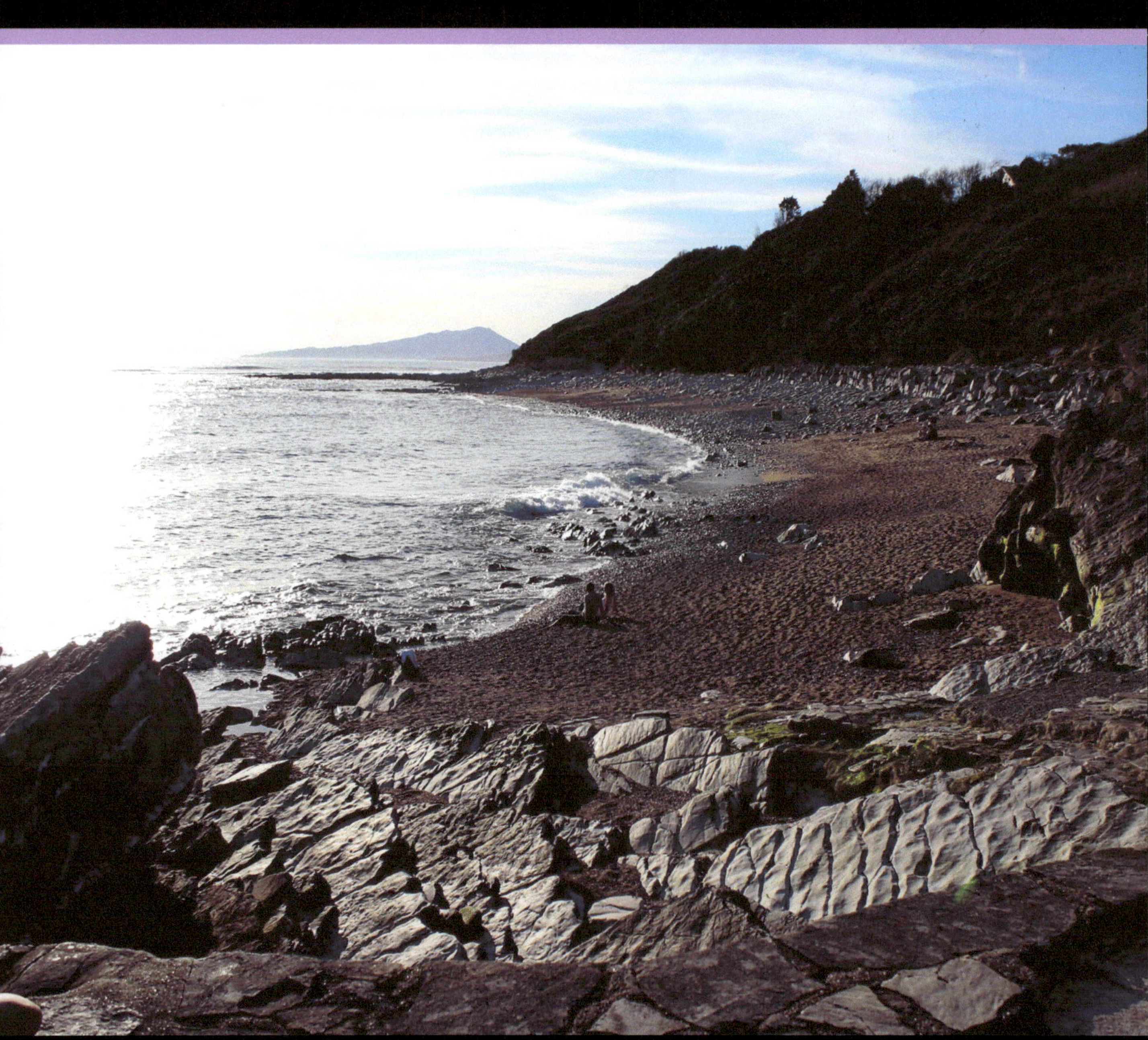

Guéthary, France - Pays Basque

Lord, thank you for letting me live to see one more day. Father God, my life is in your hands. Watch over and guide me that I may do your will. In everything I do and all that I live, let me be peaceful, loving, and happy. Guard from disease, frustration, ridicule, and anger. Bind my tongue that I may not say what I will regret. Lord, lift me when I am feeling low and bind my wounds that I may feel your blessings on my life. Amen.

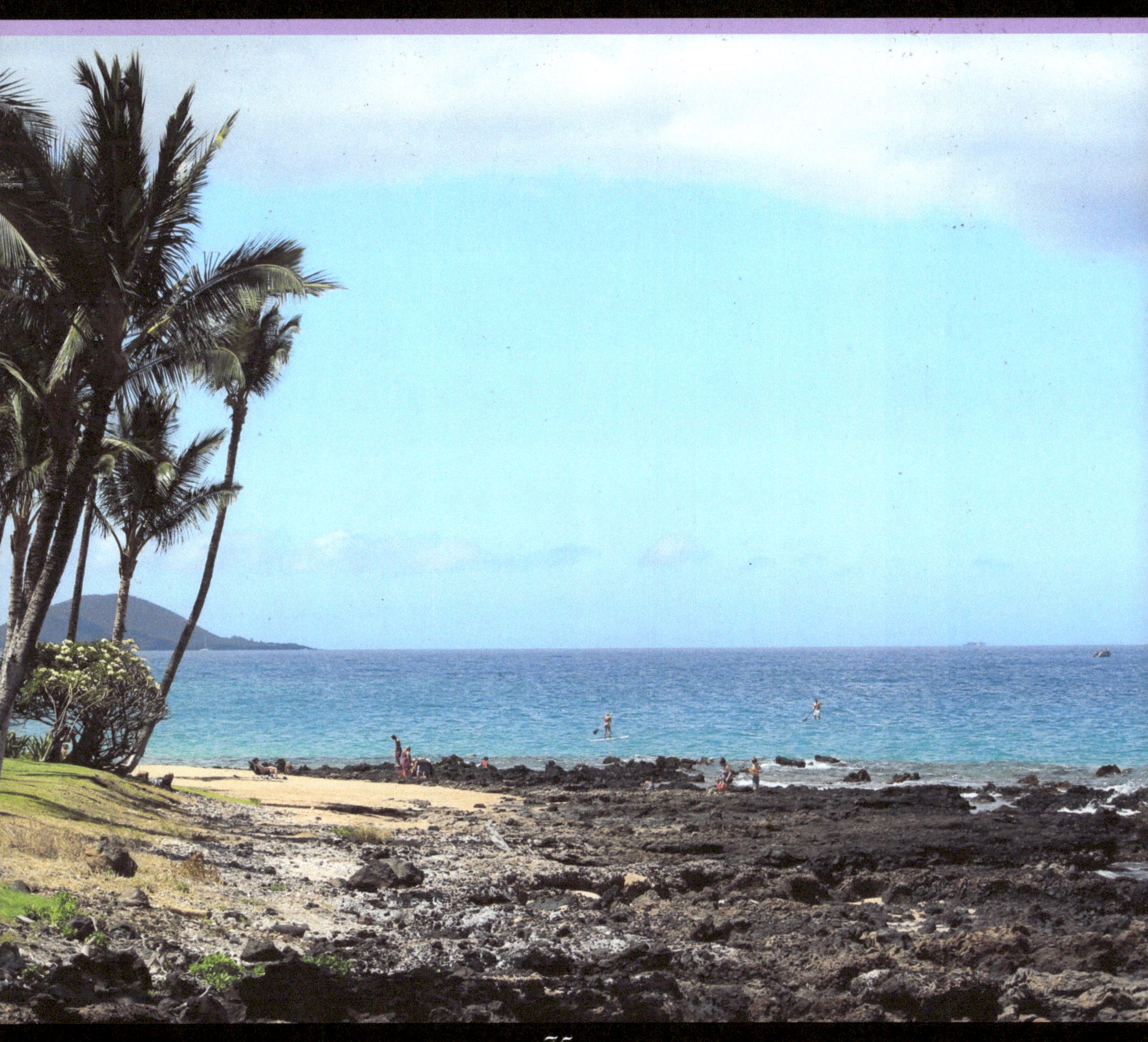

Maui, Hawaii - Kahului

Lord, let me feel your joy and your strength. Let your sun shine upon me. Let the wind blow through my hair. Let me live like love is water and have believe like my faith is bread. Let me nourish my soul in laughter and let work until dreams come true. Let me build a life of happiness without fear or worry. Let me wake with only hope for tomorrow and sleep with my heart open wide. Let me live in happiness; let me live in you...

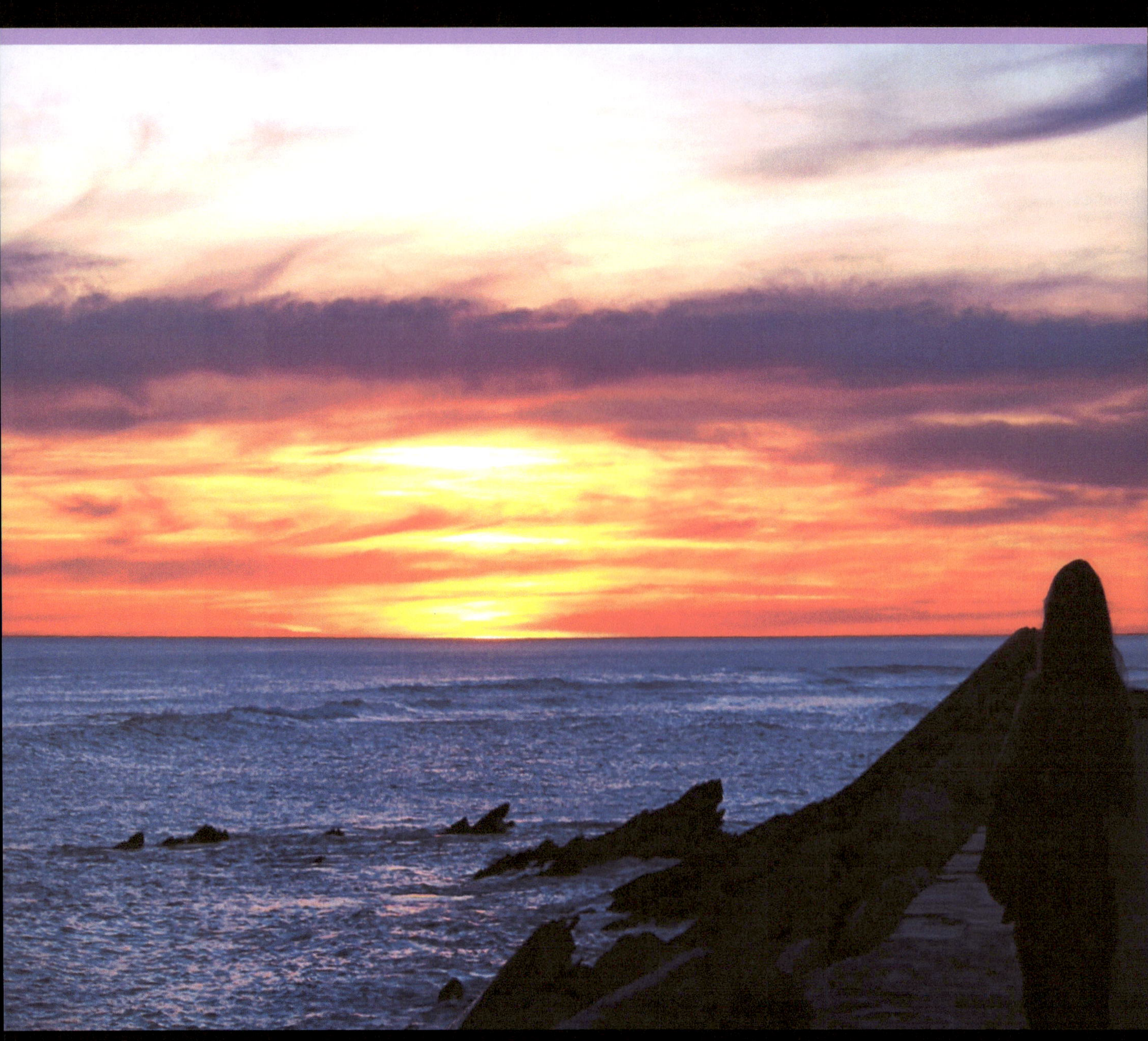

Guéthary, France - Pays Basque

Thank you for this beautiful day, Lord. Thank you for all the blessing on my life. You woke me up this morning and protected me through the night. You guided my footsteps and kept me when I went astray. Because of your grace, I can pray in my right mind. How blessed I am to have your love. This world my test my faith, but your love is everywhere. Thank you for protecting me. Only your grace have kept me safe...

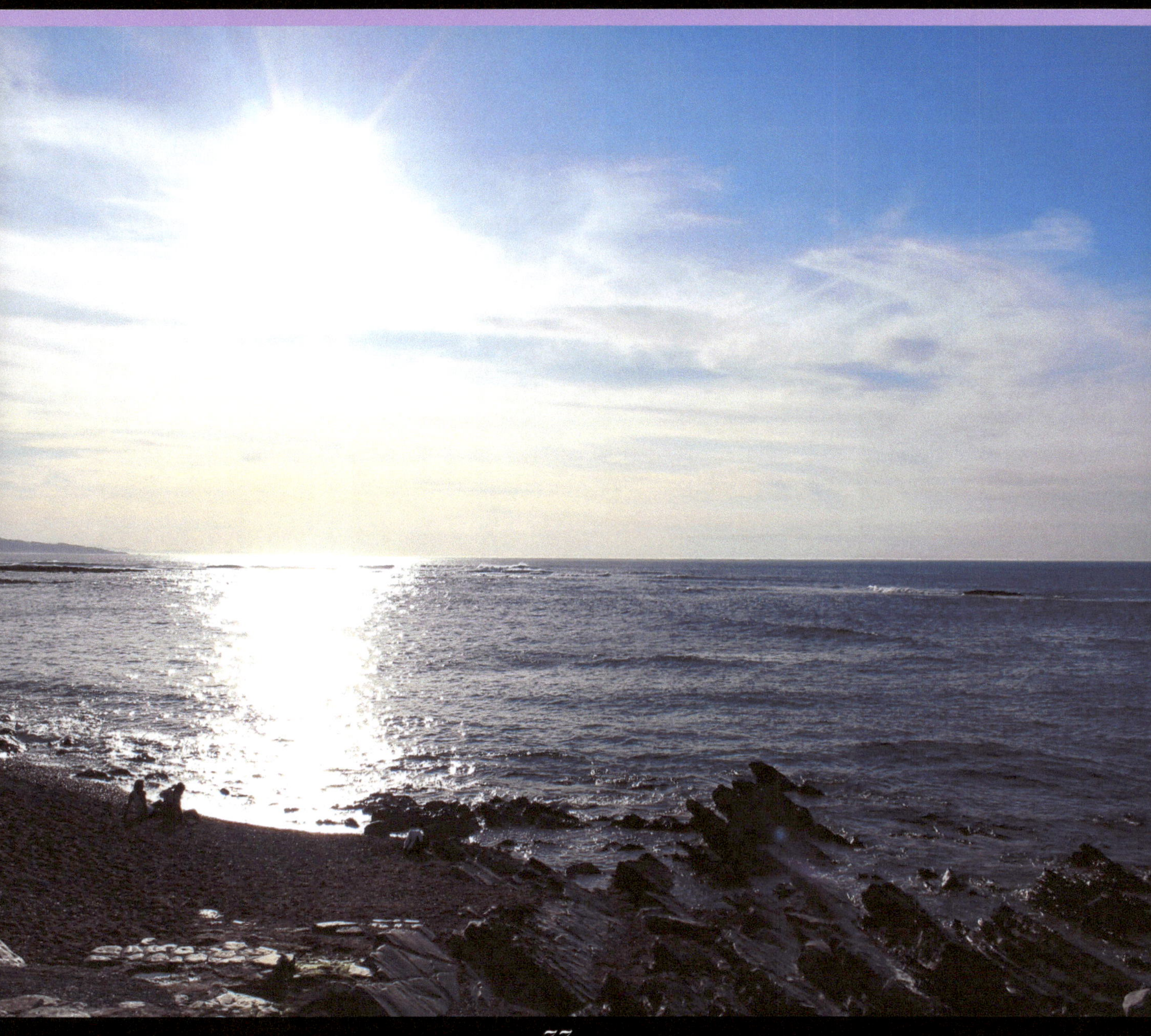

Guéthary, France - Pays Basque

My Lord, open a door to my happiness. Many have been closed in my face. Lord, you hold the key to my deliverance. Only you, Father, can get me through this difficult time. I feel like an empty wind blowing through a valley, but where ever you want me, that is where I wish to be. Please surround me with your love and bind me in your heart. I want to be forever in your will. Deliver me this day... Amen.

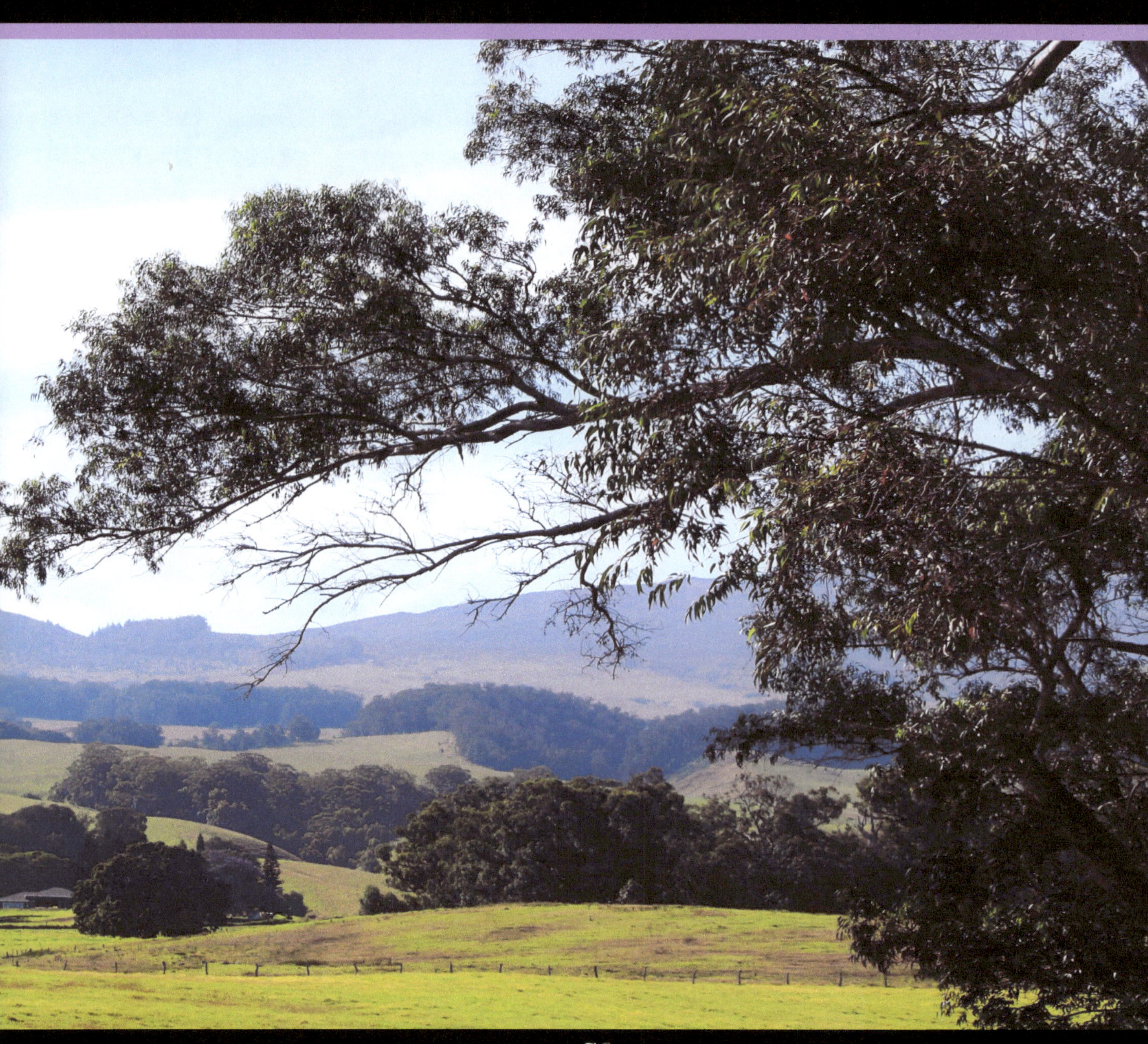

Maui, Hawaii - Kula

Safe-Keeping

Lord, keep me in your tender care... Watch over my loved ones so that we may feel your holy presence. Lord, keep us safe and free from harm. Walk with us in our daily lives, and guide us towards our dreams. Lift us up so that we may feel your glory and be secure in your arms. Father, please be with us in every way; in our hearts and in our minds that we may receive your blessings in our lives. In Jesus name I pray... Amen.

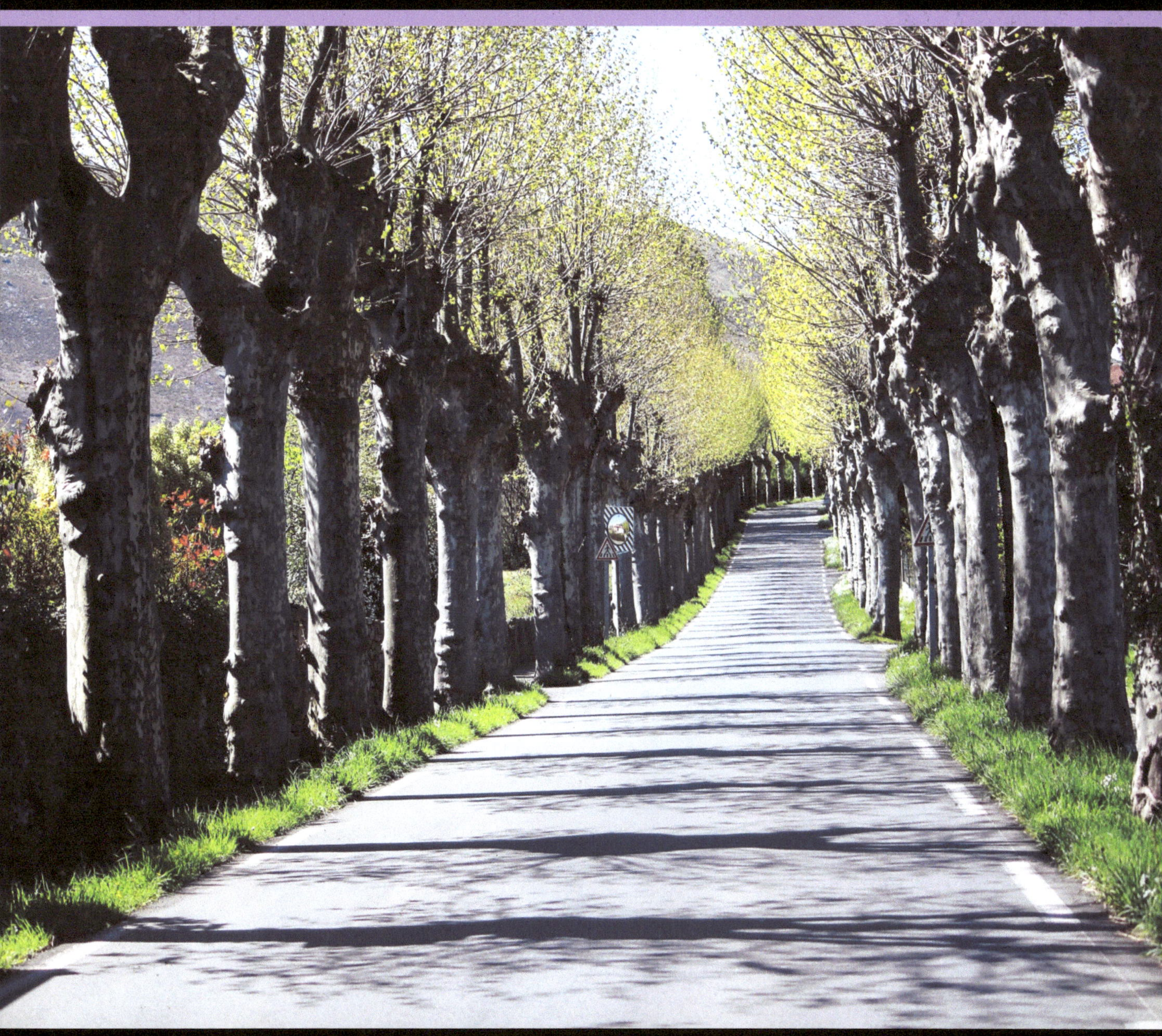

La Rhune, France - Pays Basque

Courage

Replace my loneliness with love, my frailty with strength, my fears with faith, my doubts with courage, and my tears with joy. Wrap me in your arms of love and surround me with your grace. Heavenly Father, touch my heart and my life, so that I may live in peace. Let hope be my battle cry and strength be my armor. Gird me with courage and let me be unafraid of what lies ahead. Grant me this blessing in Jesus name... Amen.

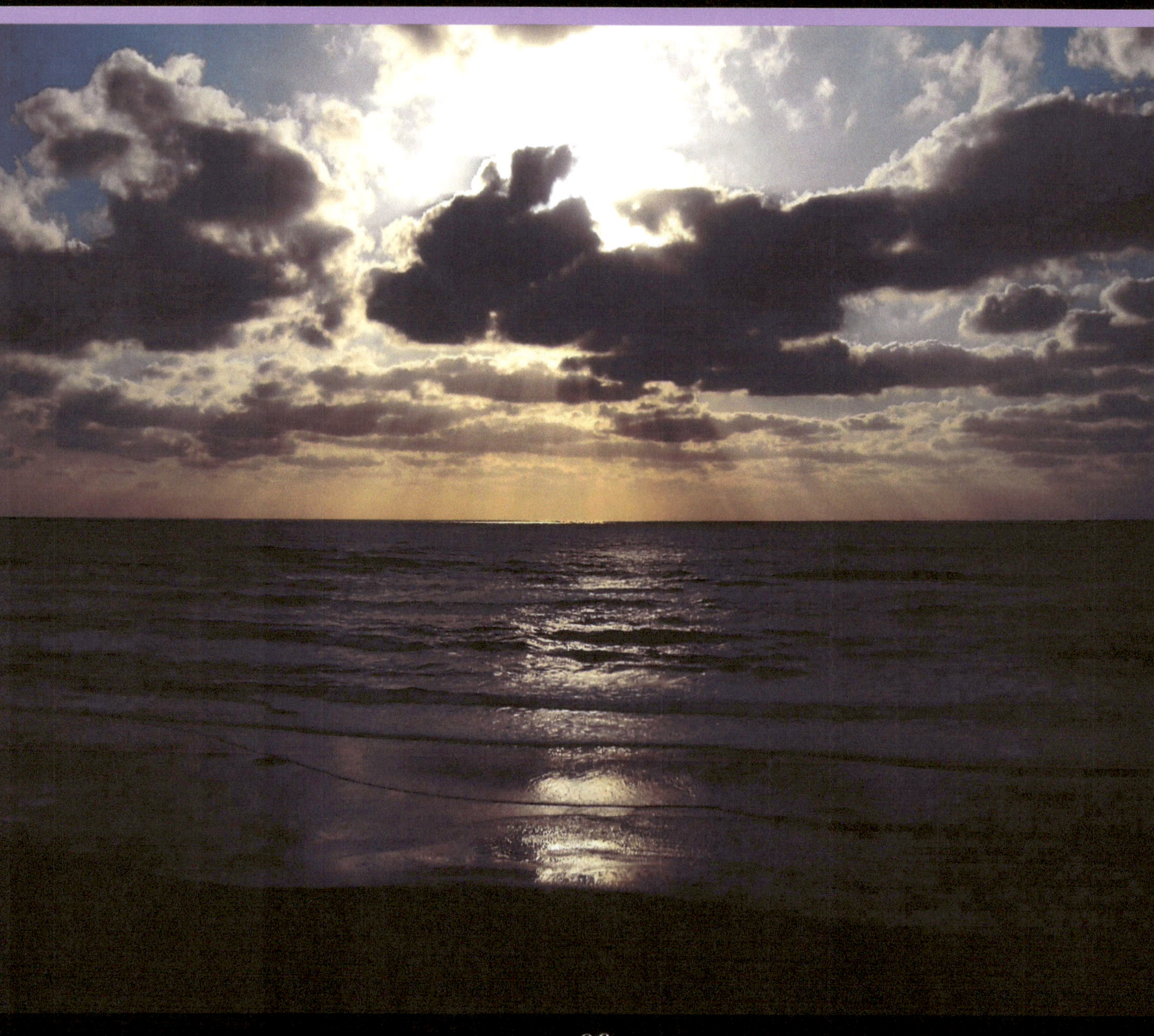

Biarritz, France - Plage de Milady

Protection

Lord, watch over my children... Make them vessels of your love. Keep them safe from their enemies. Give them wisdom, courage, and love. Let them be guided by their faith and protected from their fears. Let them be saved by your amazing grace. Let their anger dissolve into empathy and their character be beyond reproach. Let them know where to turn when they need help and let them turn to you. In Jesus name...Amen.

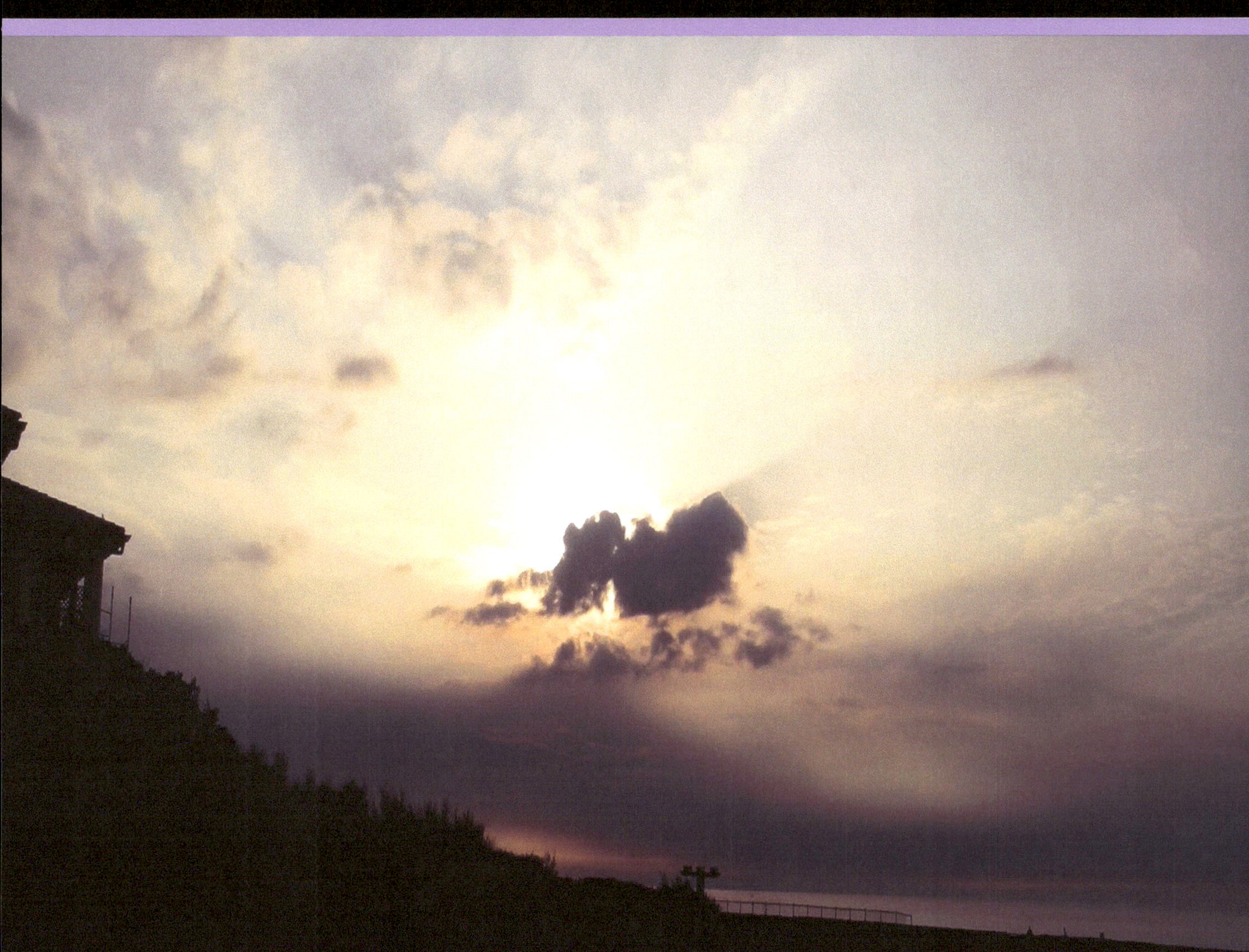

Almighty redeemer, cover me with your grace. When pain overtakes me and life overwhelms me, I know you won't forsake me. And I know that you are there, because every time I call you, I feel you draw near. You send the angels to comfort me and they watch over me as I pray. You are so good to me, Lord. You help me through the bad times and I endure. With you, I rise again, even after I fall. Thank you, for loving me...

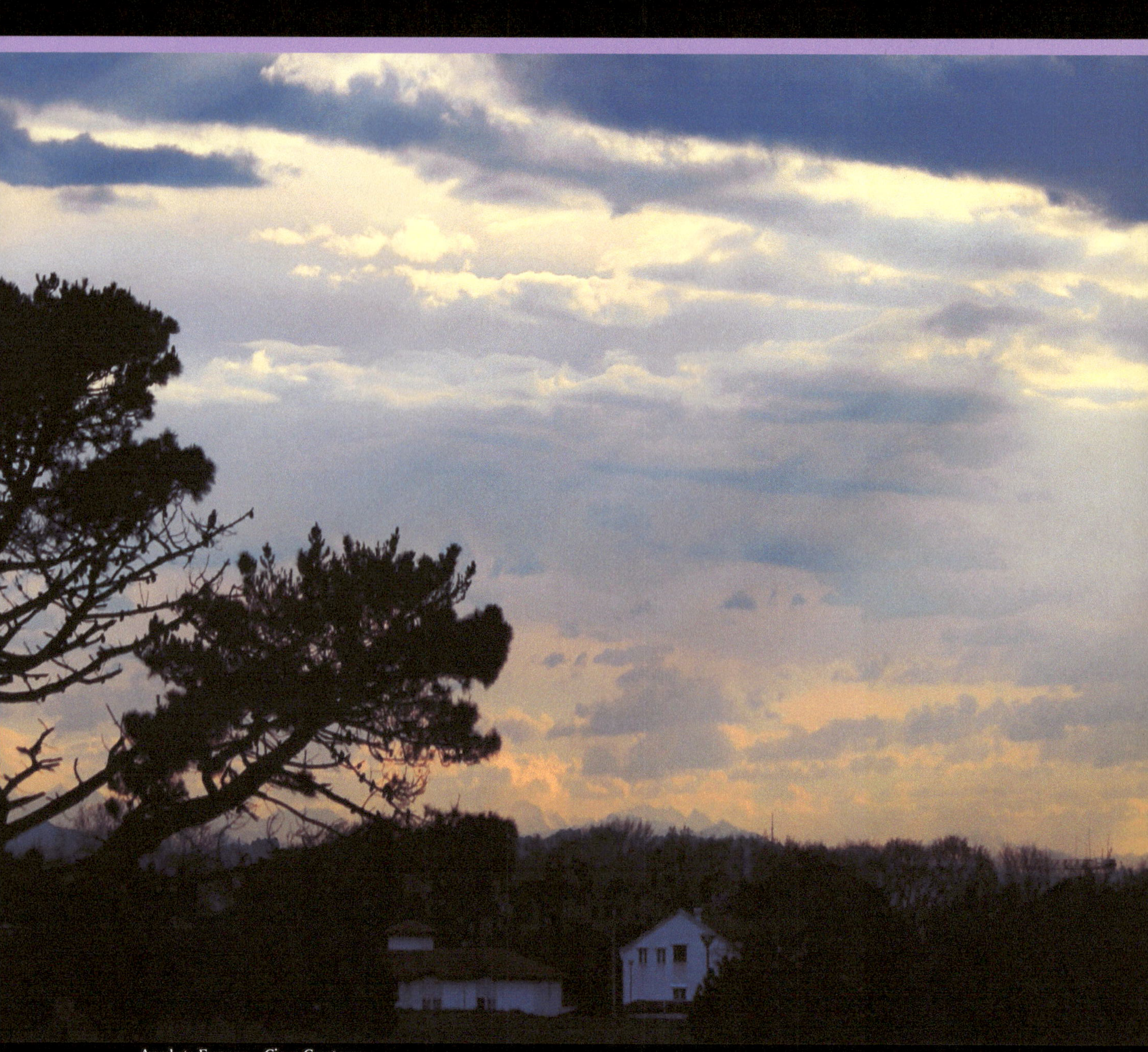

Anglet, France - Cinq Cantons

Heavenly Father, I raise my hands in praise to you. There is no one like you in all the earth, for only you can heal my pain so I sing praises to your name for your love and power are great. My voice cries out, though I am worn from the fight. You, Lord, are my hope. Where else can I turn, but to your everlasting love? Who else can hear my suffering? For you are my God and only you can deliver. I pray for eternal peace... Amen

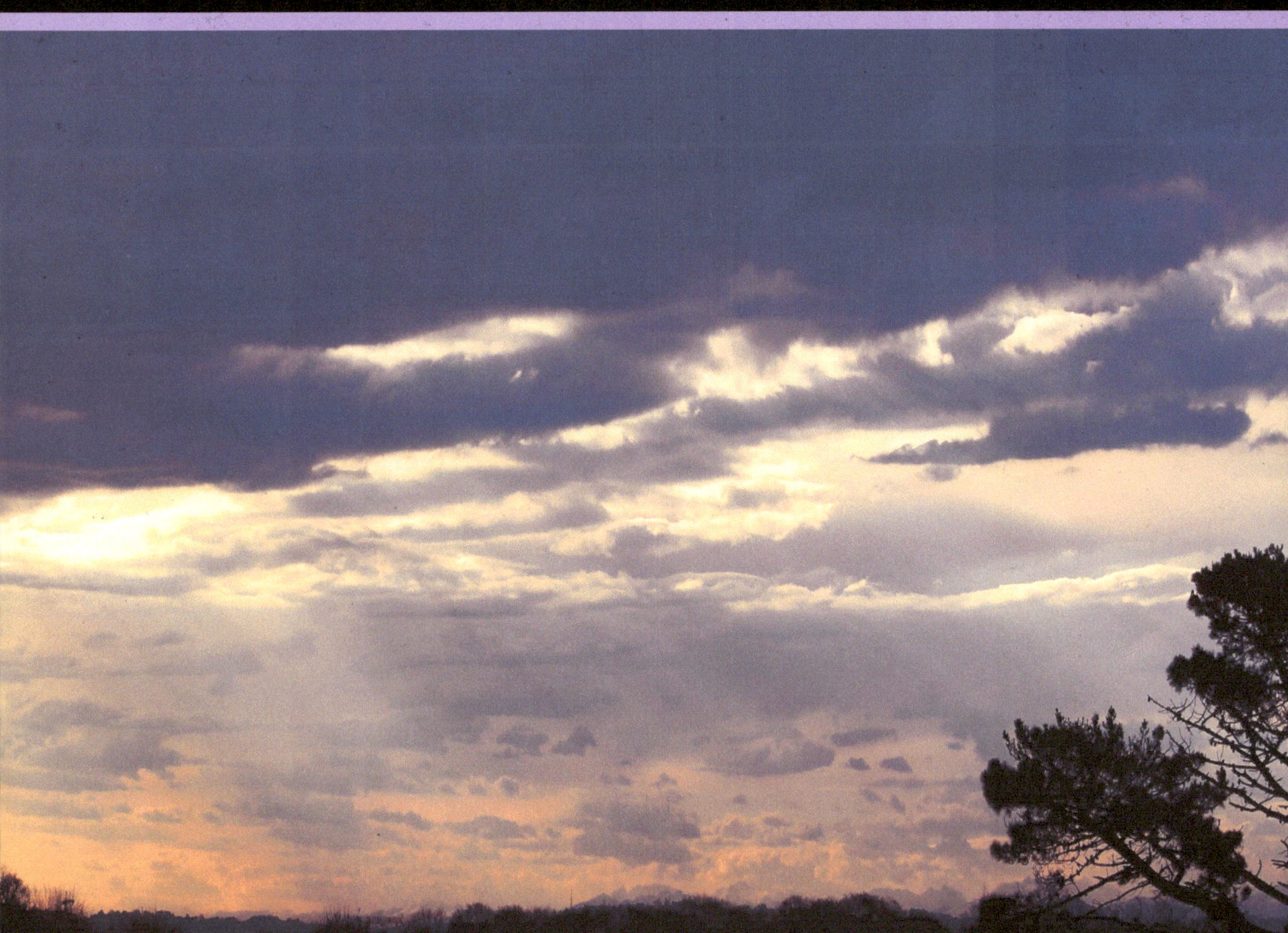

I give my all to you, Lord; to walk in faith and leave behind my tears. Lord, let me be inside your mercy and live inside your love. Deliver my soul from sorrow. Grant me a miracle by faith. Lift my head that I may see the promises life holds for me. Open my heart to the present and close the door to the painful past. I need a miracle in my life. I put all my trust in you. Please grant me my heart's desire. I will always praise you. Amen.

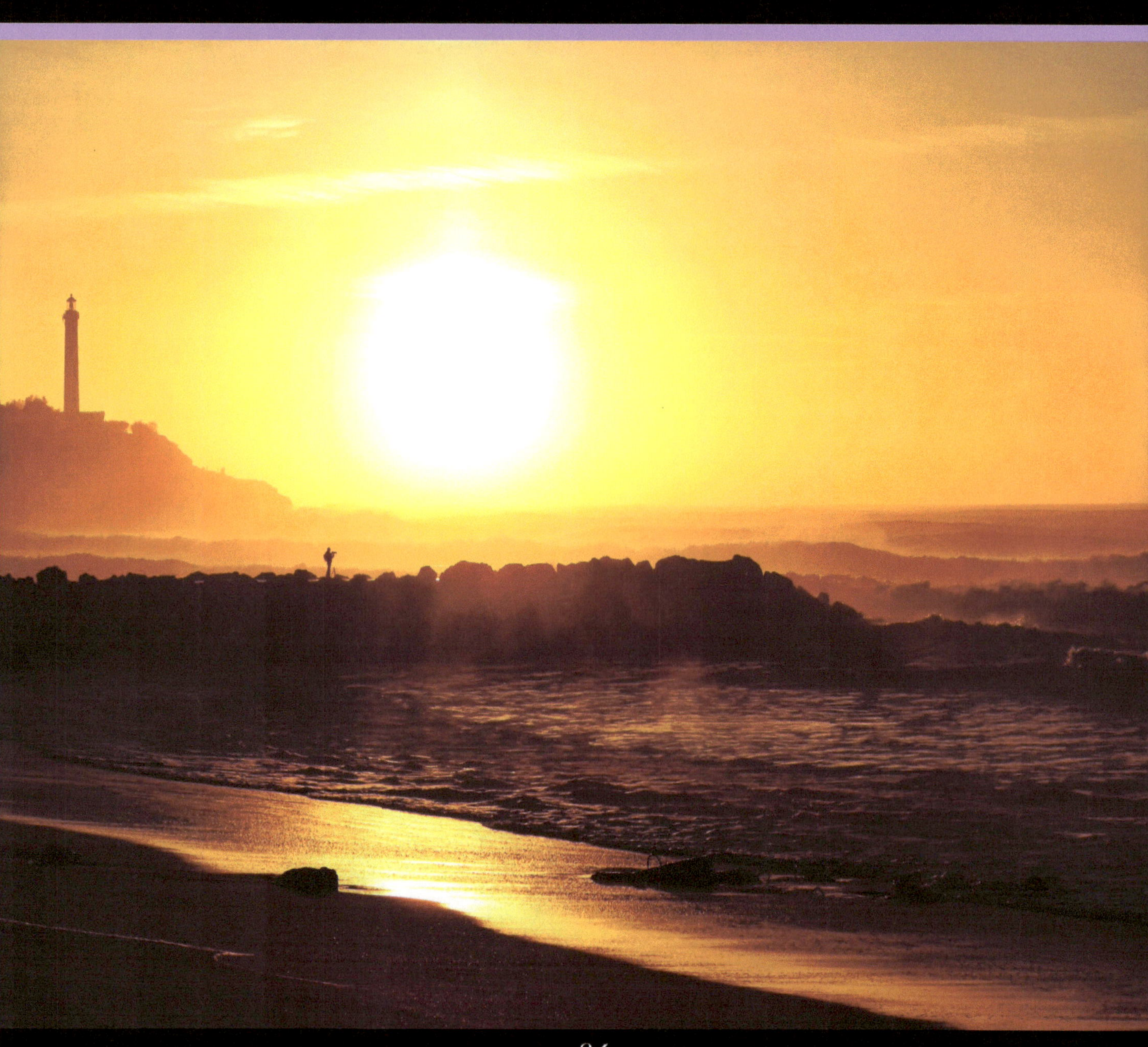

Anglet, France - Chambre d'Amour

MESSAGES OF

INSPIRATION FROM THE HOLY BIBLE

HOPE

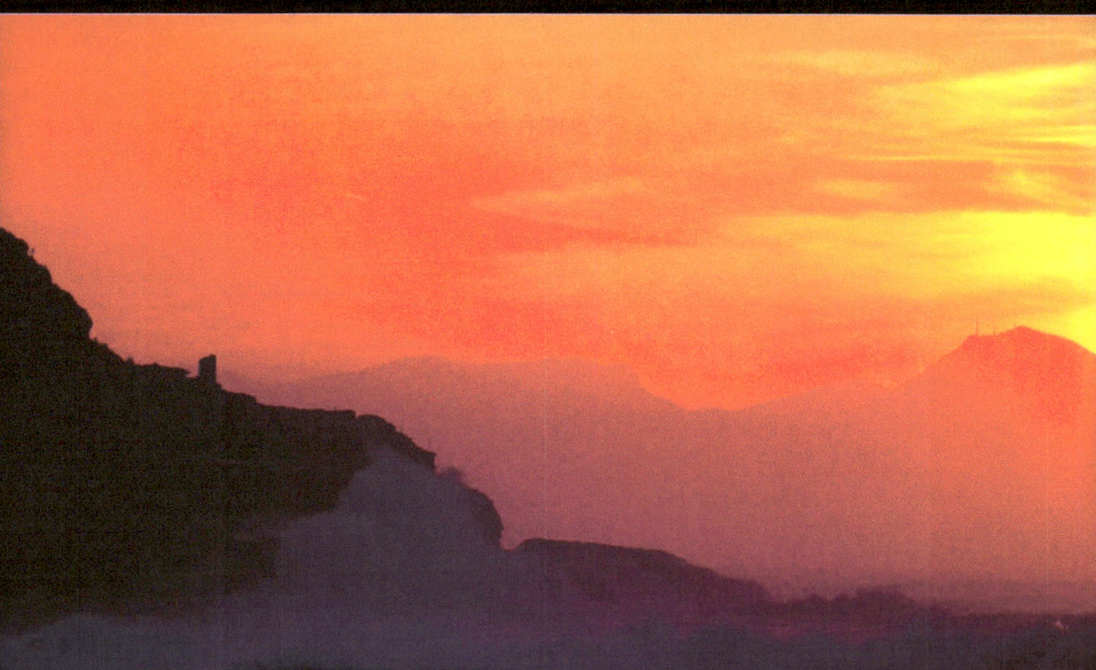

"May the LORD bless you and keep you. May the LORD shine his face upon you and be merciful unto you. May the LORD look upon your face and give you peace".

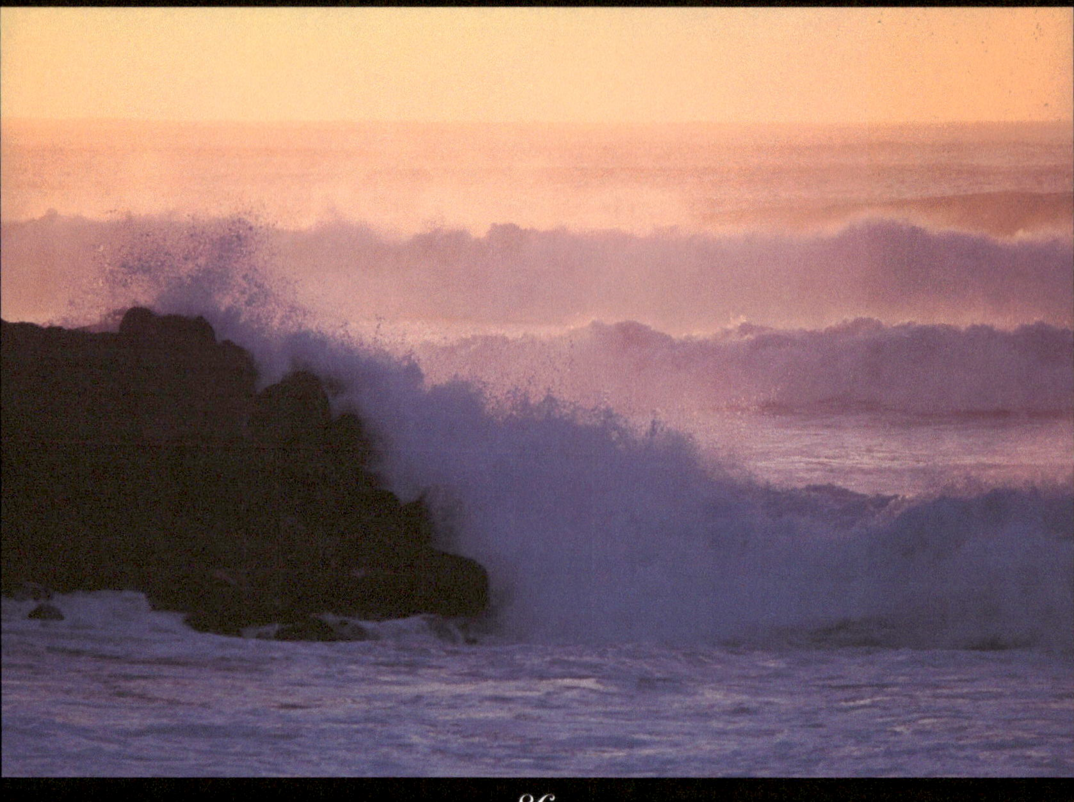

Anglet, France - Chambre d'Amour

1 Thessalonians 5:16-18

No mater what happens in your life, whatever you are going though, rejoice.

Pray without ceasing through every storm and every drop of rain.

There is a miracle in keeping your faith. This is what GOD wants for your life. Be positive.

"Rejoice always. Pray at all times, because this is what GOD wants from you during your life, when you believe in Yeshua, Christ Jesus."

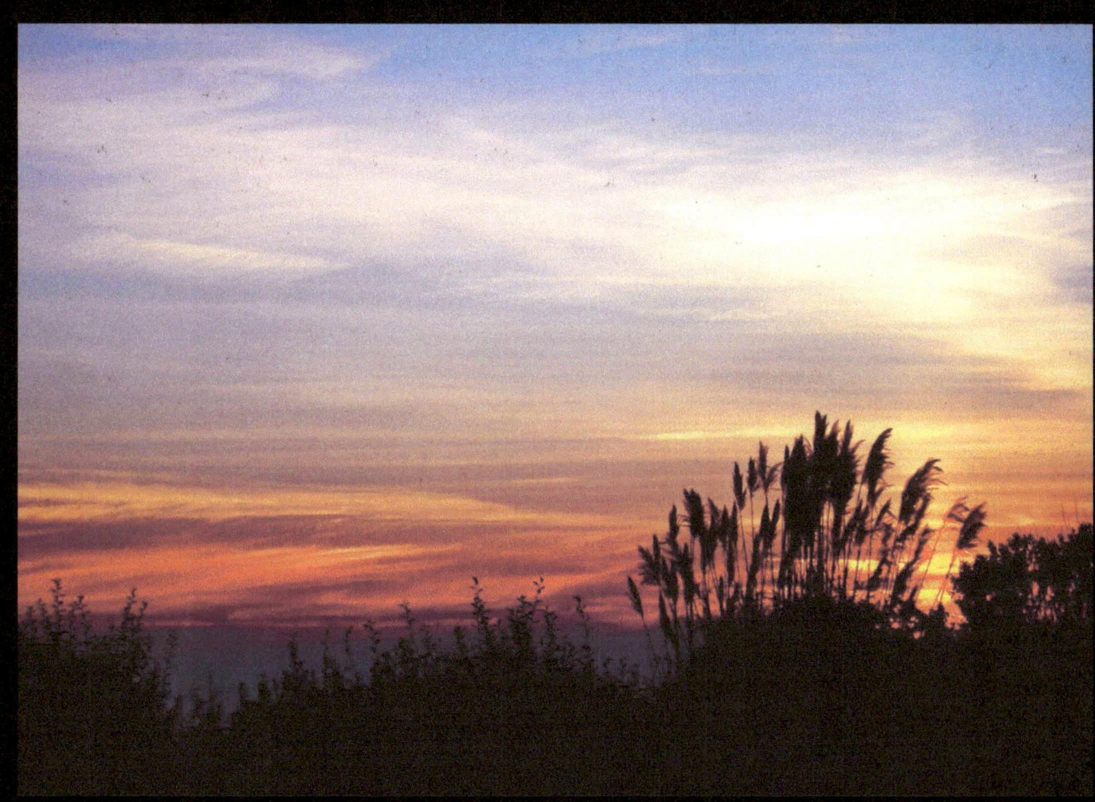

Anglet, France - Golfe de Chiberta

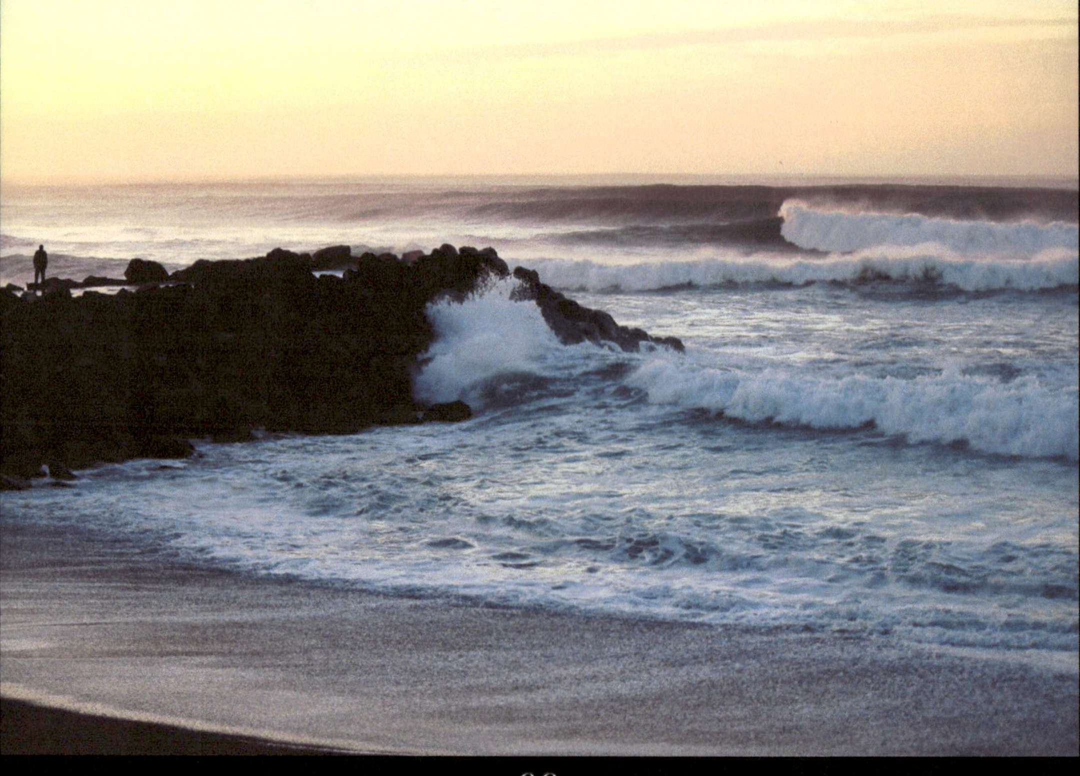

Anglet, France - Chambre d'Amou

In the midst of trouble, call on the Divine, and do not be afraid.

God is your hope. Have faith.

"GOD is our hope and strength and our help in times of trouble. Therefore, we will not be afraid, though the earth trembles and the mountains tumble into the midst of the sea, and the oceans rage and toss and the mountains quake from their thunderous rage."

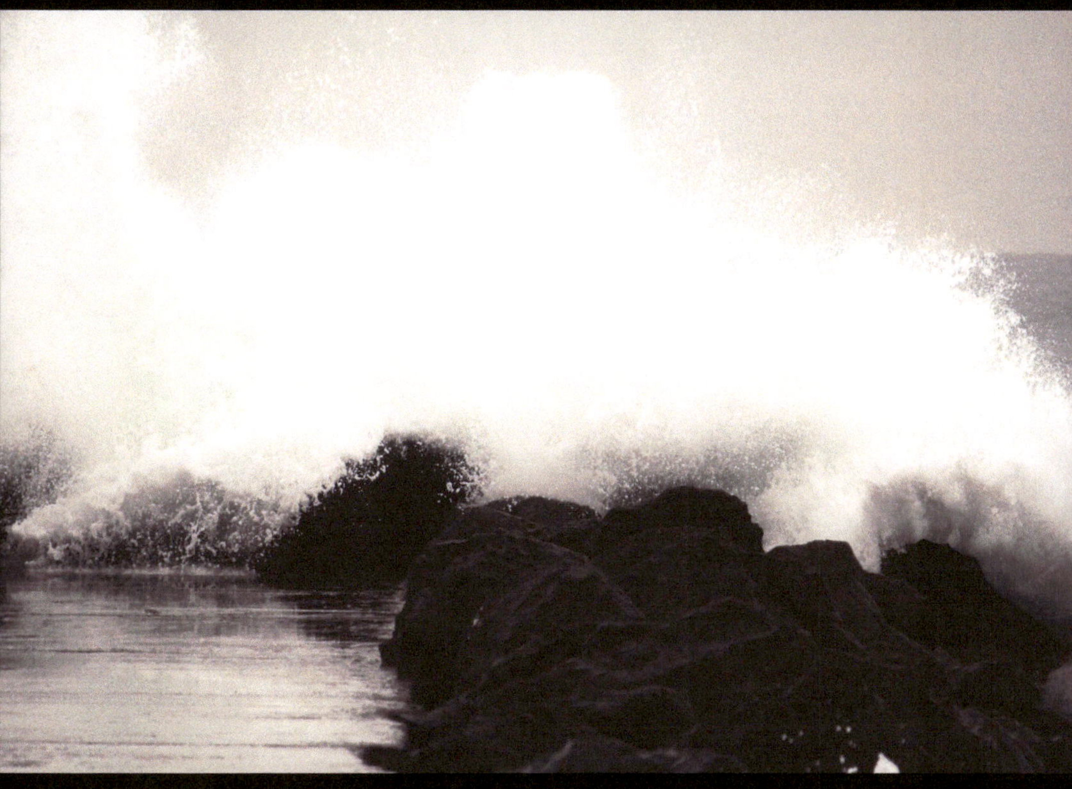

Anglet, France - Chambre d'Amour

Mathew 7:7-11

The Divine will give you everything that is good for you.
Ask for what you want.

"Ask, and you shall receive; seek, and you shall find; knock, and the door shall be opened. For everyone who asks receives, he who seeks finds, and to him who knocks, the door shall be opened. Is there a man among you who will offer his son a stone when he asks for bread, or a snake when he asks for a fish? If then, as bad as you are, know how to give your children what is good for them, how much more will your heavenly Father give good things to those who ask Him!"

(Jesus Christ)

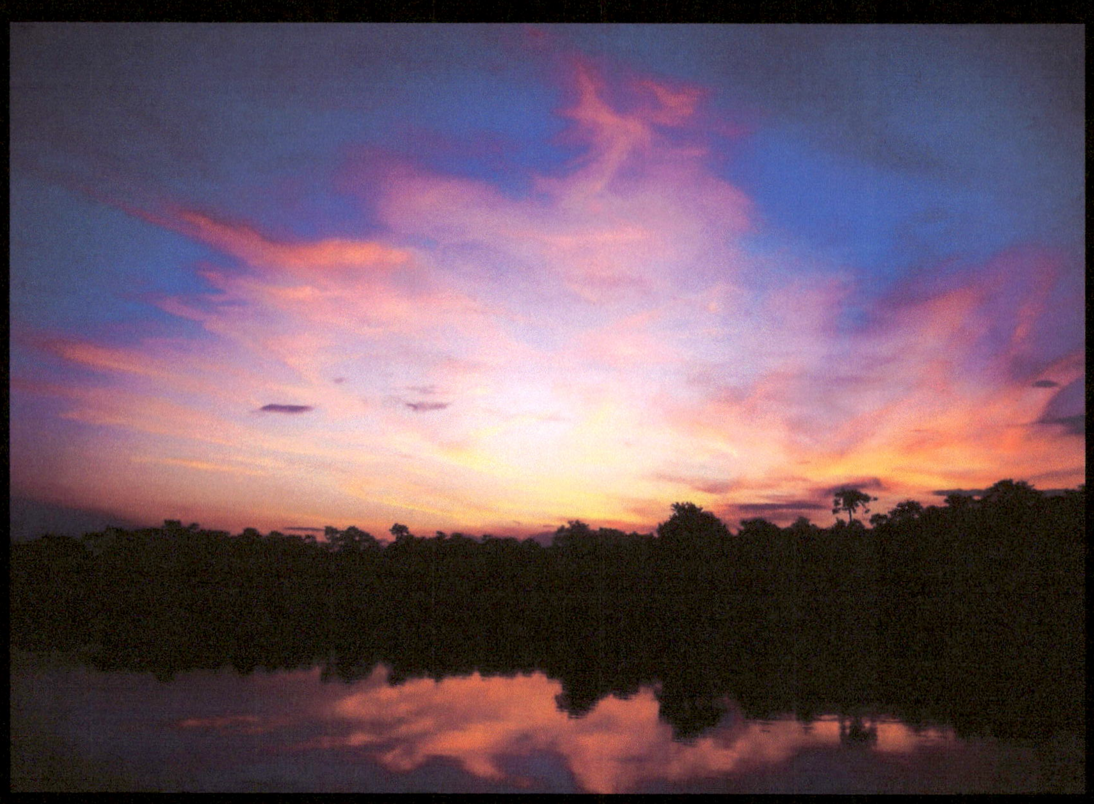

Hossegor, France - Pays Basque

Mathew 6:25-34

The Divine will provide all of your needs.

"...I tell you, do not worry about your life, what you will eat, or what you will drink: nor about your body, or what you will wear. Is life more than just eating, how you look or feel? Is it more than clothes? Look at the birds in the air... They do not work in the fields for money nor store food in pantries, yet your Heavenly Father feeds them. Are you not worth more than birds? ...Why worry about clothes? Consider how the lilies grow in the fields; they do not work, they do not weave; and yet, I tell you, even Solomon and all his luxuries was not dressed like one of these. But if that is how GOD clothes the grass in the fields, which is there today, and is thrown in the oven tomorrow, then will he not all the more clothe you? How little faith you have! No, do not worry and ask, 'What are we going to eat? or, What are we going to drink?' or, 'What will we wear for clothes?' ...Your Heavenly Father knows that you need all of those things. First search the kingdom of GOD, and all that is just and right; and all these things shall be given to you. Therefore, don't worry about tomorrow; because tomorrow will look after itself. Each day has enough problems of its own."

(Jesus Christ)

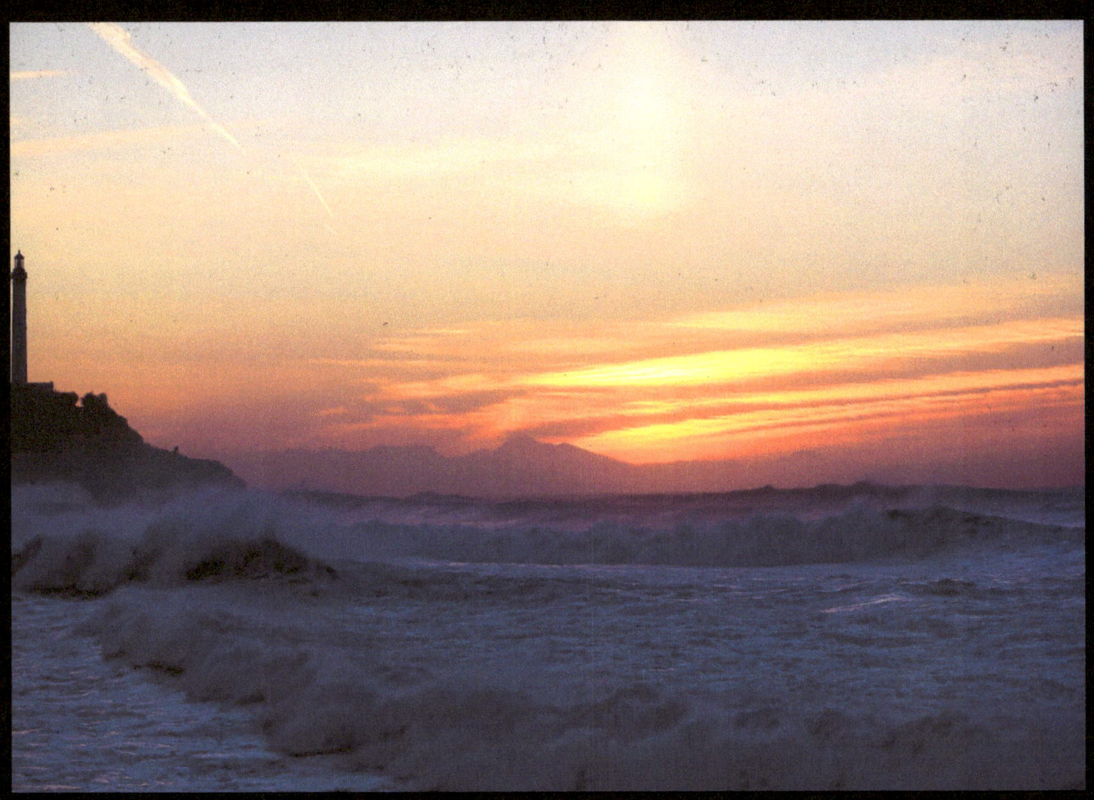

Anglet, France - Chambre d'Amour

Don't cry... GOD cares or you.

He will heal you and raise you up.

"When they came to the gate of the city, there was a young man being carried out who had died. He was the only son of his mother who was a widow and many people from the city was with her. And when the Lord saw her, he had compassion for her. He said to her, 'Don't cry'. Then he went over and touched the stretcher; the men who was carrying it stopped. Then he said, "Young man, arise." And the woman's son sat up and began talking. (Jesus) then gave him to his mother.

(Jesus Christ)

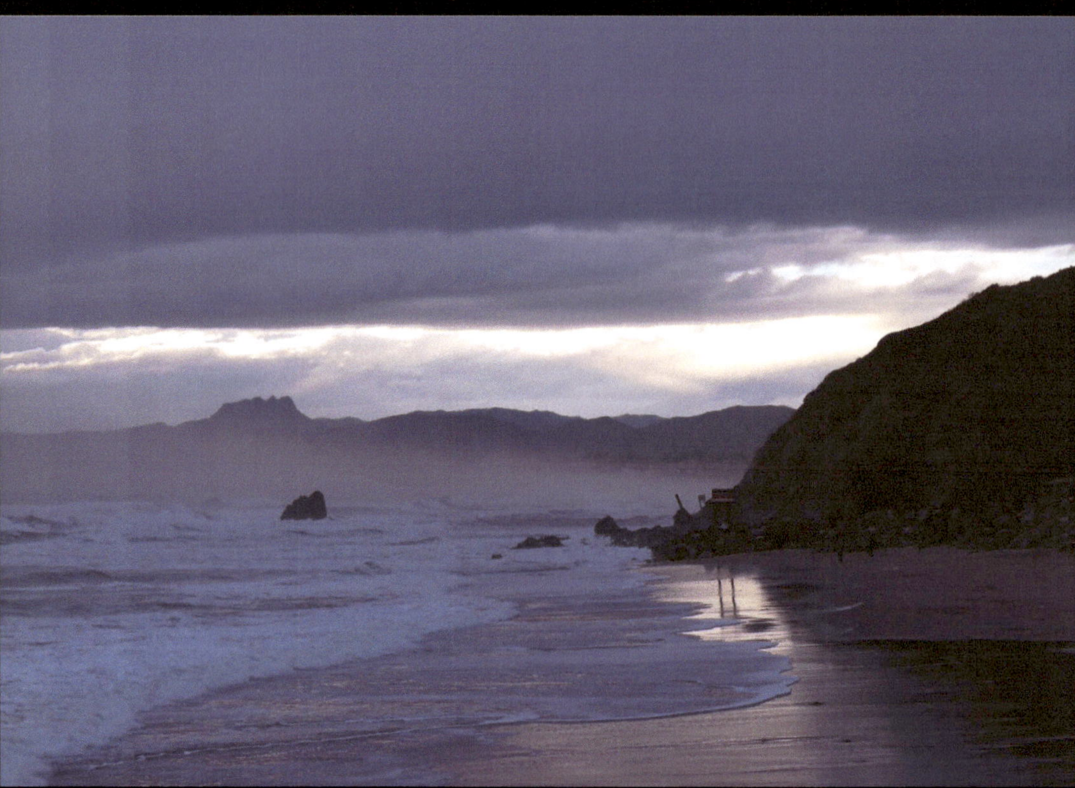

Biarritz, France - Plage de Milady

Psalms 23

The Divine will guide and protect you.

He will provide your every need.

"The LORD is my shepherd, I shall not want. He makes me to lie down in green pastures. He leads me beside the still waters. He restores my soul. He guides me on the path of righteousness for His name's sake. Even if I walk through the valley of shadows and death, I will fear no evil; for You are with me. Your shepherd's rod and staff protect me. You prepare a table before me in the presence of my enemies. You anoint my head with oil; my cup runs over. Surely, goodness, and mercy shall follow me all the days of my life, and I will dwell in the house of The LORD forever."

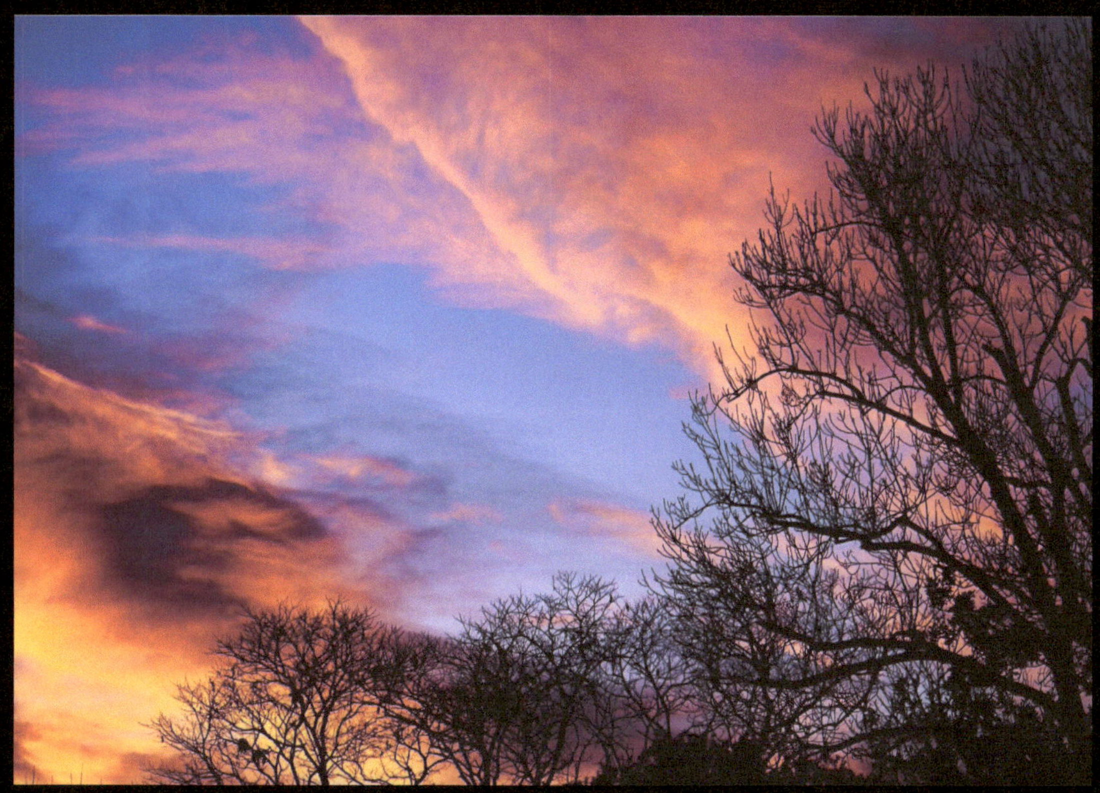

Anglet, France - Cinq Cantons

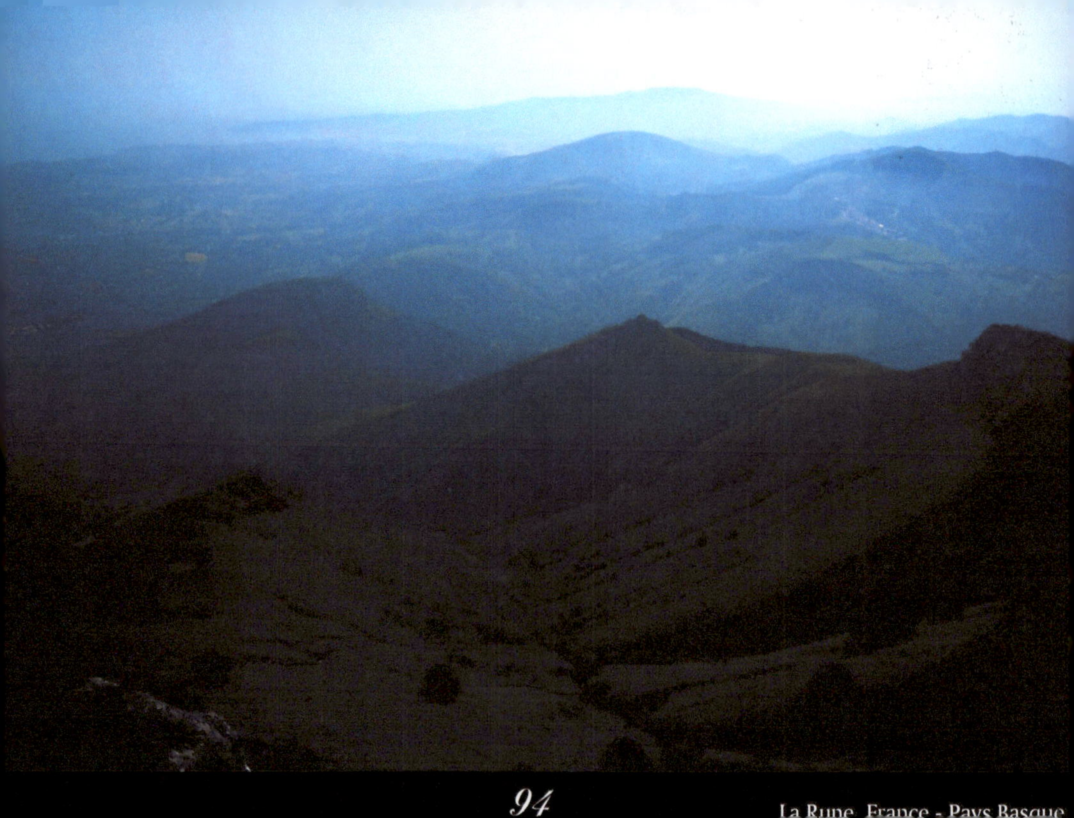

La Rune, France - Pays Basque

Forgive, be patient, and be angry no more.

The Divine will grant your heart's desire.

"Do not strive to out do the evildoers or emulate those who do wrong. For like the grass, they soon wither and fade like the green of spring. Trust in the LORD and do good... Depend upon the LORD, and He will grant you your heart's desire. Commit your life to the LORD; trust in Him and He will bring it to pass. He will make your righteousness shine forth as the light, and the right of your cause, like the sun at noonday. Wait quietly for the LORD, be patient until He comes... Be angry no more, and put away your vengeance; and do not worry - it only causes harm... For evildoers will be destroyed; but those that wait on the LORD, they shall inherit the earth."

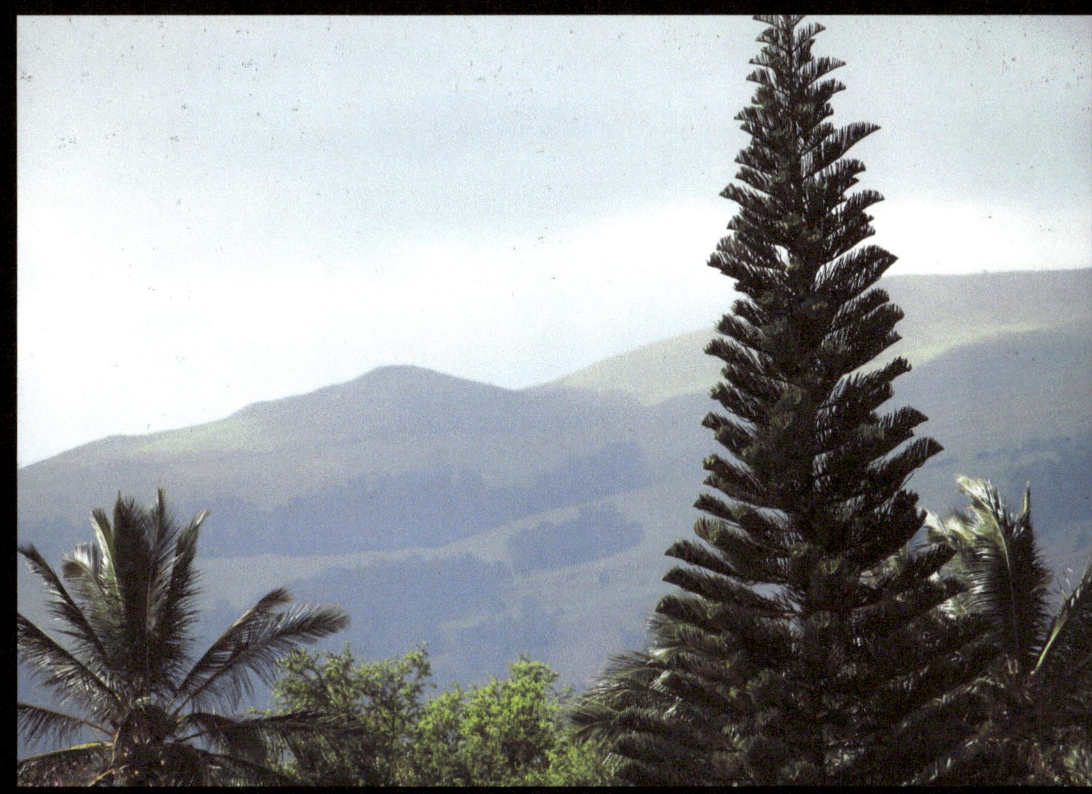

Maui, Hawai'i - Kihei

Isaiah 43:19

Begin something new.

What you can perceive can be achieved. Lay your plans.

"Here and now I do a new thing; this moment it will spring forth. Can you not perceive it? I will even make a way through the wilderness, and rivers in the barren desert..."

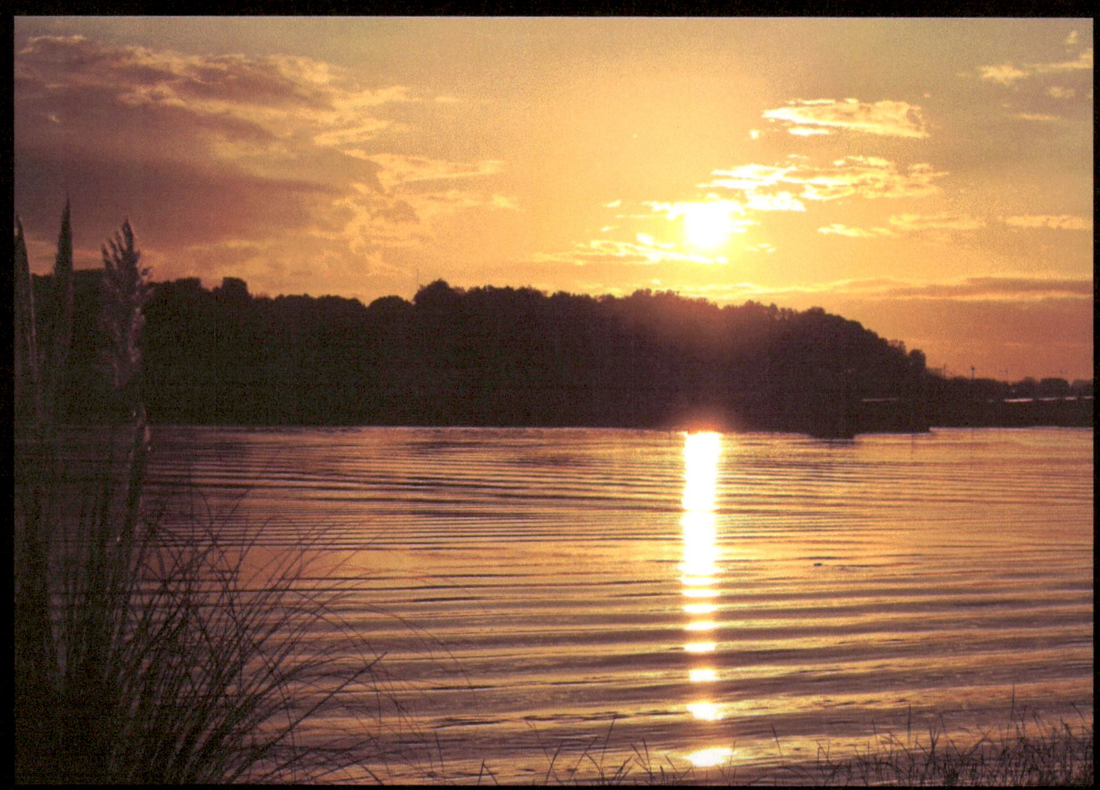

Bayonne, France - L'Ardour

Persevere in your struggles and always have hope.

"Therefore, since we have been justified through faith, we have peace with The Divine GOD through our Lord, Yeshua, Jesus Christ; through whom we have gained access by faith into this grace in which we stand. And we rejoice in the hope of the glory of GOD. And so, we also rejoice in our suffering, because we know that suffering produces perseverance; perseverance character, and character - hope. And hope does not disappoint us, because the love of GOD has been poured out into our hearts by the Holy Spirit."

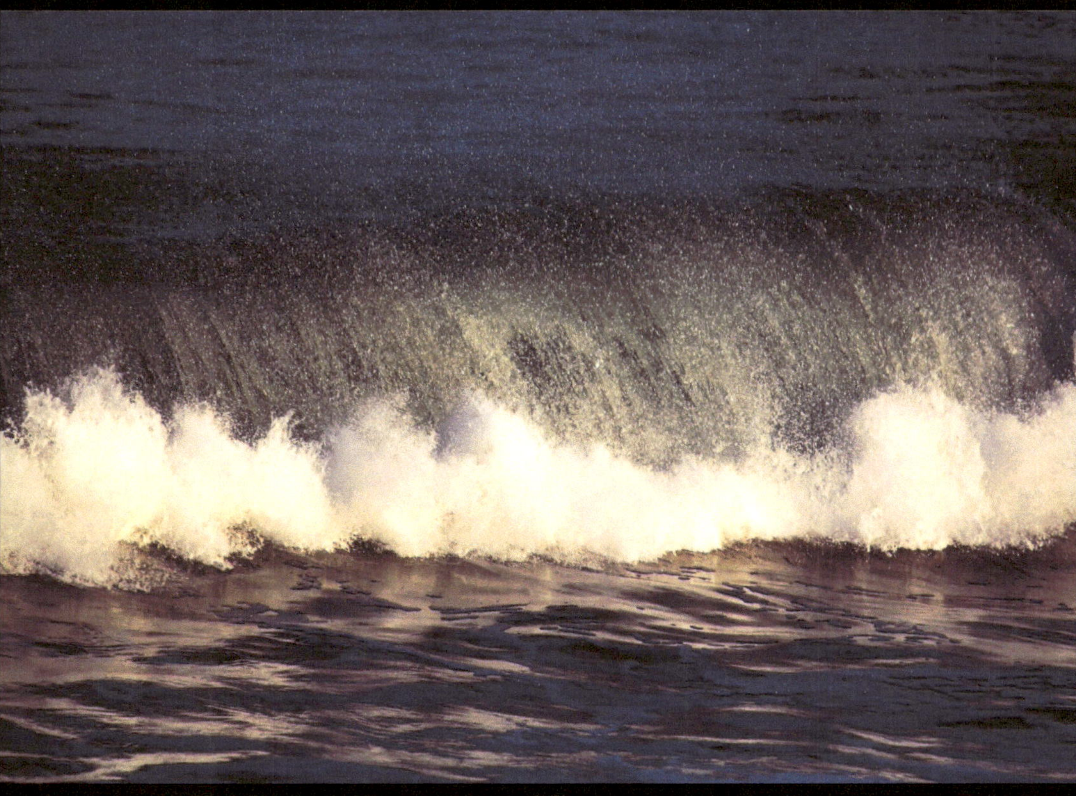

Anglet, France - Chambre d'Amour

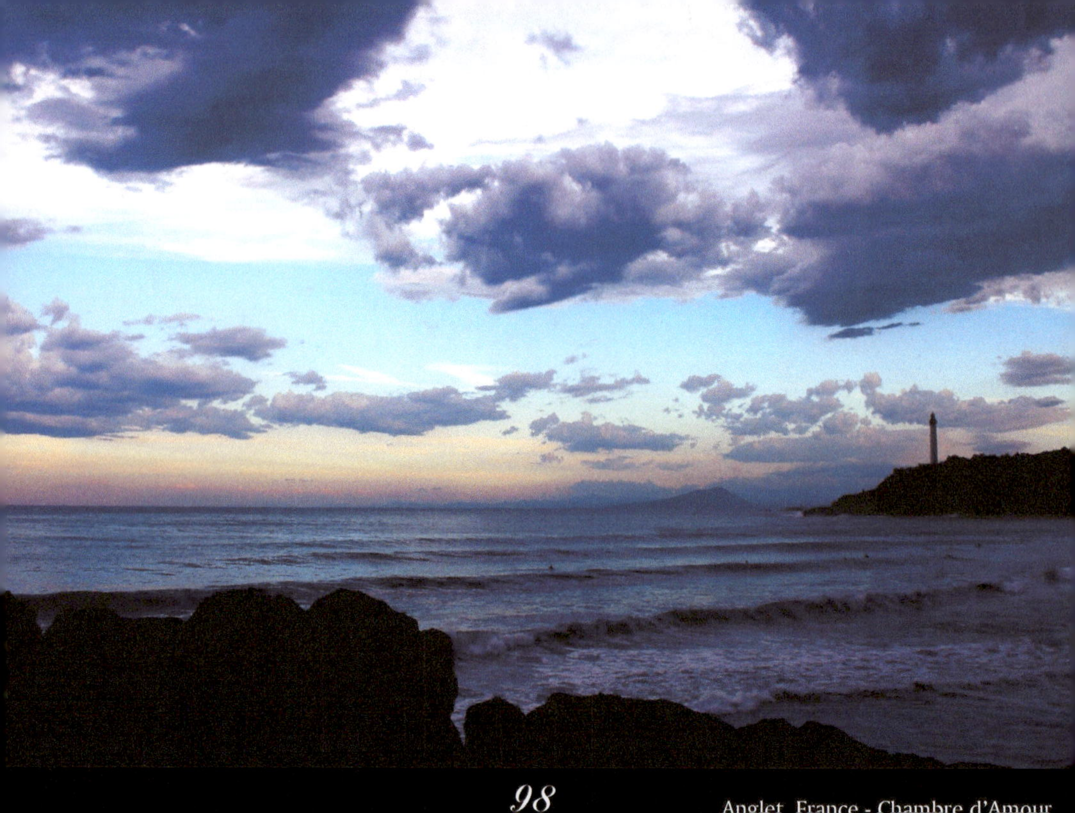

Anglet, France - Chambre d'Amour

The Divine gives you strength and courage.

"The LORD, the everlasting GOD, creator of the wide world, grows neither weary nor faint. No man can fathom his understanding. He gives power to the weak, and to those who are exhausted, He gives strength. Even the young will get tired and become weary, and the young men shall truly fall; but they that wait on the LORD shall renew their strength, they shall mount up with wings as eagles, they shall run and not be weary; they shall walk and not faint."

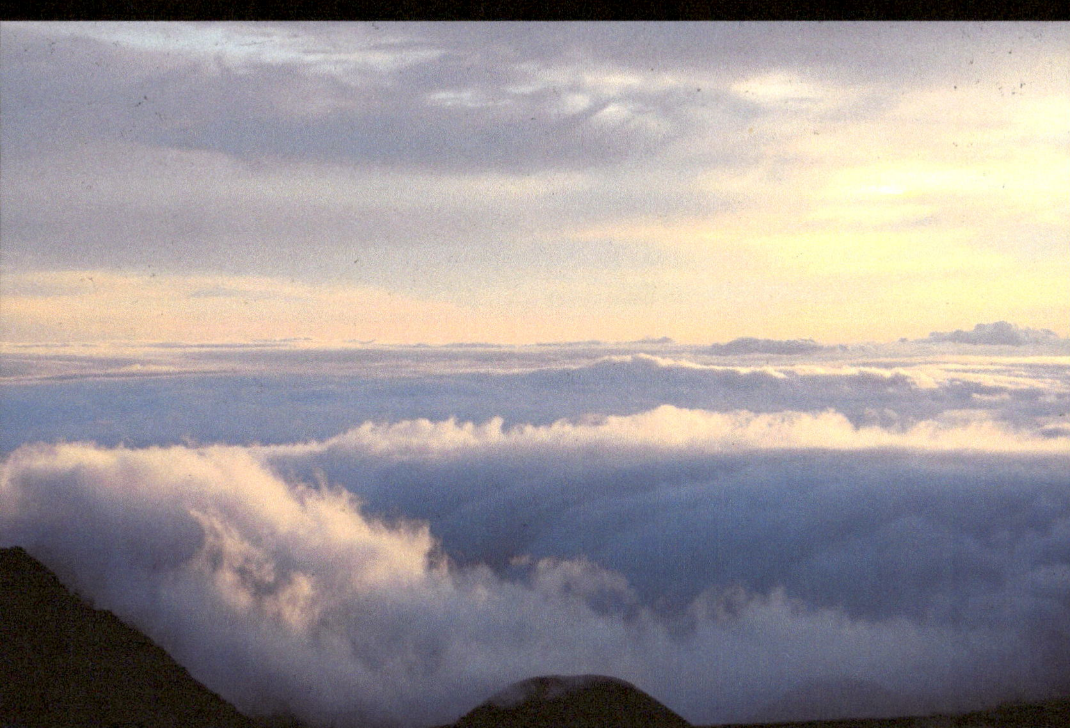

John 14:13-14

Your prayers will be granted.

"Whatever you shall ask in My name that I will do, so that the Father may be glorified in the Son. If you ask anything in my name I will do it."
(Jesus Christ)

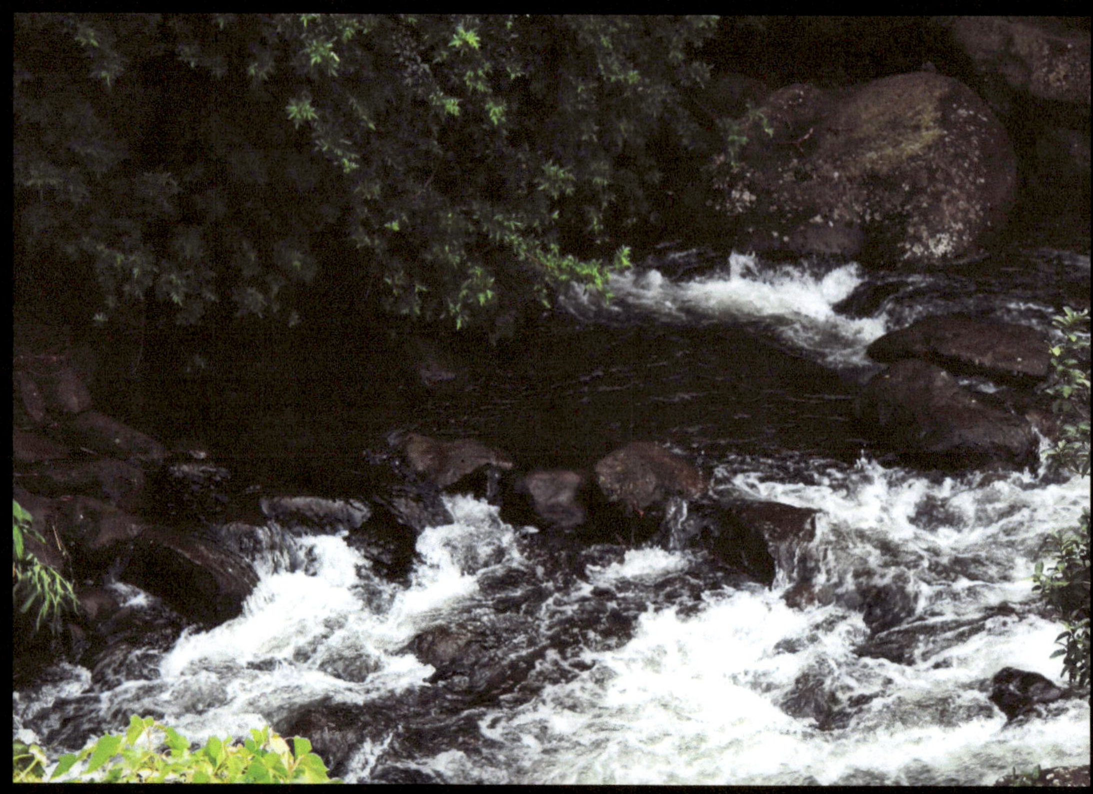

Maui, Hawai'i - Iao Valley

Hebrews 11:1, 6

Faith is the substance of things hoped for,
and the evidence of things unseen.

"Without Faith it is impossible to please GOD, for he who comes to The LORD must believe that He is, and that He rewards those who diligently seek Him."

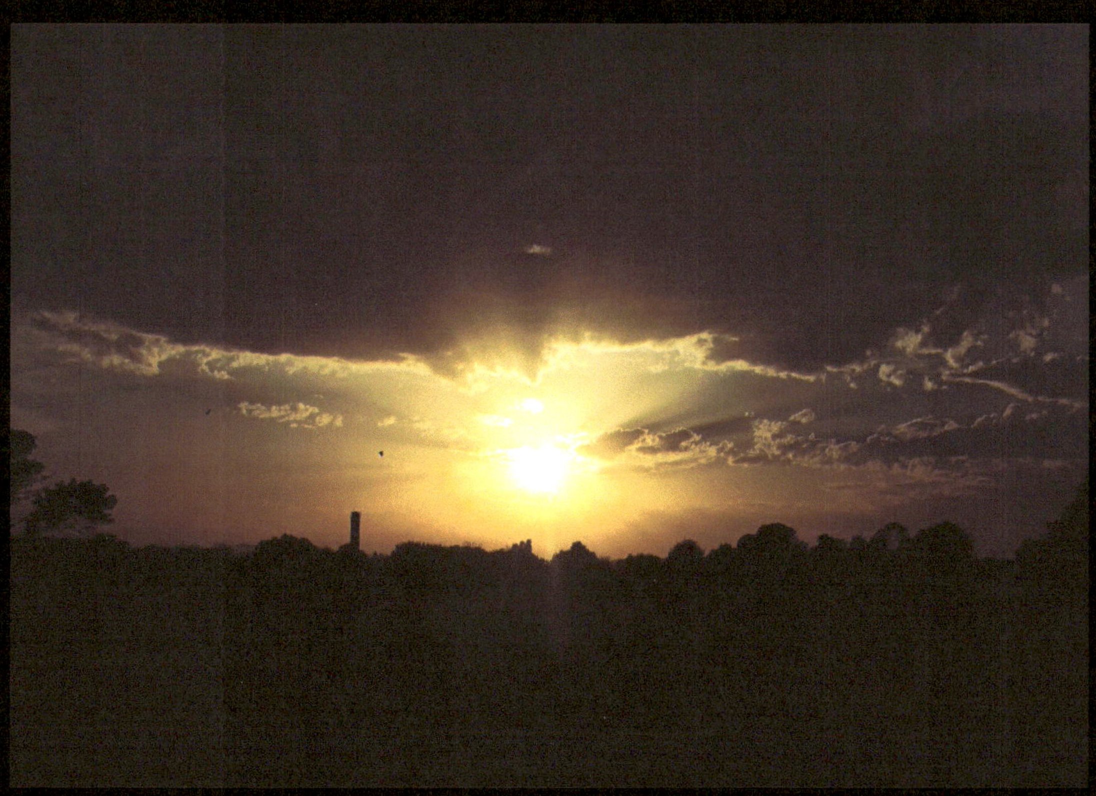

Anglet, France - Cinq Cantons

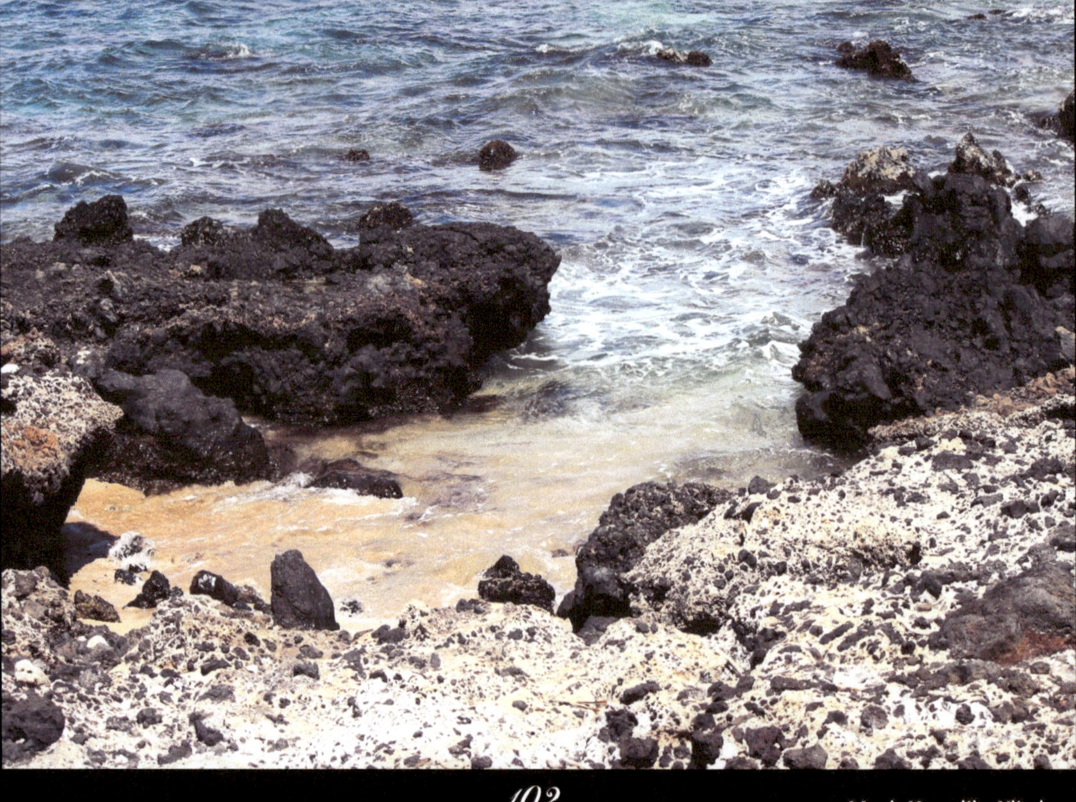

Maui, Hawai'i - Kihei

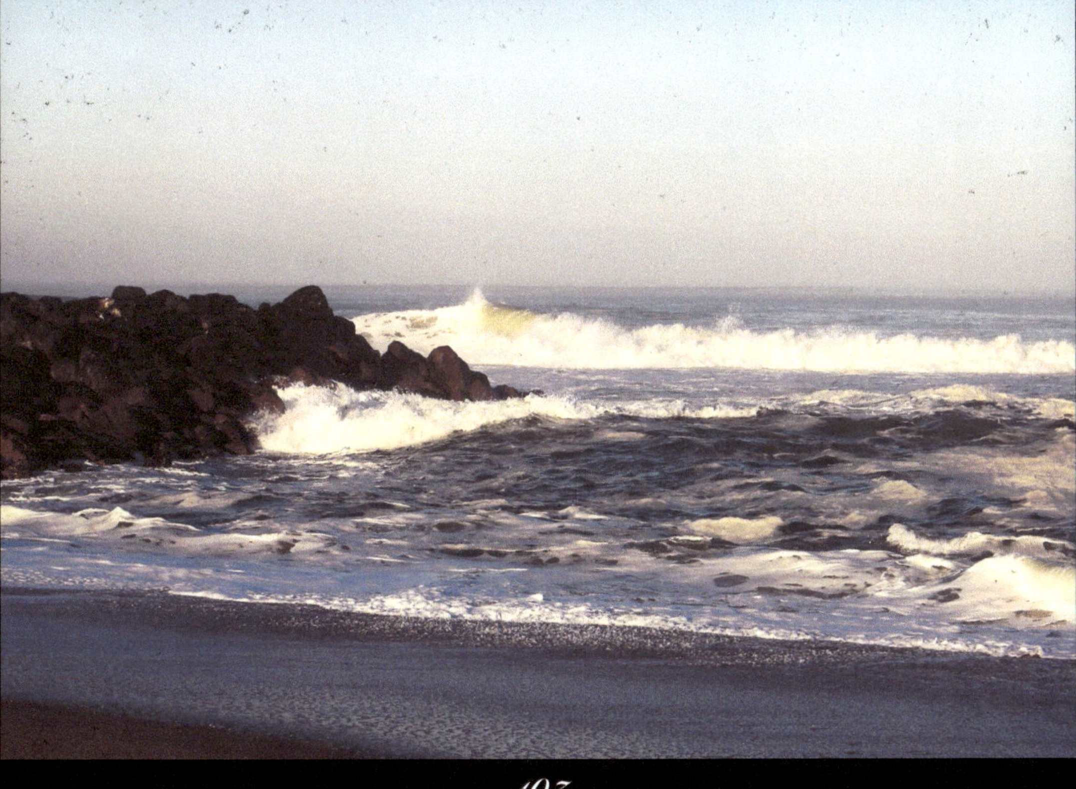

Anglet, France - Chambre d'Amour

"...Then a woman who suffered from hemorrhages for twe[illegible] years came from behind, and touched the hem of his garment; for she said to herself, 'If I can only touch his cloak, I shall be healed.' But Yeshua (Jesus) turned and when he saw her, he said, 'Take heart, my daughter; your faith has made you whole.' And the woman was healed from that hour."

(Jesus Christ)

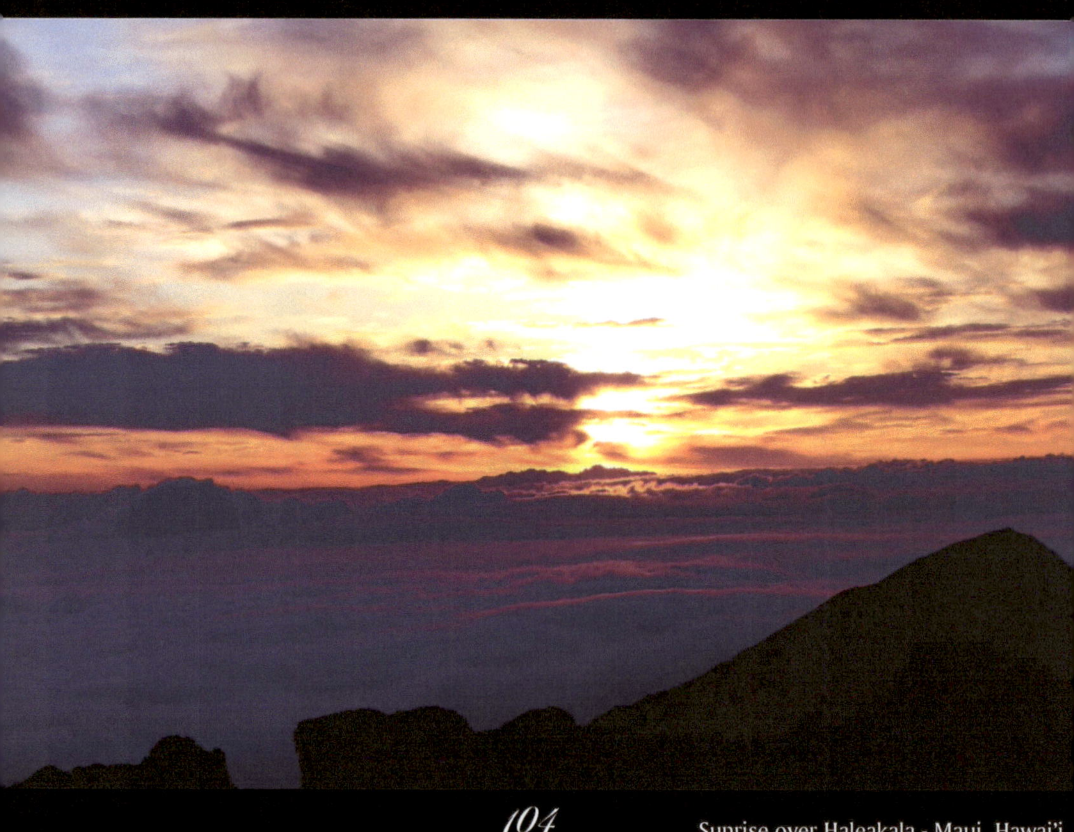

Sunrise over Haleakala - Maui, Hawai'i

"For I alone know the thoughts that I think towards you... Thoughts of peace and not of evil; but to give you a future and a hope. Then you will call upon Me and pray to Me, and I will listen to you. And when you seek Me, you shall find Me; when you search for Me with all your heart, I will let you find Me... I will restore your fortunes and gather you again..."

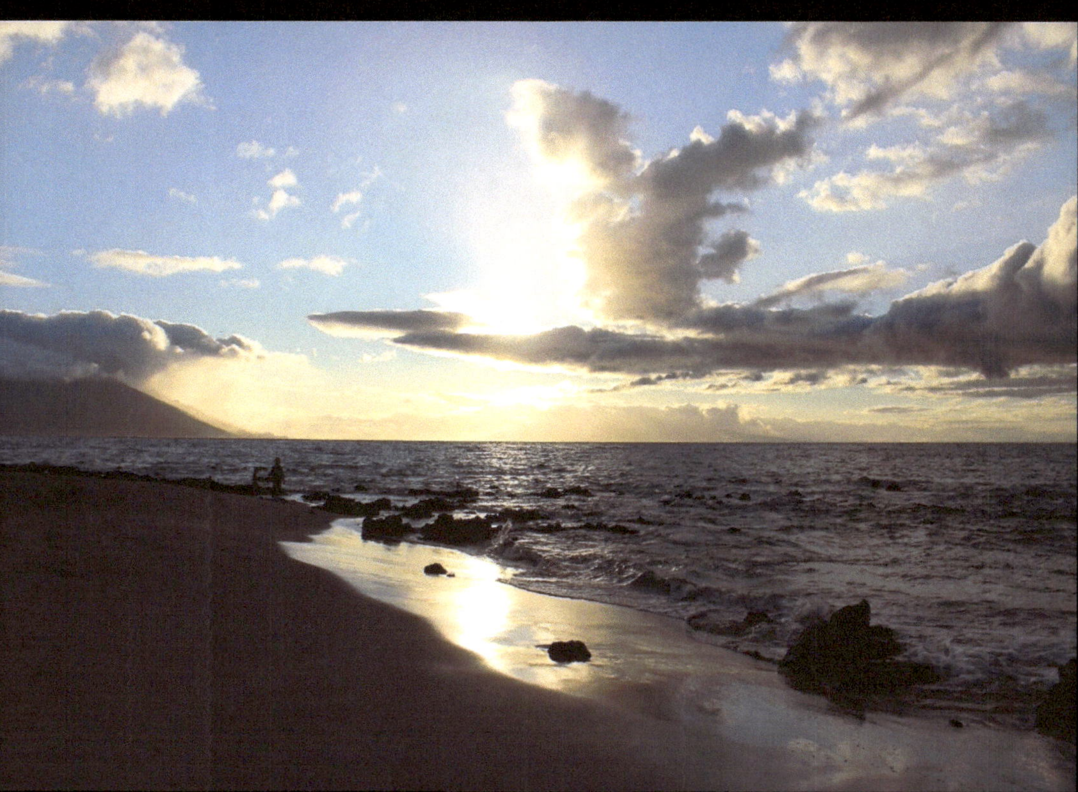

"The LORD GOD is with me, therefore, I am not afraid of what any man can do to me."

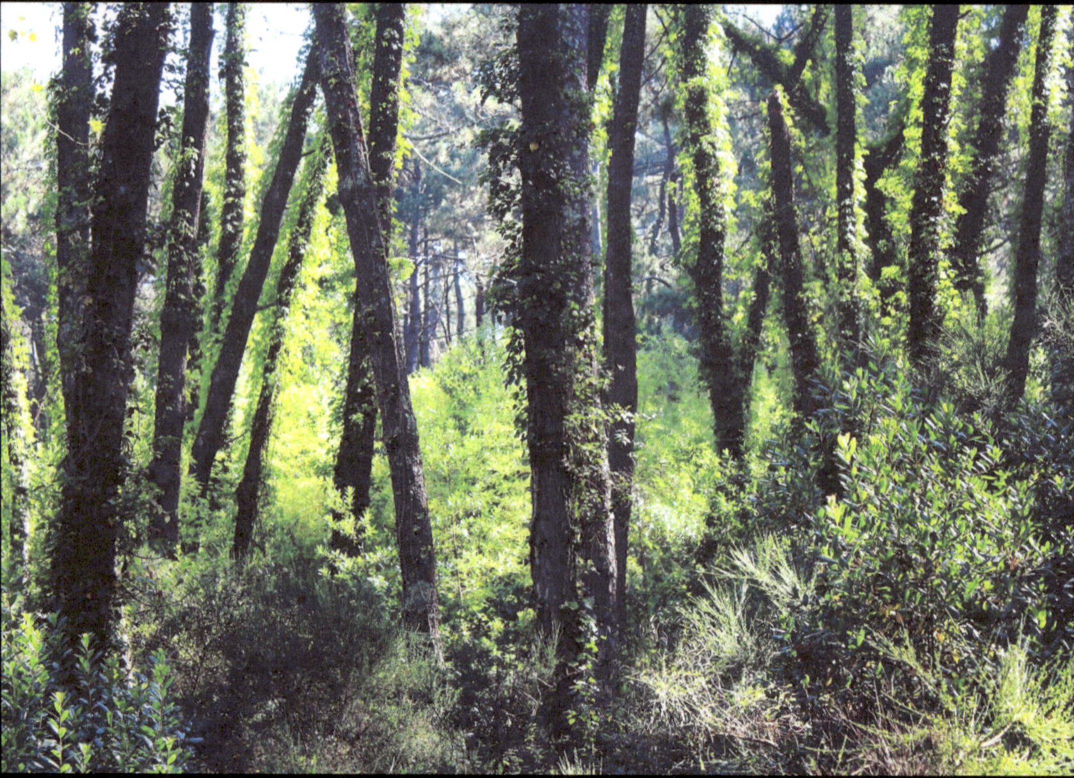

Anglet, France - Forêt de Chiberta

Mathew 17:20-21

Faith, prayer, and fasting, makes the impossible, possible.

"Your faith is too small. I tell you this: If you have faith no bigger than a mustard seed, you can say to this mountain, 'Move from here to there!', and it will move. Nothing will prove impossible for you. However, this can only be manifested by prayer and fasting."

(Jesus Christ)

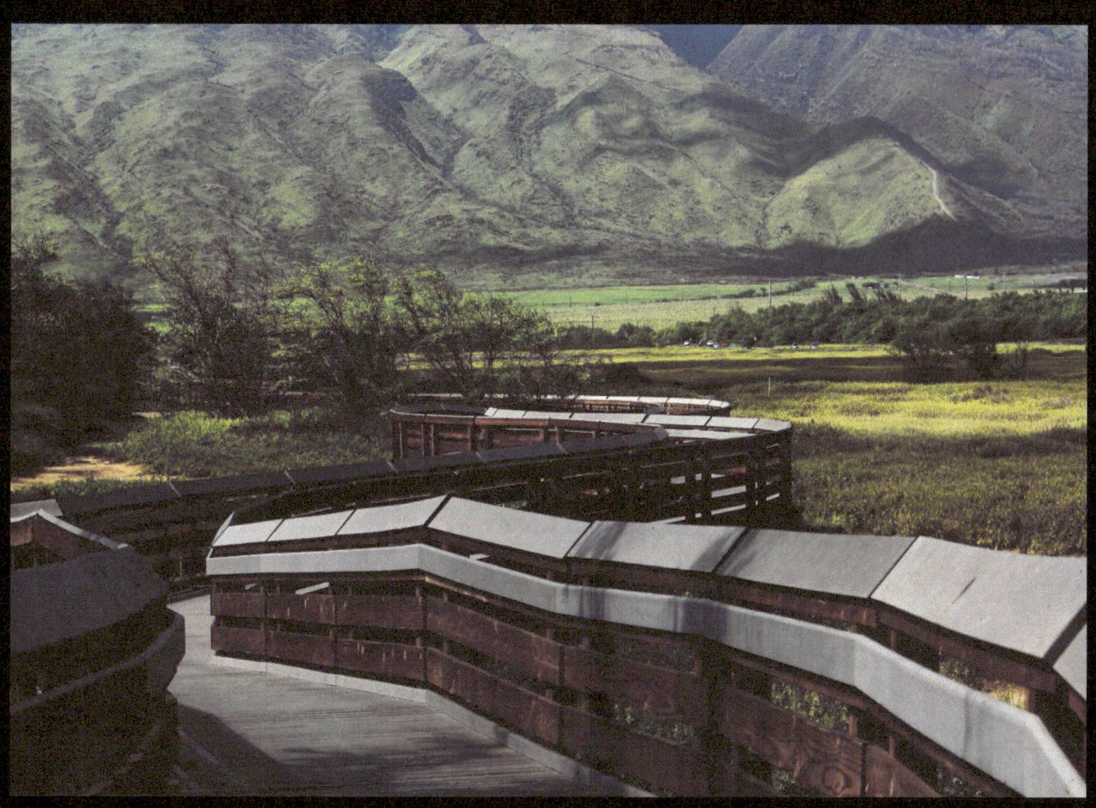

Maui, Hawai'i - Nature Preserve

Romans 8:24-25

The Divine will sustain you. Be courageous.
Never be afraid.

"But You, Oh LORD, are a shield for me, My glory, and the One who lifts up my head. I cried to the LORD with my voice, and He heard me from His holy hill. I laid down and slept. I awoke, because the LORD kept me. I will not be afraid of ten thousands men surrounding me."

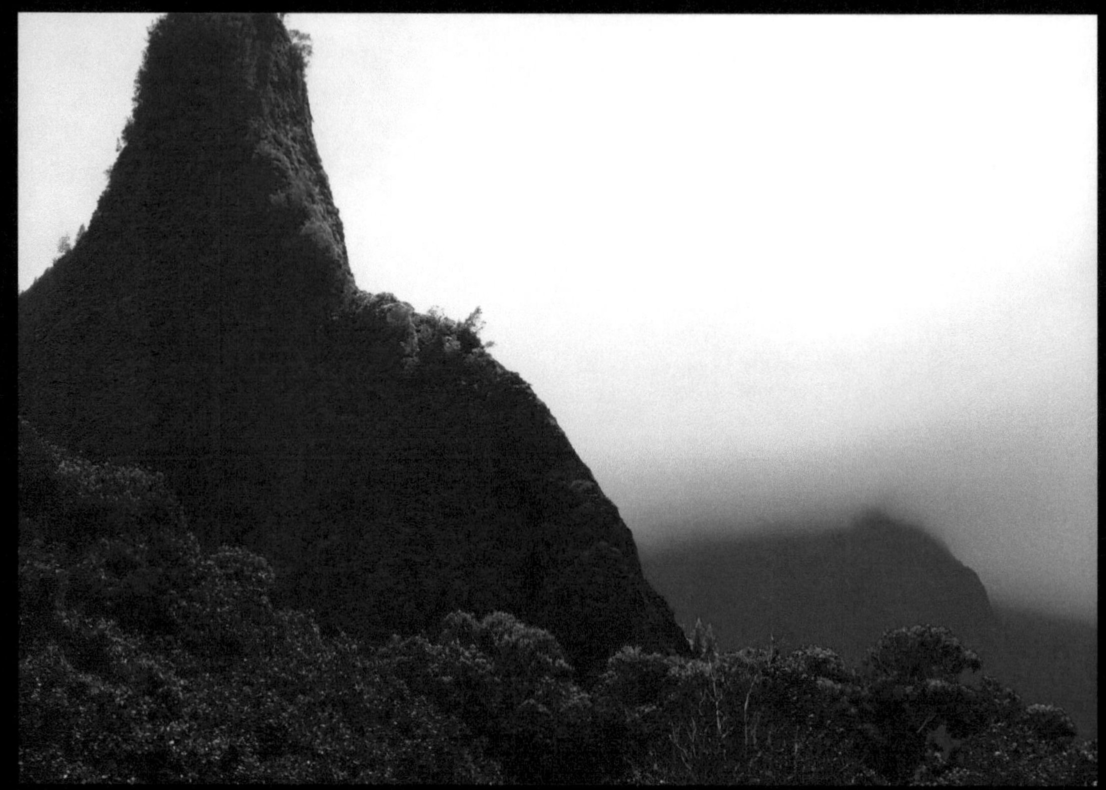

Iao Valley - Maui, Hawai'i

Isaiah 41:13, 17-20

The Divine will help you, the needy, and the poor.

"For I the LORD your GOD will hold your right hand, and say to you, 'Don't be afraid; I will help you'." When the poor and needy search for water and there is none, and they are suffering from thirst, I, The LORD, will hear them. I, The GOD of Israel - will not forsake them. I will open rivers in high places and fountains in the midst of the valleys: I will make the wilderness a pool of water, and dry lands springs of water. I will plant in the wilderness the cedar tree... and the myrtle, and the oil tree; I will set in the desert the fir tree, and the pine, and the box tree ensemble: That you may see, and know, reason, and understand together that the hand of The LORD has done this, and that the HOLY ONE... created it."

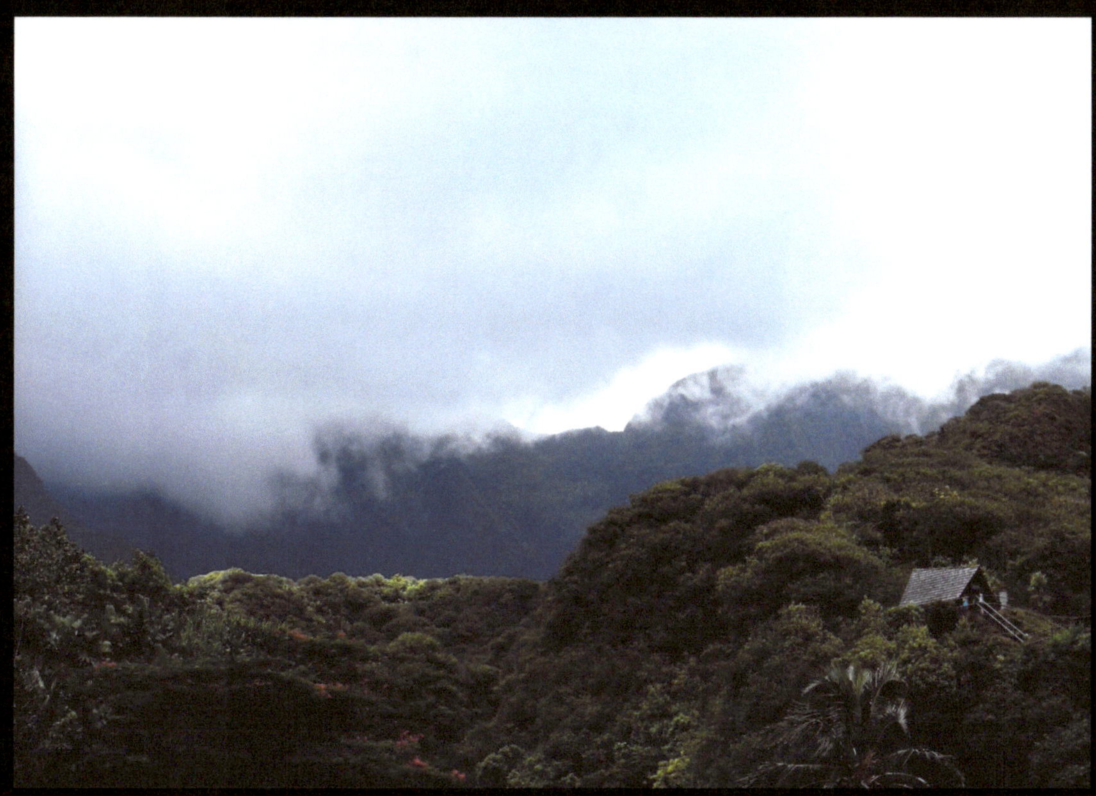

Maui, Hawai'i - Iao Valley

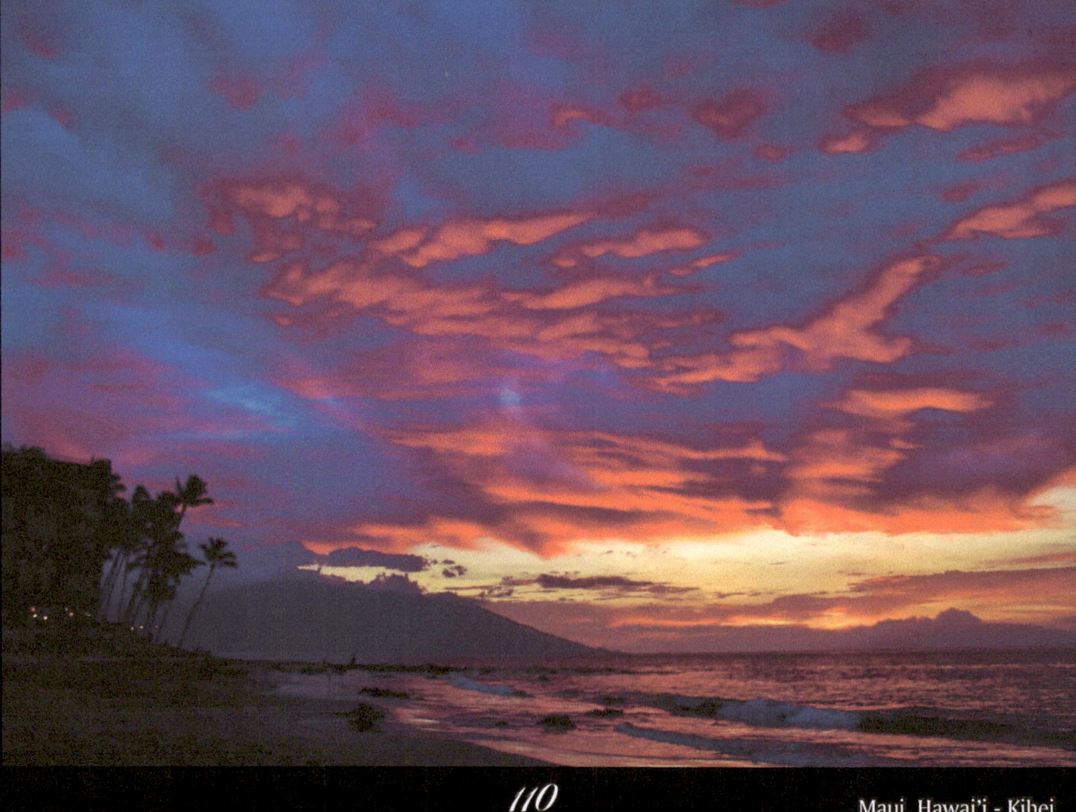

Maui, Hawai'i - Kihei

"Love suffers patiently and is kind. Love envies no one. Love is never boastful, nor conceited, nor rude. It is never selfish nor quick to take offense. Love keeps no score of wrongs. And it does not gloat over other men's sins, but delights in the truth. Love bears all things, believes all things, hopes all things, and endures all things. There is nothing love cannot face. There is no limit to its faith, its hope, and its endurance. Love never comes to an end, even when all testimonies stop, or all tongues cease to speak, or knowledge vanishes away. For we know only a part and can only foretell only a part, but when what is perfect has come, then all will be made clear. When I was a child, I spoke like a child, I had the understanding of a child, and thought like a child; but when I became a man, I put away childish things. Now we see through a dark glass, but then we shall see face to face. Now my knowledge is only partial; but then I shall know even as I am known. In a word, there are three things that last forever; faith, hope and love, but the greatest of them all is love."

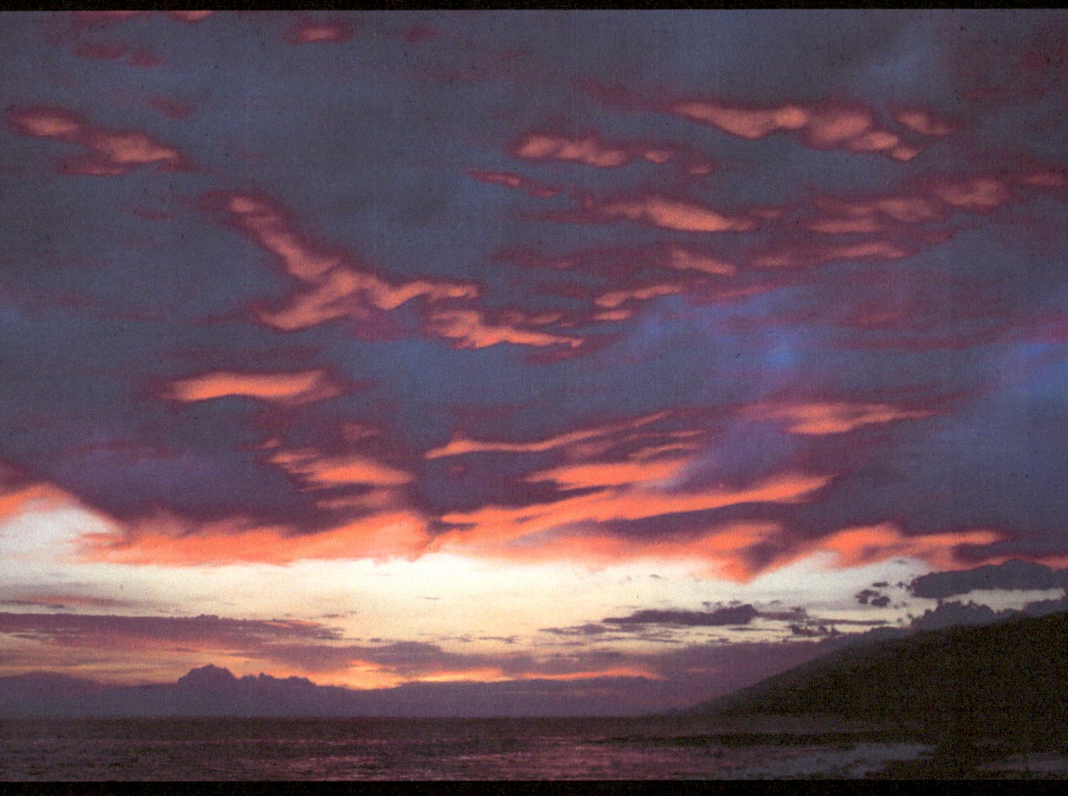

Maui, Hawai'i - Kihei

Mark 5:36

Believe and don't be afraid...
There is nothing GOD cannot do.

"When Jesus heard the words that were said, he turned to the leader of the synagogue and said, ' Do not be afraid; believe."
(Jesus Christ)

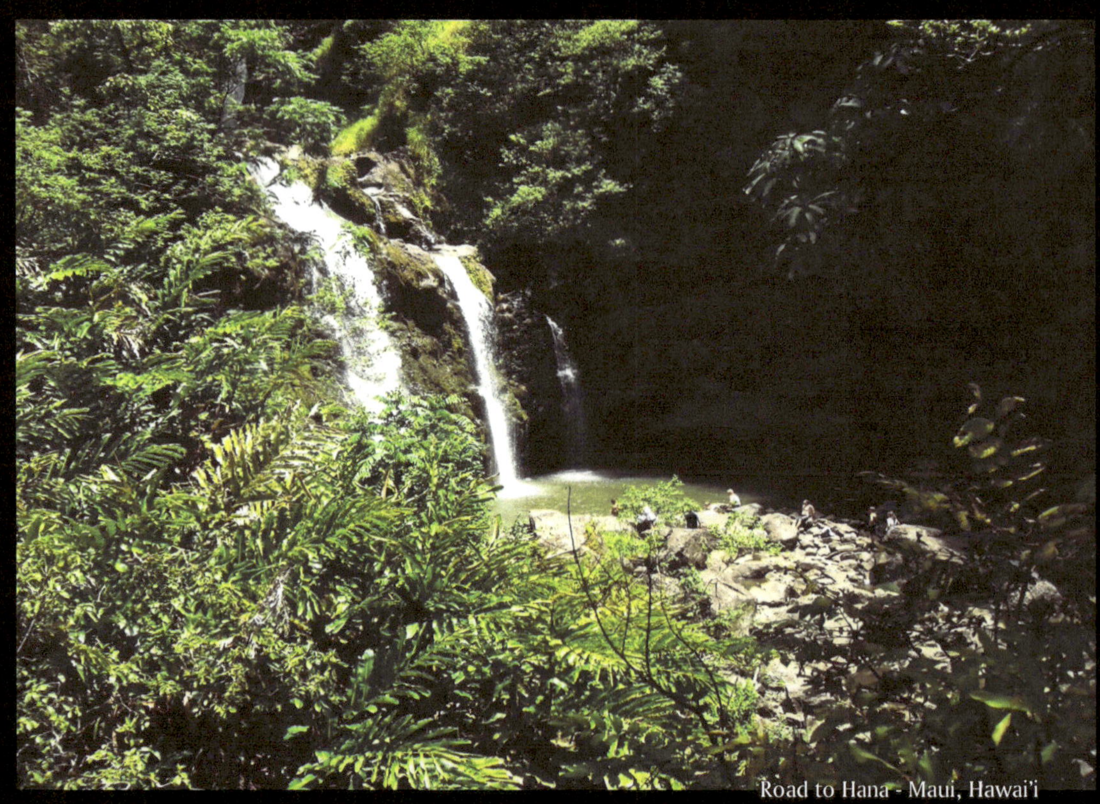

Road to Hana - Maui, Hawai'i

John 14:27

The Divine gives us peace of heart and mind.

"Peace I leave with you. My peace I give to you, such as the world cannot give. Don't let your heart be troubled, nor let it be afraid."

(Jesus Christ)

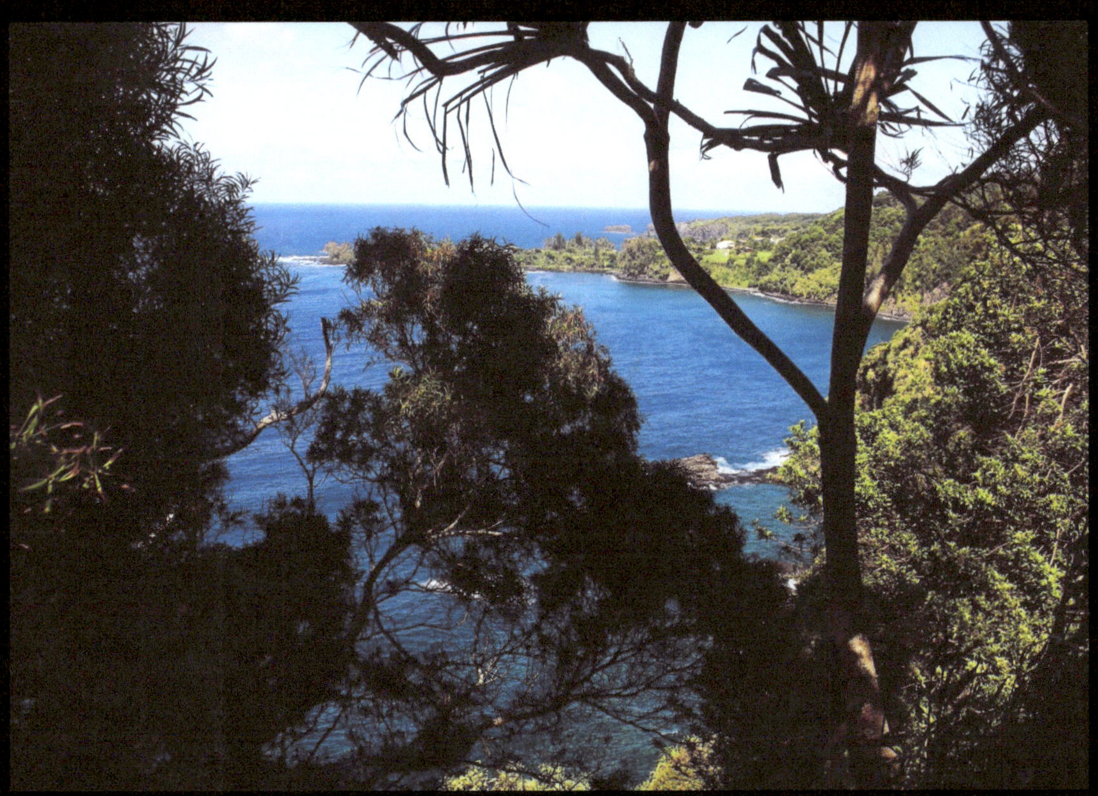

Maui, Hawai'i

Isaiah 43:2

Through fire, the rain, and the stormy seas,
GOD will see you through.

"When you travel through the seas, I will be with you. And when you pass through the floods, they will not overtake you. And when you walk through the very fire, you shall not be burned, neither will the flames set you on fire."

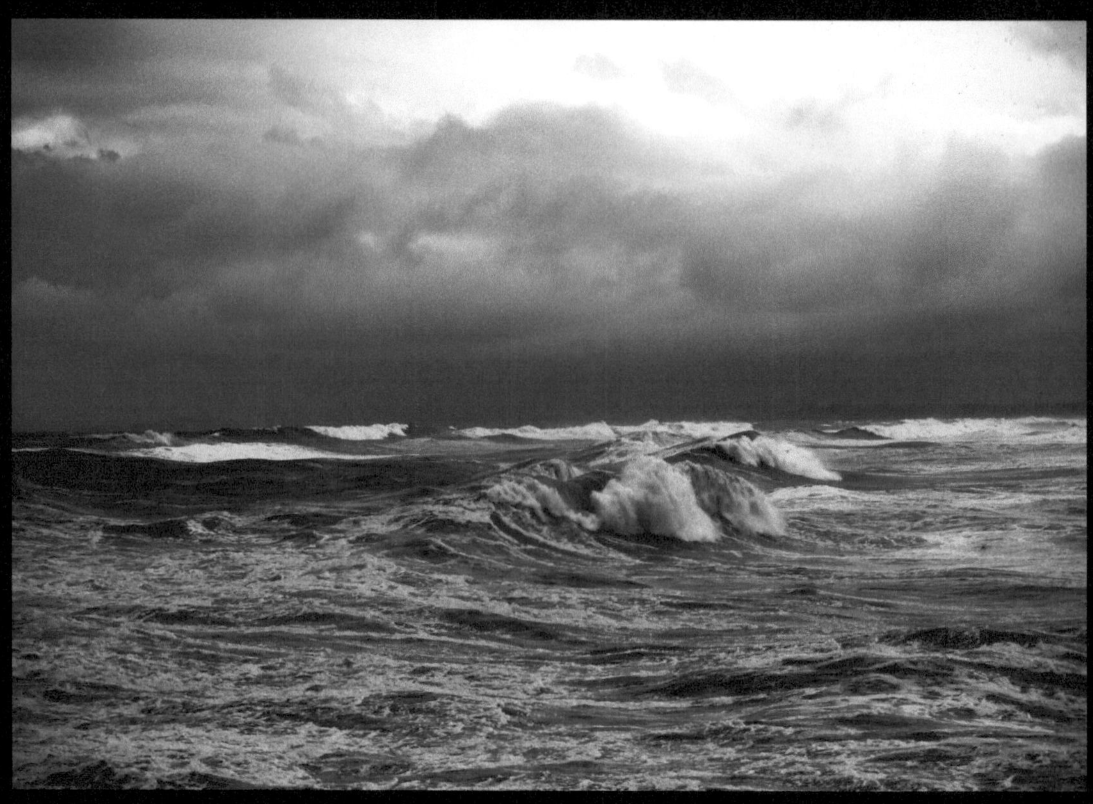

Anglet, France - Chambre d'Amour

Be strong and courageous for GOD is with you.

"Be of a positive spirit and be strong. Do not worry or be afraid of any person, because GOD Himself goes with you, and He will not fail you, nor abandon you. The Divine personally walks in front of you. He is by your side. Never be afraid or discouraged."

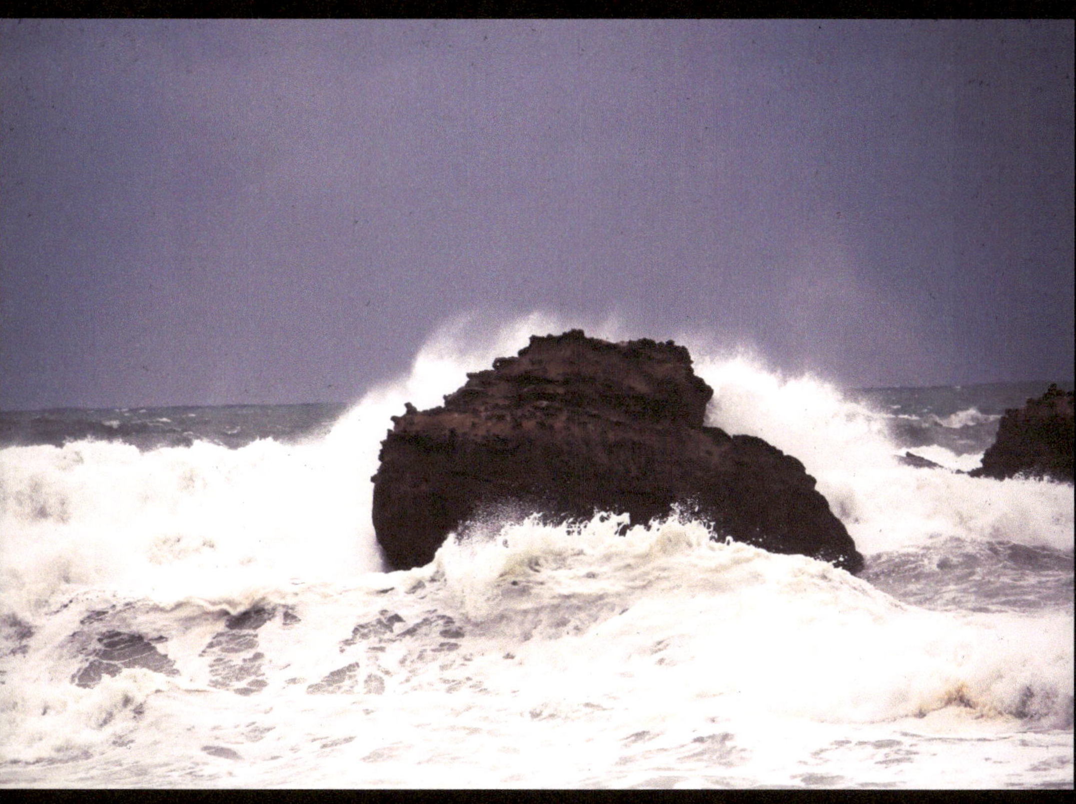

Anglet, France - Chambre d'Amour

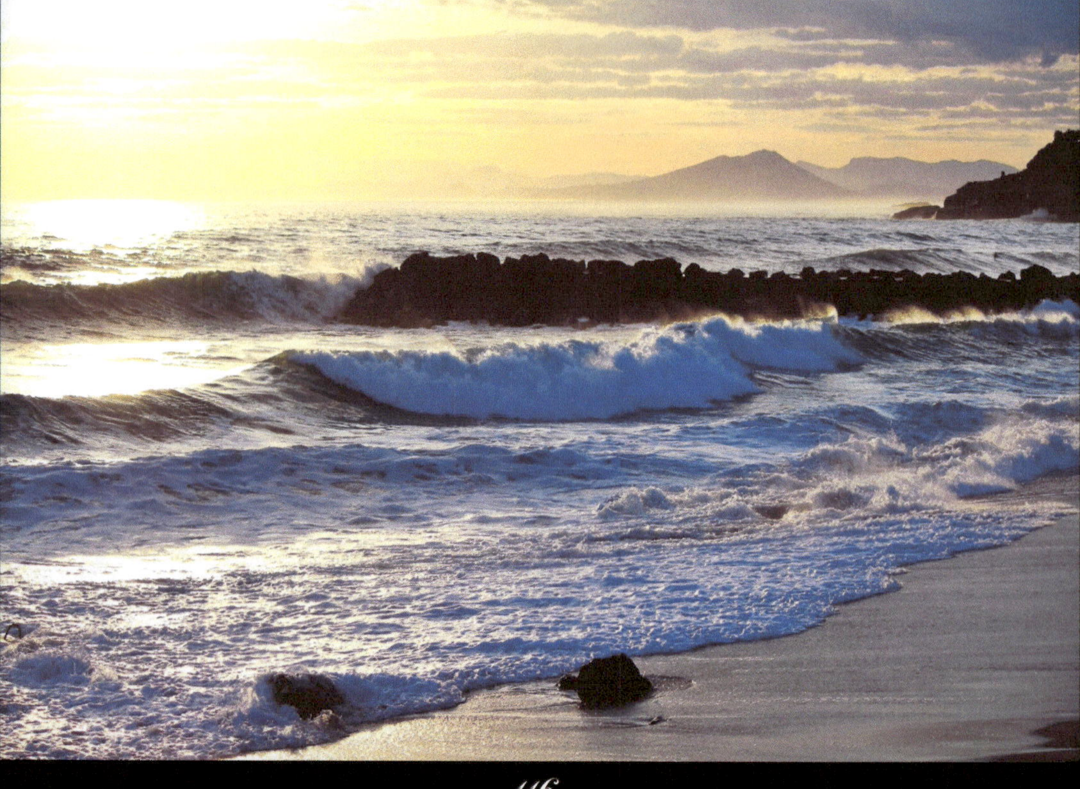

Anglet, France - Chambre d'Amour

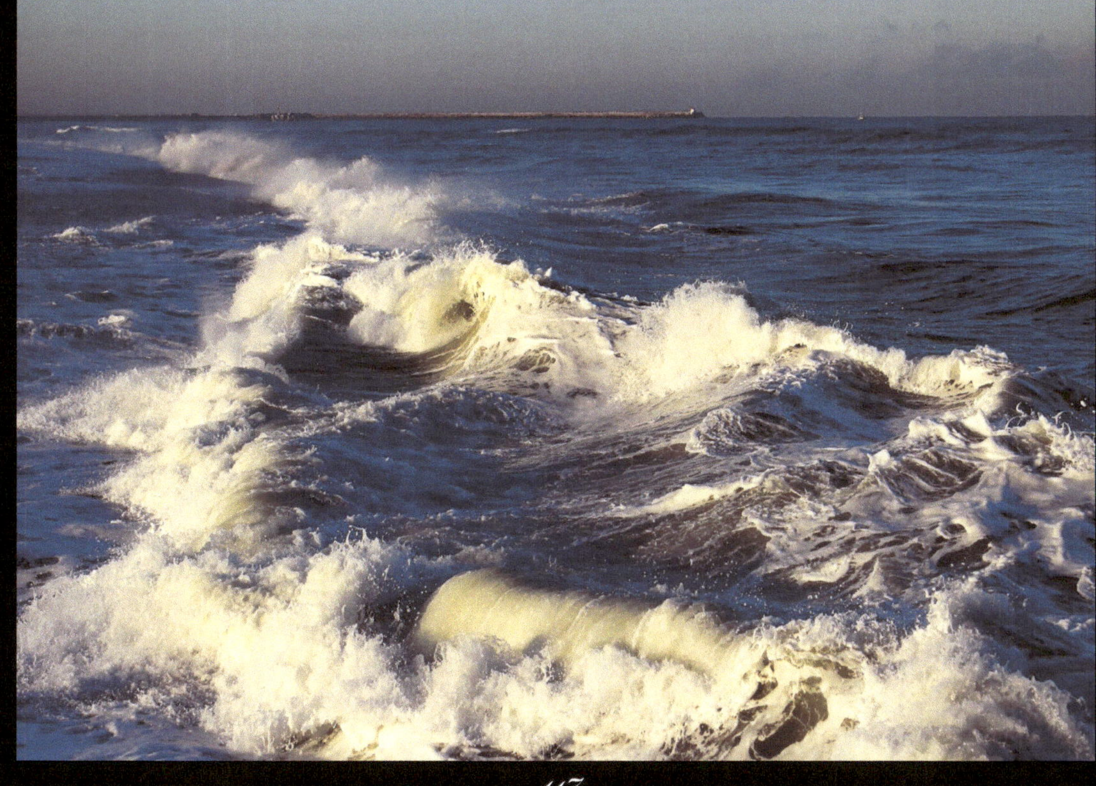

Anglet, France - Chambre d'Amour

Never be afraid to love and never be ashamed that you loved,

for true love comes from GOD. Love is Divine.

"My Beloved, let us love one another, for love comes from GOD. And everyone that loves is born of GOD and knows GOD. But a person who doesn't love, does not know GOD; for GOD is LOVE."

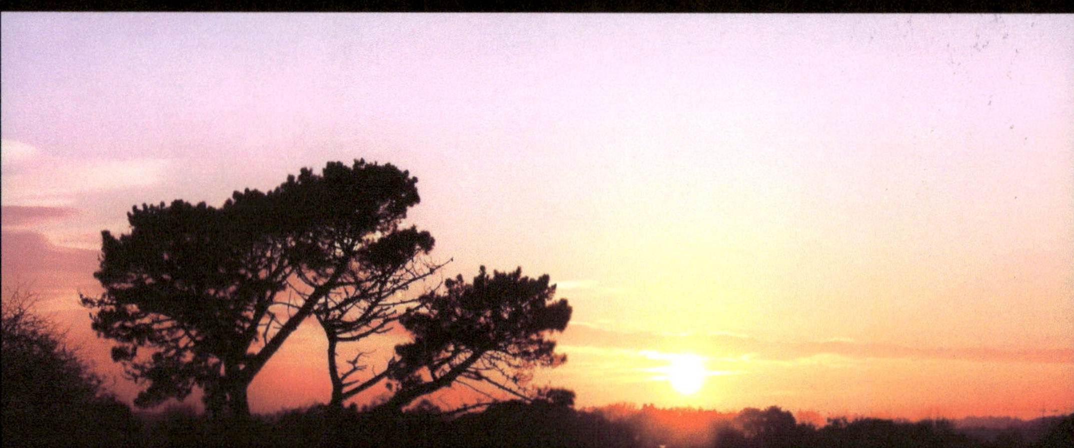

Micah 7:8

You shall overcome; even the darkness.

"Do not think that you can gloat over me, my enemies; even though I have fallen, I will rise! And if ever I sit in a place of darkness, The LORD shall be my light."

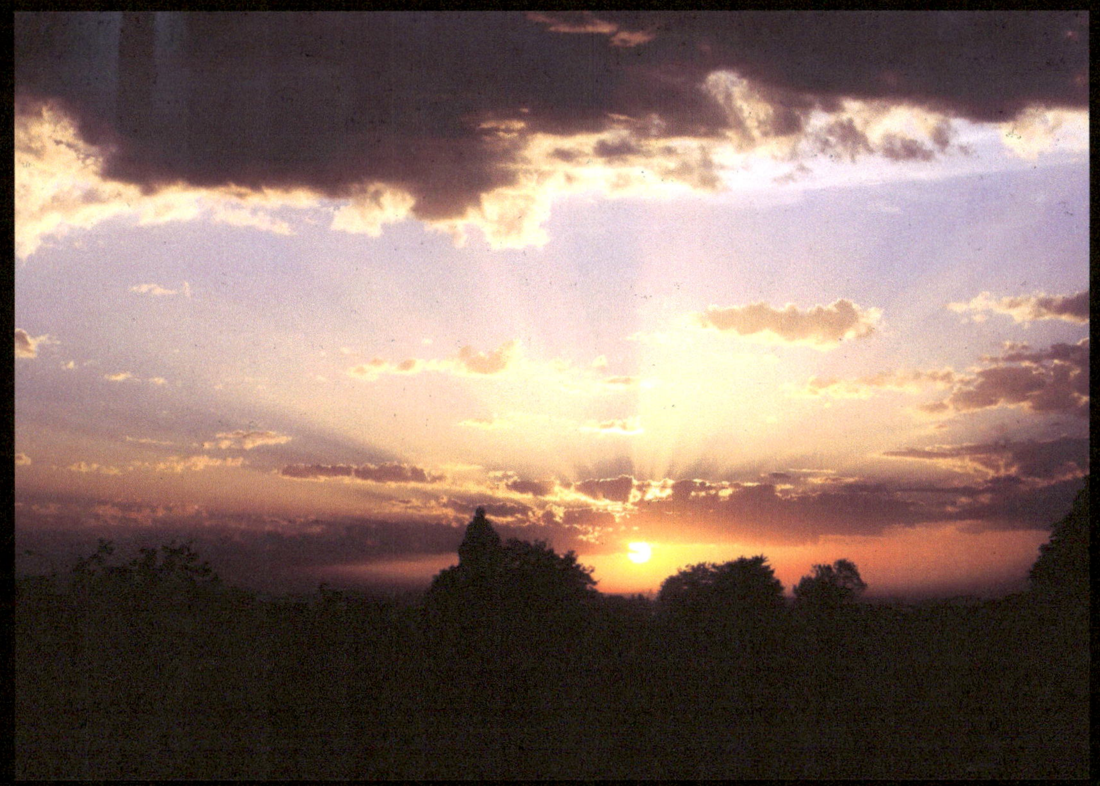

Anglet, France - Sunrise at Cinq Cantons

The Divine will give you what you believe.

'"...Do you believe that I have the power to do what you want?" "Yes, sir," they said. Then he touched their eyes and said, "As you have believed, so let it be," and their sight was restored."

(Jesus Christ)

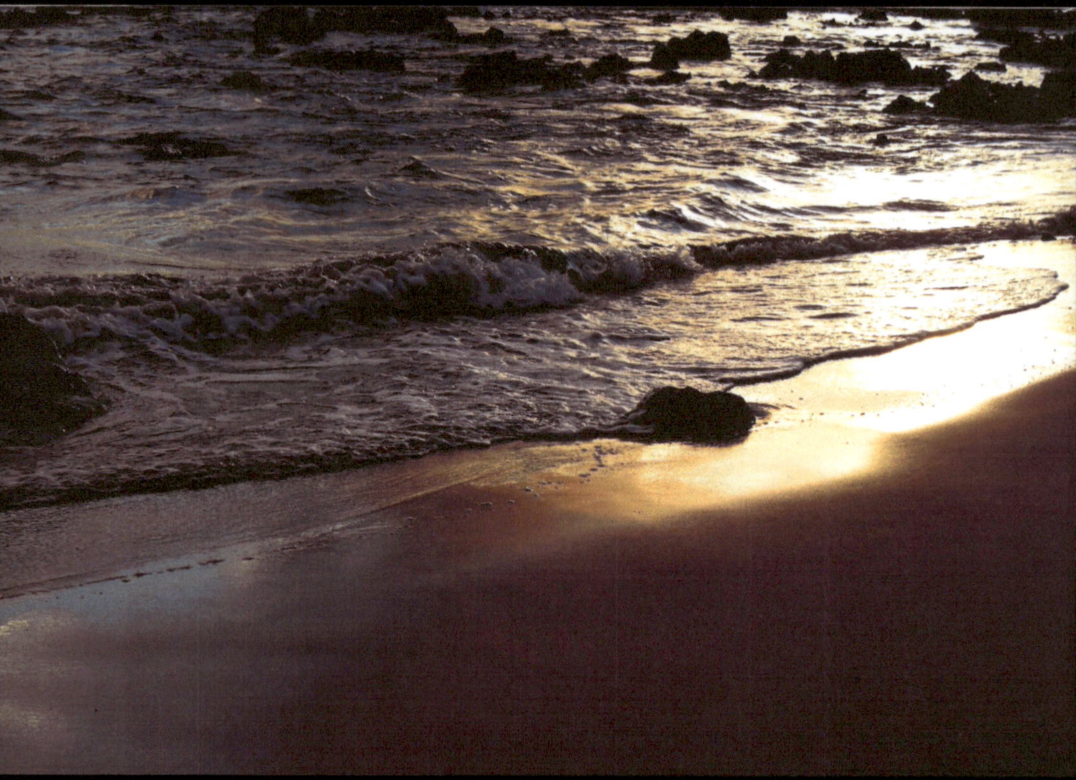

Maui, Hawai'i, Kihei

"No one will be able to stand against you, through all the days of you life, for I will be with you as I was with Moses. I will not leave you, nor ever fail you."

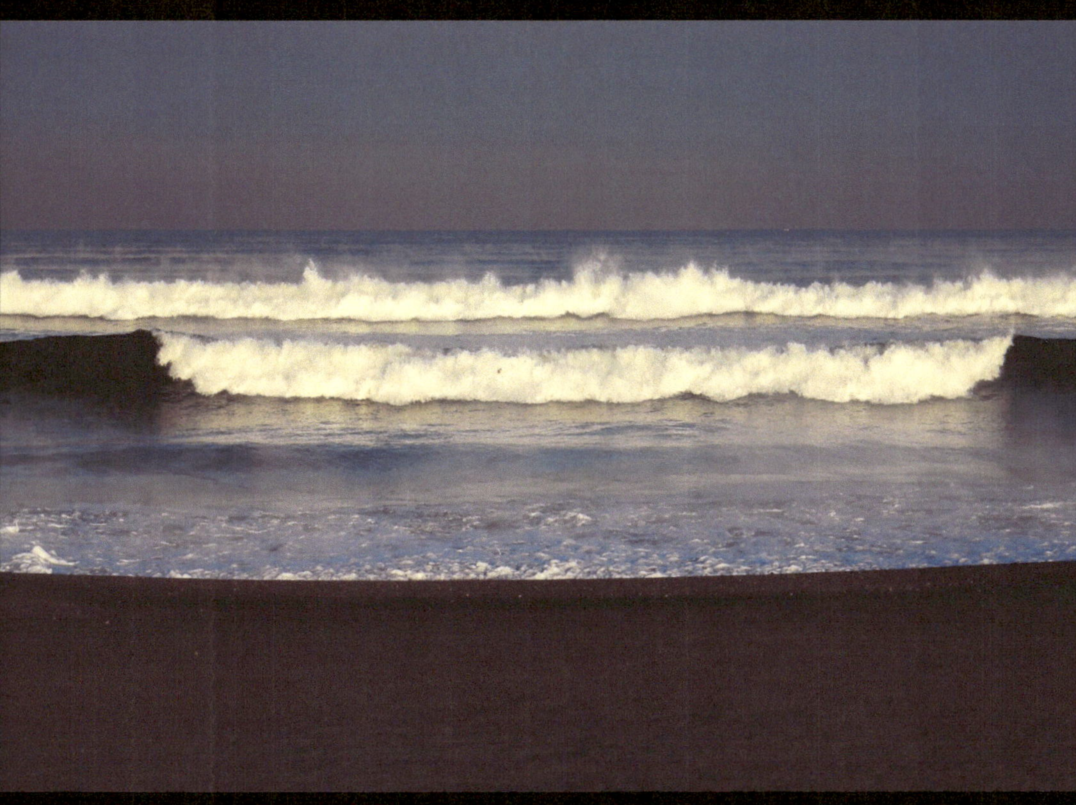

Anglet, France - Chambre d'Amour

Have faith in the Divine and believe you have power to manifest.

"Have faith in GOD. For as sure as I say to you, whoever tells this mountain, 'Move and be fall into the sea' and do not doubt in their heart, but believes that what he says will happen, he will manifest whatever he says. Therefore I tell you, whatever you ask for when you pray, believe that you receive it."

(Jesus Christ)

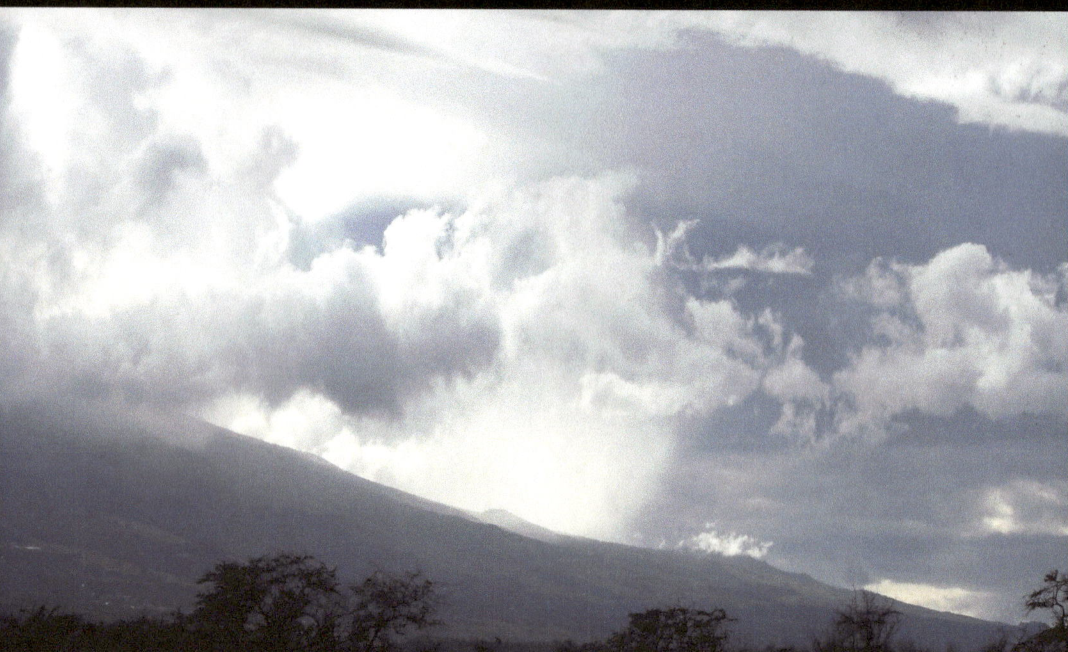

Hebrews 10:32-36, 39

Have confidence even when you've suffered loss.

"...You met the challenge of great suffering and held firm. Some of you were abused and tormented to make a public show, while others stood loyally by those who were so badly treated. And you had compassion on me in my chains, and cheerfully accepted the seizure of your possessions, knowing that you possessed something more lasting in Heaven. Do not then throw away your confidence, for it carries great reward. Because you need patience, so after you have done the will of GOD, you may receive what He has promised. ...We are not among those who shrink back and are lost; we have the faith to make life our own."

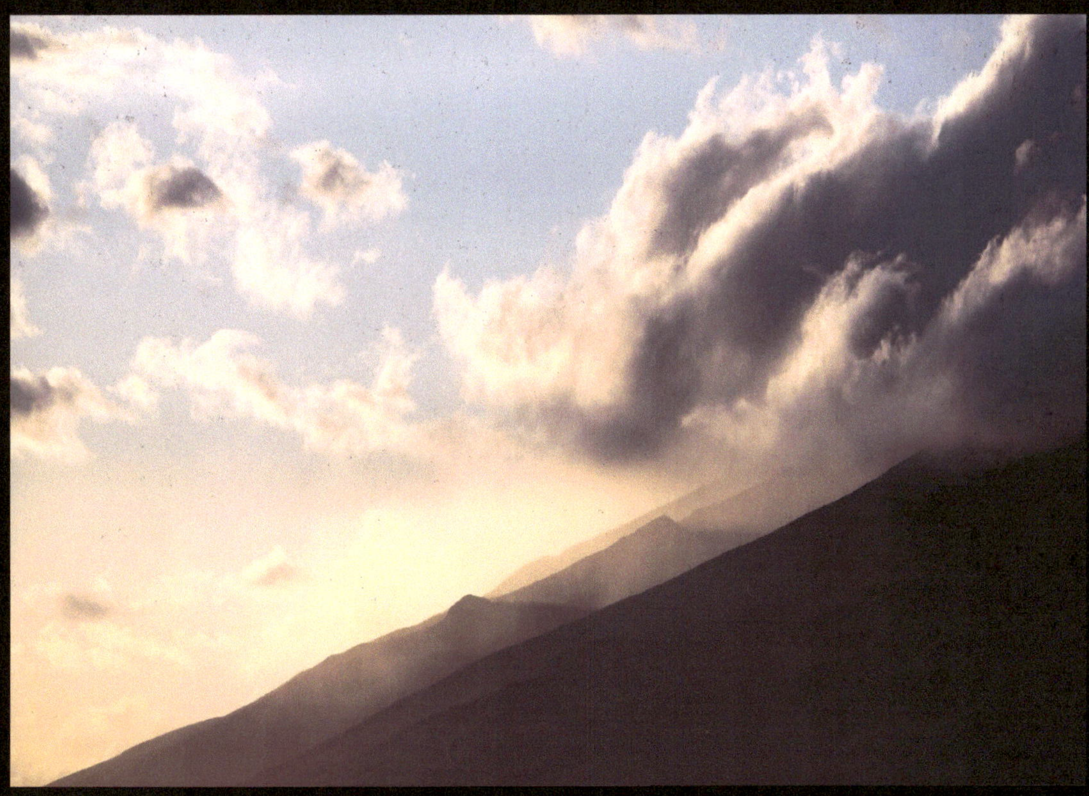

Maui, Hawai'i

Be fierce, and know that GOD is with you.

"The Lord is my light and my salvation. Whom shall I fear?The LORD is the keeper of my life, so who should I be afraid of? NO one!"

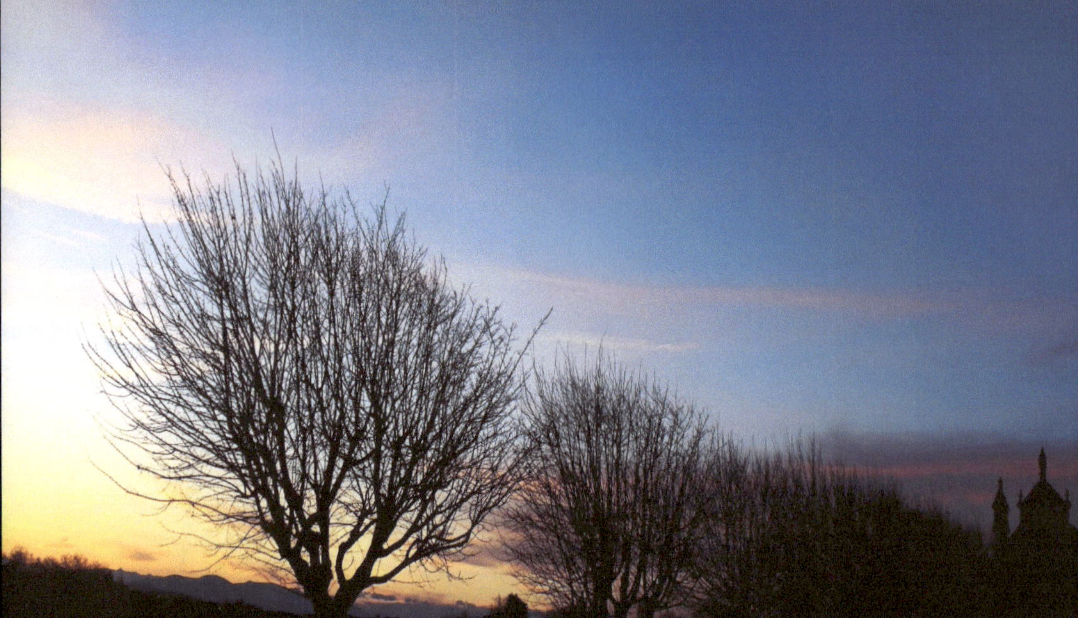

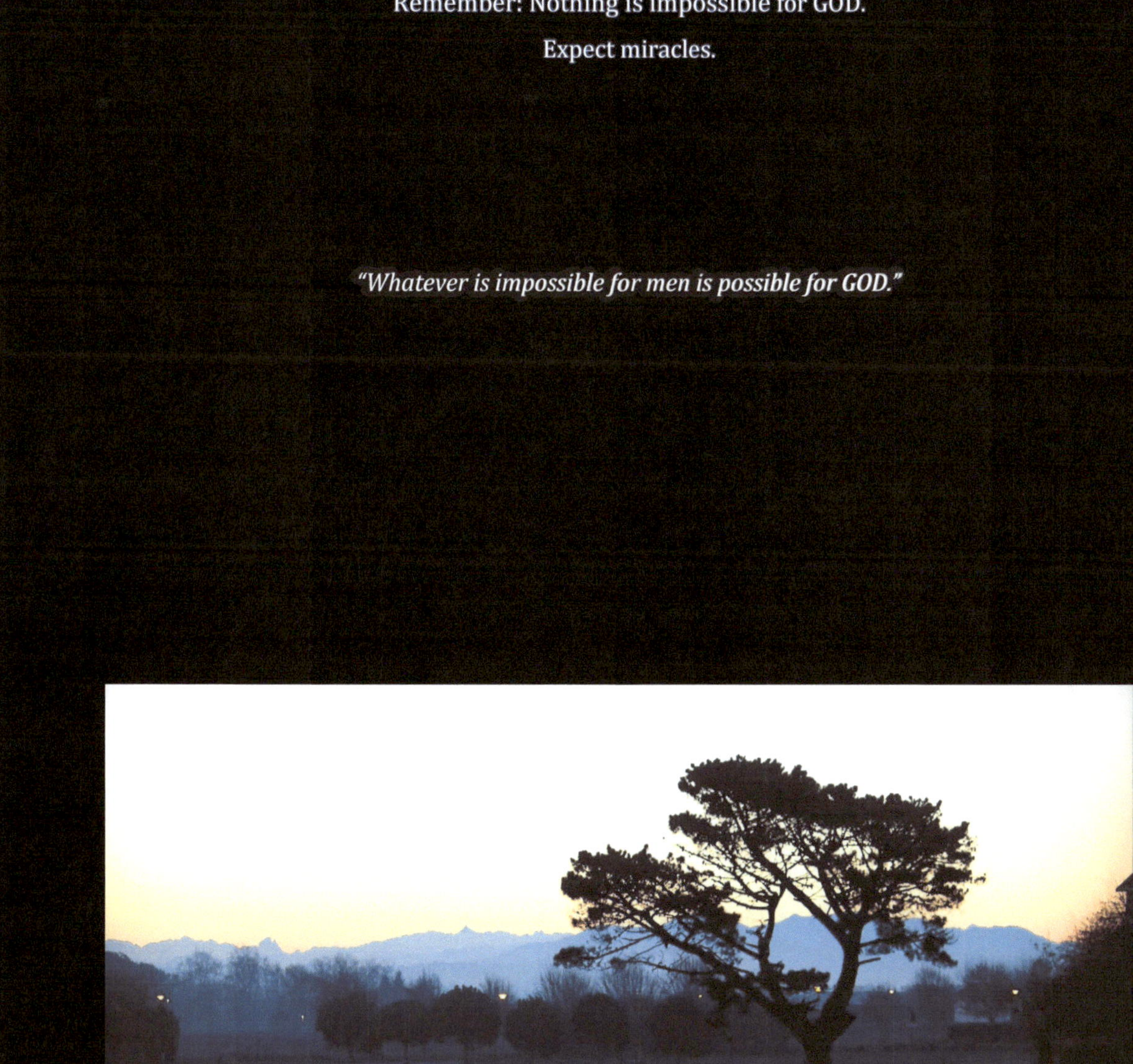
Remember: Nothing is impossible for GOD.
Expect miracles.
"Whatever is impossible for men is possible for GOD."

If I can inspire a heart to beat again, or breathe life into a dream;
hearten those who cry in the night and bring them the morning sun,
then my journey was worth the tears, and I triumphed in the midst of them all.

-D. Ashanti-Dubois

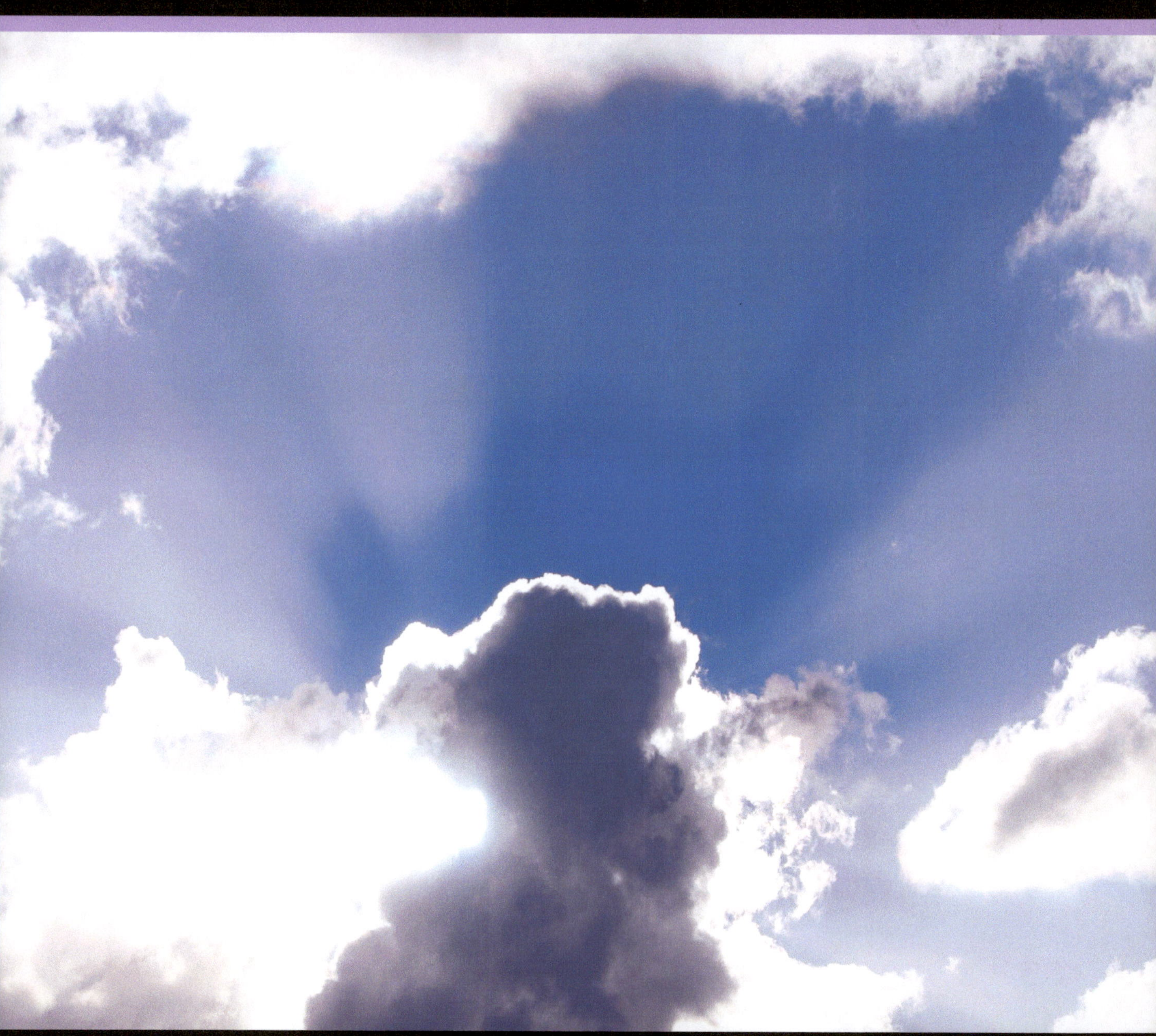

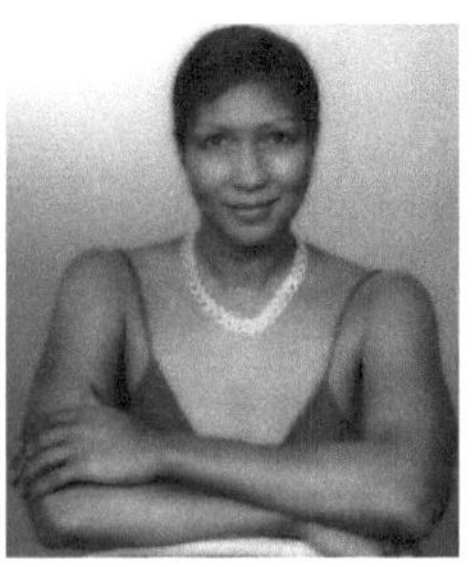

ABOUT THE AUTHOR

Author and creative artist, D. Ashanti-Dubois, brings light and love to the universe of literature through her latest edition, Messages of Hope – A Spiritual Trinity, Messages Affirmations & Prayers. As a multifaceted writer, photographer, vocalist, composer, graphic artist, and inspirational speaker, D. Ashanti-Dubois brings a unique perspective to the world of spiritual enlightenment. After nearly two decades of living internationally and in Hawaii, her intrepid journey has emboldened her belief in the spirit of hope, love, and humanity.

Born and raised in St. Louis, Missouri where she began her creative journey writing poetry, prose, and songs at the tender age of five, D. Ashanti-Dubois continues her artistic odyssey producing various genres of books, music, photography, and art.

Her spiritual anthology, *Messages of Hope,* is a collection of beautifully written spiritual insights to inspire and empower your life. The entire Messages of Hope series can be purchased online through Amazon.com and other vendors. Also available: *Messages of Hope – Words to Uplift the Human Spirit:* An uplifting book of 33 inspirational messages and 36 exercises to change in your life along with more than 150 gorgeous original photographs. *Messages d'Amour–Reflections of Love:* A romantic diary of love poems with gorgeous floral photography to inspire love and romance. *Heaven & Earth:* A magnificent collection of spiritual poetry and nature photography.

For more books available by D. Ashanti-Dubois visit www.mydovesong.com. Look for other editions scheduled to be released in the coming years.

www.ingramcontent.com/pod-product-compliance
Lightning Source LLC
LaVergne TN
LVHW070127110826
845147LV00002B/200